Discovery Travel Adventures

BIRDWATCHING

Judith Dunham
Editor

John Gattuso
Series Editor

D1410553

Discovery Communications, Inc.

INSIGHT GUIDES

Discovery Communications, Inc.
John S. Hendricks, *Founder, Chairman, and Chief Executive Officer*
Judith A. McHale, *President and Chief Operating Officer*
Michela English, *President, Discovery Enterprises Worldwide*
Judy L. Harris, *Senior Vice President, Discovery Enterprises Worldwide*

Discovery Publishing
Natalie Chapman, *Vice President, Publishing*
Rita Thievon Mullin, *Editorial Director*
Mary Kalamaras, *Senior Editor*
Maria Mihalik Higgins, *Editor*
Heather Quinlan, *Editorial Coordinator*
Chris Alvarez, *Business Development*
Jill Gordon, *Marketing Specialist*

Discovery Channel Retail
Tracy Fortini, *Product Development*
Steve Manning, *Naturalist*

Insight Guides
Jeremy Westwood, *Managing Director*
Brian Bell, *Editorial Director*
John Gattuso, *Series Editor*
Siu-Li Low, *General Manager, Books*

Distribution
United States
Langenscheidt Publishers, Inc.
46–35 54th Road, Maspeth, NY 11378
Fax: 718-784-0640

Worldwide
APA Publications GmbH & Co.
Verlag KG Singapore Branch, Singapore
38 Joo Koon Road, Singapore 628990
Tel: 65-865-1600. Fax: 65-861-6438

Discovery Communications produces high-quality nonfiction television programming, interactive media, books, films, and consumer products. Discovery Networks, a division of Discovery Communications, Inc., operates and manages the Discovery Channel, TLC, Animal Planet, Travel Channel, and Discovery Health Channel. Visit Discovery Channel Online at www.discovery.com.

Although every effort is made to provide accurate information in this publication, we would appreciate readers calling our attention to any errors or outdated information by writing us at: Insight Guides, PO Box 7910, London SE1 1WE, England; fax: 44-20-7403-0290; e-mail: insight@apaguide.demon.co.uk

Printed by Insight Print Services (Pte) Ltd, 38 Joo Koon Road, Singapore 628990.

Birdwatching/Judith Dunham, editor; John Gattuso, series editor.
    p. cm.—(Discovery travel adventures)
    Includes bibliographical references (p.).
    ISBN 1-56331-928-4 (pbk.)
      1. Birding sites—United States—Guidebooks.
2. Birding sites—Canada—Guidebooks. 3. Bird watching—United States—Guidebooks. 4. Bird watching—Canada—Guidebooks. 5. United States—Guidebooks. 6. Canada—Guidebooks. I. Dunham, Judith. II. Series.
QL682 .B62 2000
598'.07'23473—dc21   99-058196

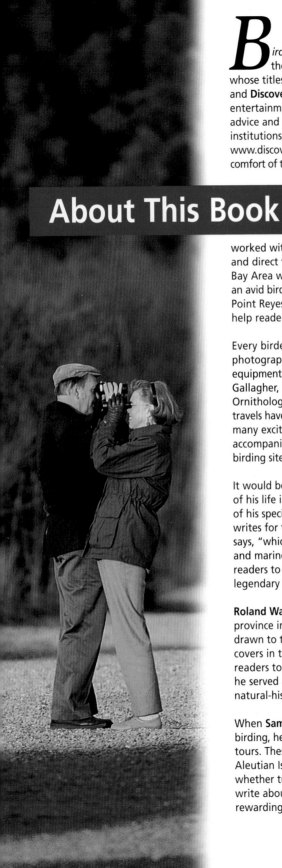

*B*irdwatching combines the interests and enthusiasm of two of the world's best-known information providers: **Insight Guides**, whose titles have set the standard for visual travel guides since 1970, and **Discovery Communications**, the world's premier source of nonfiction entertainment. The editors of Insight Guides provide both practical advice and general understanding about a destination's history, culture, institutions, and people. Discovery Communications and its website, www.discovery.com, help millions of viewers explore their world from the comfort of their home and encourage them to discover it firsthand.

About This Book

This book reflects the contributions of dedicated editors and writers familiar with the top birding destinations in North America. Series editor **John Gattuso**, of Stone Creek Publications in New Jersey, worked with Insight Guides and Discovery Communications to conceive and direct the series. Gattuso called on **Judith Dunham**, a San Francisco Bay Area writer and editor, to serve as project editor. Dunham, herself an avid birder, offers a tour of one of her favorite West Coast destinations, Point Reyes National Seashore, and also shares tips and techniques to help readers enjoy their time in the field.

Every birder leaves home with binoculars in hand, and writer and photographer **Tim Gallagher** sorts through the wide range of optical equipment available today and gets readers started in bird photography. Gallagher, director of publications for the Cornell Laboratory of Ornithology, is also editor-in-chief of the Lab's quarterly, *Living Bird*. His travels have taken him to the Arctic, Central America, and Iceland, among many exciting places, and his articles on his experiences are always accompanied by his top-notch photography. Here, Gallagher covers two birding sites: Churchill, Manitoba, and Point Pelee National Park, Ontario.

It would be hard not to envy naturalist **Clay Sutton**, who has lived most of his life in Cape May, New Jersey, a crossroads for migratory birds. One of his specialties is, in fact, avian migration, the subject of a chapter he writes for this book. "It was fascinating to grow up in Cape May," he says, "which fueled my interest in migration in all its forms, from birds and marine mammals to dragonflies and butterflies." Sutton introduces readers to Cape May's spectacular migrations and describes two other legendary birding spots, Hawk Mountain Sanctuary and South Florida.

Roland Wauer has birded in every state in the United States and every province in Canada. He first started birding in the northern Rockies, drawn to the majesty of Grand Teton National Park, a destination he covers in this guide. Wauer is also uniquely suited for introducing readers to Big Bend National Park and the Lower Rio Grande Valley: he served as chief park naturalist at Big Bend and leads birding and natural-history tours of the national park and the valley.

When **Sam Fried** is not at his Connecticut home base writing about birding, he is out in the field photographing or leading small, customized tours. These pursuits have taken him across North America, from the Aleutian Islands to the Dry Tortugas. Drawn to wide, open spaces, whether tundra, desert, or prairie, Fried welcomed the occasion to write about Pawnee National Grassland. He also recommends a host of rewarding activities for traveling birders.

Few aspects of birding are as simultaneously rewarding and frustrating as identifying birds. **Jules Evens**, a wildlife biologist living in Northern California, demystifies bird identification, showing how even beginners know more than they think they do. He has been a research associate at the Point Reyes Bird Observatory since 1974 and has led field trips and taught natural history to adults and children. **Glen Martin**, a San Francisco Bay Area writer specializing in wildlife and the environment, covers Klamath Basin, a place he explored extensively while living in the northern part of the state. Other projects have taken him to Alaska, down the entire Sacramento River by kayak, and throughout the Sierra Nevada.

The wetlands and sandhills of south-central Nebraska were among the places that **Michael Furtman** explored when he followed the waterfowl migration from Saskatchewan to Louisiana. He has written extensively about wildlife habitats and is the author of books on geese and bald eagles. **Rose Houk**, a former park ranger and author of several books on nature travel, ventured to the birding hot spot of southeast Arizona. "The wonder of so many hummingbirds and my first sighting of an elegant trogon," she says, "underscored the fantastic bird life found in my home state of Arizona."

Alaska is a destination on most birders' wish list. **David Cline**, based in Anchorage, is fortunate to live within an easy drive of the Kenai Peninsula, an area he has birded on land and at sea – and even by airplane. Cline has devoted his life to conservation, working to protect wildlife such as the brown bears of Kodiak Island. Central Park in New York City, perhaps the antithesis of Alaska, was a place that **John Turner** first birded as a youngster growing up on Long Island. He continues to return to the park, not only for this guide but to lead field trips, and has written extensively about his home turf. Turner also covers Acadia National Park.

The birds of Hawaii serenade **Rita Ariyoshi** just outside her window as she writes about nature travel and the natural history of the Hawaiian Islands, from endemic birds and botany to whales and other undersea life. For this guide, she takes readers to Hawaii Volcanoes National Park.

Les Line was honored in the 100th anniversary issue of *Audubon*, the magazine he edited for 25 years, as one of 100 "Champions of Conservation" who most influenced the 20th-century environmental movement. Line has authored, edited, and provided photographs for more than 30 books on natural history, including *The Sea Has Wings*, which features Bonaventure Island, the destination he covers for this guide.

Thanks to the many park rangers and naturalists who reviewed the text. Thanks also to members of the Stone Creek Publications editorial team – Edward A. Jardim, Michael Castagna, Sallie Graziano, and Nicole Buchenholz.

Birdwatching (opposite) offers an opportunity to learn about all aspects of nature.

The tufted titmouse (above) feeds on berries and insects and is seen year-round throughout the eastern United States.

Sandhill cranes (below) gather in spectacular flocks during migration and on their wintering grounds.

Previous pages: A Lucifer hummingbird feeds at an agave blossom in Texas.

Following pages: Caspian terns feed their young on a Michigan lakeshore.

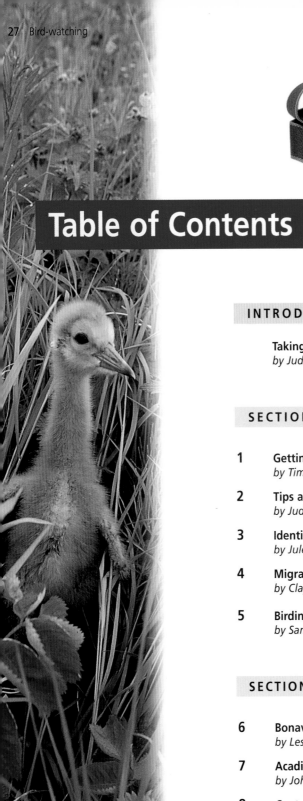

Table of Contents

MAPS

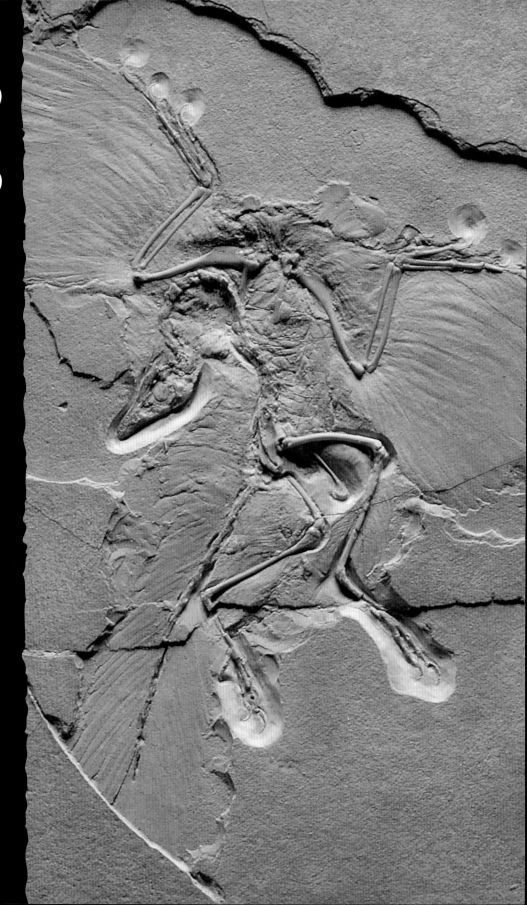

Birds first took to the air about 150 million years ago. The earliest known bird, *Archaeopteryx*, a close cousin of the dinosaurs, was about the size of a crow and had sharp teeth and claws protruding from its wings. It was in all likelihood a poor flier, able perhaps to elude predators by flapping between trees or briefly lifting off the ground, but incapable of extended flight. ◆ Primitive though it was, *Archaeopteryx* was the beginning of a dynasty that would survive mass extinctions and ecological turmoil and inhabit every corner of the globe. As our planet whirls into the 21st century, it supports more than 9,000 species of birds in territories as diverse as remote icefields unmarked by human footprints, ocean expanses with nary a perch in sight, and city parks where birdsong competes with the urban din. ◆ About 900 of the world's species reside in or visit North America: seabirds and shorebirds, waterfowl and wading birds, raptors, and songbirds.

As birds share the secrets of their lives, they reveal the ebbs and flows of nature's rhythms.

Given their considerable number, birds are among the creatures we are most likely to encounter in the wild. They sail through forests and fields and flock by the hundreds and thousands in wetlands and at seashores. As if boldly announcing their presence, they regale us with a wide repertoire of songs and calls. Just when we think we can predict their comings and goings, birds become secretive and elusive. After all, they can fly – high, fast, and far beyond our view. And they can dive and swim, vanishing into watery darkness. These two polar qualities – ubiquity and mystery – begin to explain why tens of millions of watchers revel in the challenges and rewards of birding.

Archaeopteryx, often described as a feathered dinosaur, may have been a precursor to modern birds.

Previous pages: Black tern chicks on lily pads; a common loon on a Maine pond; snow geese in Washington.

The feathered wings and tails of dinosaurs called *Caudipteryx* (left) may have been more useful for display than for flight.

A bald eagle (right) extends its powerful talons as it takes aim on a fish.

The eastern kingbird (below) is fascinating to observe as it sallies out from a perch to hawk insects.

Seeing a faraway speck, we turn a hopeful gaze to the sky, urging the creature to glide our way so we may admire its beauty up close and give it a name. We cock an ear toward the song of an invisible avian vocalist, at once appreciating the serenade and rifling our mental inventory for the songster's identity. Sometimes a bird refuses to give us a good look; identification is beyond our grasp. Then it's enough just to watch and listen, enthralled by beings endowed with the magic of flight, whose vocalizations sound full of lofty purpose and meaning.

Rare is the birder who has not longed to exchange arms for wings. "I like especially the idea of floating among the clouds all day," writes Edward Abbey, "seldom stirring a feather, meditating on whatever it is that vultures meditate about. It looks like a good life, from down here." Yet bound to the earth as we are, we must be content learning about birds one glimpse at a time. If we are attentive, every look at a vulture or sparrow or hummingbird brings insight into subtle variations of appearance and behavior. And as our knowledge grows, each species becomes singular in its complexities.

Birds mature, breed, and change plumages, each species according to its own specialized calendar. Most impressively, many species migrate epic distances, from continent to continent, hemisphere to hemisphere. Recognizing and observing their cycles connects us with nature's grand rhythms. "There is symbolic as well as actual beauty in the migration of the birds," Rachel Carson wrote, "the ebb and flow of the tides, the folded bud ready for spring. There is something infinitely healing in the repeated refrains of nature – the assurance that dawn comes after night, and spring after winter."

The extraordinary mobility of birds makes them dependent on a network of habitats where they can nest and raise their young, obtain sustenance in winter, and find refuge during migrations fraught with peril. Though birds are constantly threatened by habitat loss, many wildlands, including the outstanding places in this book, have been preserved from Alaska to Florida, Quebec to California. Once you are enraptured by birds, you will want to make your own epic journey to see streams of raptors following the wind, a hummingbird sampling the nectar of a desert blossom, or seabirds nesting on a surf-lashed island. You will find rewards wherever your own migration takes you.

◆

Preparing For the Field

◆

A little planning goes a long way. Before your trip, get comfortable seeing the natural world with binoculars, and learn about bird behavior. Participating in field trips or other activities can enhance your traveling experiences.

Getting Equipped

One of the great appeals of birding is that you don't have to spend a lot of money to get started. For less than the price of a ski weekend, you can acquire essential items that will last for years. Actually, all you really need are binoculars – "binos," "binocs," or "bins" in birder parlance – and a good, up-to-date field guide. Eventually, when you become addicted to birding, you'll probably want to upgrade your binos or buy a high-powered spotting scope for scrutinizing the feather detail on distant shorebirds. But for now, a decent pair of binoculars will be more than enough. ◆ Even if you're an experienced birder and have been using binoculars for years, buying new ones can be a daunting task. There are so many makes, models, and types available, at prices ranging from less than $100 to more than $2,000. How can you ever hope to find the right ones? The only way is to do a little research and shop around. ◆ Begin by taking a close-up look at binoculars. At the most basic level, binoculars consist of two low-powered telescopes mounted side by side. Because you're using both eyes, viewing is more natural and comfortable, and you see a more three-dimensional image than through a scope. Each individual telescope, or barrel, of a pair of binoculars has a set of prisms between the objective (front) lens and the ocular (eyepiece) lens. The light rays are bent back and forth as they travel through the prisms, which makes it possible to have a long focal length, and hence high magnification, with a relatively short barrel. Prisms also correct the upside-down image your eye would otherwise receive. ◆ Modern binoculars have three basic prism

Choose binoculars that suit your needs, then buy a good field guide. You're ready to go birding.

Experienced birders like to take a spotting scope, as well as binoculars, into the field.

Previous pages: An indigo bunting perches on the stem of a thistle.

designs – porro prism, roof prism, and reverse porro prism. Porro prism binoculars are the traditional wide, short, relatively heavy binos many people grew up with. You can distinguish them easily because the eyepieces are closer together than the objective lenses. Roof prism binoculars employ smaller prisms placed in-line in the binocular barrels, and thus the eyepieces and objective lenses are directly aligned. They're longer, slimmer, and generally much lighter and more weather-resistant than porro prism binos – also significantly more expensive. The reverse porro prism, a common design in compact binos, inverts the standard porro prism so that the objective lenses are closer together than the eyepieces. Your choice depends on your needs and budget.

Bino Basics

Pick up virtually any pair of binoculars and you'll find numbers such as 7x35, 8x56, or 10x40 stamped on the exterior. These numbers refer to the magnification and the size of the objective lenses in millimeters. For example, 7x35 binoculars magnify the image seven times and have objective lenses 35 millimeters in diameter. Binoculars often have another figure representing field of view. It may be listed in degrees, from a narrow 3.5 degrees to a wide 11 degrees, or it might just state the width of the area you will see – for example, 300 feet at 1,000 yards. In most cases, the greater the magnification, the smaller the field of view.

Magnification is a major consideration when choosing binoculars. You want enough power to bring a bird's image close enough to identify; however, the higher the magnification, the more difficult it is to hold binoculars steady. The effects of hand vibration are greatly intensified by high magnification, which can lead to eye fatigue and headaches. Maximum mag-nification for comfortable handheld viewing is probably 10x. If you're planning to buy budget binoculars costing $150 or less, don't go above 7x or 8x. Optical imperfections show up more in inexpensive models.

Another consideration is relative brightness. This is determined by the size of the exit pupil – the diameter of the beam of light that exits the eyepiece and enters your eye. If you do a lot of birding in low-light conditions, such as dawn or dusk, you want as bright an image as possible, and therefore exit pupil size becomes a major factor. You can determine the exit pupil with this simple formula: Divide the magnification of the binoculars into the size of the objective lens. Thus, 10x40 binoculars have an exit pupil of four millimeters. The pupil of a human eye is approximately seven millimeters when completely open, so the closer you can get to that figure, the better the particular optical instrument will be in dim light. Of course, binoculars

Porro prism binoculars (above) have eyepieces that are closer together than the objective lenses.

Sunglasses offering protection from the sun's ultraviolet rays (right) make a good addition to the birder's inventory of gear.

Optical equipment needs to be portable (opposite, top). Carefully assess the weight of binoculars and scopes before you purchase them.

A curious sandhill crane (opposite, bottom) approaches a photographer. For more skittish subjects, you may need a blind.

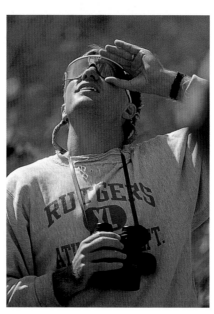

with larger exit pupils have larger – and heavier and more costly – objective lenses.

The Fine Points

Now, it's time to start defining your needs. Are you mostly interested in pelagic (deep-sea) birding? If so, you want highly water-resistant, rubber-armored binoculars. Is your birding mostly at close range? Then be sure to get binoculars with a minimum close focus adequate for your needs. Do you bird frequently in deep woods or other low-light situations? You'll value binoculars with a large exit pupil, within the limits of the amount of weight you want to carry and how much money you want to spend.

Be sure to try out as many

binoculars as possible before you buy. Talk to other birders about their preferences and check out their equipment. Look through binoculars at a local optical dealer. If you wear eyeglasses when birding, wear them when you're testing binoculars. See if the eyecups fold or pop down adequately to give you a

decent-sized image area. Many binoculars, even top-of-the-line models, are poor for eyeglass wearers, imposing a tunnel-vision view. Binoculars should adjust sufficiently to accommodate the size of the space between your eyes, called interpupillary distance. Though binos are hinged in the middle to achieve this adjustment, the barrels on some models cannot be moved close enough to create a single image for people with a narrow interpupillary distance.

If the dealer will let you, walk outside and gaze at a distant object. Put the center in sharp focus, and look at the outer edge. Is it fuzzy? This kind of vignetting is common in budget binoculars and

Birding with RTP

No one in the history of bird-watching has had a more profound influence than renowned artist, author, and all-around naturalist Roger Tory Peterson. RTP, as he was often called, single-handedly invented the modern system of field identification.

Peterson was just 25 years old in 1934 when he published his landmark work, *A Field Guide to the Birds*. The United States was mired in the Great Depression, so the publisher, Houghton Mifflin, was naturally concerned about the risks of the project. The book's first print run numbered only 2,000 copies. It sold out in a week, and Peterson's field guides have subsequently sold in the millions.

What made his field guide such an instant success? Simply that nothing like it had existed before. None of the authors of other bird books had made a meaningful effort to simplify the process of identifying the baffling array of birds seen in the field. With this new guide, Peterson noted in his introduction, "live birds may be run down by impressions, patterns, and distinctive marks, rather than by anatomical differences and measurements that the collector would find interesting."

The "Peterson System" addressed these needs admirably, providing color and black-and-white plates of birds, most on a given plate drawn in a similar pose to emphasize each bird's diagnostic features such as wing bars, eye lines, tail bars, and eye rings. To make the system simpler still, Peterson provided tiny arrows pointing to the most visible field marks that distinguished each species.

Roger Tory Peterson died in 1996, but his presence is still very much with us. In a sense, we all go birding with him each time we slip on our binoculars and set off into the field.

birding situation. What do you do when you're standing at the edge of a vast mudflat, trying to detect the subtle distinguishing features between look-alike shorebird species in a distant mixed flock? Without the greater magnification of a spotting scope, you're bound to miss some significant birds.

As with binoculars, several key differences exist between spotting scopes, including magnification, objective lens diameter, and field of view. Again, the larger the objective lens, the more light reaches your eye. Unlike binoculars, however, most scopes have removable eyepieces, allowing you to change magnification and field of view easily in the field. Even more convenient are the zoom eyepieces offered by many companies, which allow you, for example, to scan an area in 20x, then zoom to 60x to scrutinize an interesting bird. Be careful: Many zoom eyepieces fail to produce as sharp an image as a single-power lens.

Prices of scopes vary widely, from about $100 to several thousand dollars. You can expect to pay at least $300 to $400 for a decent one. When you're shopping around, you may notice a substantial price difference between two look-alike scopes manufactured by the same company. In most cases, one model has better optical glass, which enhances clarity and minimizes color aberrations. Scope manufacturers

will cause headaches. Next, focus on an object with long straight lines, such as a building. Are the lines bent or distorted? If so, move on to the next pair.

Ask about lens coatings. Due to reflection, a great deal of light, and consequently image brightness, is lost before reaching your eyes. Fully coated lenses significantly reduce loss of light,

providing crisp detail and contrast. If you hold the binoculars at arm's length and tilt them until the light hits at the proper angle, you should be able to see the purplish or greenish sheen of the lens coating.

Moving Up, Optically

At some point, most birders discover that binoculars are not adequate for every usually place the letters ED (extra low dispersion) or HD (high density) after product names to indicate that higher-quality glass was used, or they state that the scope has a fluorite objective lens.

In general, if a scope has superior optical glass, it will cost roughly twice as much as the standard model. Is it worth the extra cost? If you're an ace birder who needs all the advantages that top-notch optics can supply (or if you have the money), then the answer is yes. But for average birding, the less costly models are fine.

When you buy a spotting scope, you'll need a good tripod to hold it steady. Two of the top brands are Gitzo, which is almost prohibitively expensive, and Bogen. Get one with a panning arm and preferably a fluid head, which will allow you to pan smoothly as you search for birds across a wide area.

Completing the Outfit

It would be difficult to overestimate the value of a first-class field guide. Binoculars and spotting scopes bring a bird's image up close. But to make sense of all the characteristics – bill shape, eye color, presence or absence of wing bars and eye lines, and so on – you need to compare what you see with an accurate reference guide.

In general, field guides that have photographs of birds are not as useful as those with illustrations. In an illustration, an artist can compose the image of a species to show its distinguishing features to best advantage.

An inventive birder (above) has fashioned her own method of steadying her binoculars.

Roger Tory Peterson (opposite) traveled the world in pursuit of birds, including this nesting royal albatross on Campbell Island in the South Pacific.

A sturdy tripod (below) keeps a spotting scope stable. The tripod's head should permit fluid movement over a broad viewing area.

Capturing Birds on Film

Photographing birds is not a hobby for the fainthearted or impatient. It can involve lugging heavy equipment through mosquito-infested marshes or up lung-searing mountainsides, and you can count on spending long hours cramped in a blind, waiting for something to happen. Yet when that graceful arctic tern brings a fish to its mate, or that stunning, male rose-breasted grosbeak lifts his head in song, nothing is more exciting than capturing the moment on film.

Unless you intend to take pictures only of backyard birds, you'll need a rugged, dependable camera and a telephoto lens. A 35mm SLR (single-lens-reflex) camera is the best choice. The unique design allows you to see the exact image that will appear in your photograph, and most models can use a wide variety of lenses.

Many manufacturers produce 35mm SLR cameras suitable for bird photography. But consider a few factors before making your choice. Do a company's products have a reputation for reliability, or are they known for breaking down frequently? Your equipment will be exposed to extremes of heat, cold, moisture, and dust, so you want the most durable camera you can afford. And does the manufacturer offer an extensive line of lenses? Remember, you're buying not only a camera body but a lens system. You want something that can grow as you become more proficient.

For photographing birds in the field, a good 400mm f/5.6 lens is hard to beat. It will magnify what you see approximately eight times, giving you a large image without forcing you to approach your subject too closely. The f/5.6 refers to the maximum size of the lens aperture when fully open. Basically, the lower the f/stop number, the "faster" the lens – that is, the more light it will allow into your camera. A faster lens, such as an f/2.8, will let you use a faster shutter speed, but to achieve that extra speed, the camera manufacturer has to put an enormous objective lens at the front of the telephoto, which greatly boosts size, weight, and especially price. It makes sense to start with the slower lens.

Don't leave home without a tripod, and buy the best one you can afford. A flimsy tripod isn't the safest support for your camera equipment and will cause blurred photographs. Most bird photographers opt for a ball-joint-style tripod head, or "ball head," because it is much quicker and easier to follow birds with a ball head than a panning head.

Once you're equipped, you might want to build a simple portable blind, using a framework of one-by-one wooden stakes, about four feet square, and attaching burlap or another drab material with a staple gun. You'll be amazed how quickly birds accept a structure like this in their environment. Or you can look at the ads for ready-made blinds in nature photography magazines. With the right equipment, before long you'll eventually be creating excellent images of wild birds in the field.

Beginners can take excellent photographs using a 35 mm single-lens-reflex camera and a telephoto lens (below). As their skill and ambition increase, they can graduate to more versatile and expensive equipment (left and bottom), including a wide range of powerful lenses.

A youngster (opposite, top) scans Jones Beach, New York, through a spotting scope, the ideal instrument for observing distant shorebirds.

A birder (opposite, bottom) in southeastern Arizona consults a field guide. Be sure to choose a guide that covers most or all of North America.

The National Geographic Society's *Field Guide to the Birds of North America* (now in its third edition) is generally acknowledged to be one of the most comprehensive portable guides to the birds of North America. The color illustrations are generally excellent; the species accounts are well written; and the range maps are conveniently placed beside the species accounts and illustrations. Roger Tory Peterson's *A Field Guide to the Birds of Eastern and Central North America* and *A Field Guide to Western Birds* are superb as well. His innovation of using arrows to point out the main identifying features of each species is particularly valuable. On the downside, the range maps are in the back of each book instead of next to the species accounts, and you have to buy two books to have full coverage of North America.

The American Bird Conservancy's 1997 *All the Birds of North America* is an excellent guide that covers the continent and features panoramic paintings by some of the world's best bird artists. On many pages, illustrations of look-alike but unrelated species are put side by side to help birders make accurate identifications.

Another useful reference is *Birds of North America*, by Chandler S. Robbins, Bertel Bruun, and Herbert S. Zim, with illustrations by Arthur Singer. This handy guide, which fits easily into most coat pockets, covers every species found in North America, though not in as much detail as in the Peterson guides. The range maps are beside each species account. The reproduction quality of the illustrations, however, is not as good as in the other guides.

As you become more advanced, you may want to have cassette tapes or CDs that will speed your ability to learn the distinctive songs and calls of birds. A number of interesting CD-ROM guides include typical field-guide information with illustrations or photographs, as well as vocalizations.

The only other things you need are the common-sense items that will make your birding experience more enjoyable: correct shoes for the kind of terrain you'll be walking through; a hat to protect you from sun and glare; appropriate clothing to maintain your comfort; insect repellent for walking through buggy environments, and perhaps a small shoulder bag, back-pack, fanny pack, or birding vest to carry your gear. Beyond that, you just need the desire to stroll through picturesque places looking for some of the most beautiful and varied creatures in all of nature.

Tips and Techniques

"*Pshhh.*" Soft but insistent, the sound penetrates the woods. "*Pshhhh. Pshhhh. Pshhhh.*" The only similar utterance you recall hearing was issued by a rude restaurant patron summoning a waiter. As you round a bend in the trail, you see the source of the noise. ◆ As two birders aim their binoculars at a streamside willow thicket, a third, binos at the ready, accelerates the pace of the sound: "*Pshhhh-pshhhh-pshhhh.*" You then hear a more familiar language. "Male mourning warbler in the back at two o'clock." "Northern parula female at seven o'clock. Hey, there's the male. Six o'clock." "Yellow-bellied sapsucker to the right, on the snag behind the two boulders. There he goes." Catching their excitement, you reach for your binoculars and try to focus on the flutter of wings mingling with the sun-dappled leaves while the trio recites birds as if reading from a list. One of the group turns and remarks, "Real birdy today, isn't it?"

A quick course in birding basics will enable you to make the most of your time in the field.

You bob your head, grateful that the comment was a greeting rather than an actual question. ◆ To most people just discovering a passion for watching birds, experienced birders like these seem members of an arcane fraternity that communicates in code. Yet most advanced birders can recall a time when they, too, were neophytes possessing only hand-me-down binoculars and a brand-new Peterson field guide – along with the realization that hundreds of species of birds are out there, waiting to be seen and heard and identified. You may be surprised to learn how many luminaries in the birding world, the late Roger Tory Peterson among them, launched their careers with nothing more

Birding with a companion or a group enables you to spot more birds. Everyone can share his or her observations to solve identification quandaries.

Birding with Children

Of the many gifts you can bestow on your children, an interest in exploring nature belongs right up there toward the top of the list. Birders who start young accumulate practical experiences and enjoyable memories they can build on for the rest of their lives.

As for any beginner, choosing the right equipment is key. Though you may have a spare pair of old binoculars, their weight or optics may not suit young children. It's well worth investing in new binos specifically for the youngsters who will be using them. Then, make time for practice sessions in your yard and around the neighborhood so the children get used to focusing on objects near and far.

On your initial forays, try to concentrate on bigger birds. Identifying fast-moving warblers or look-alike flycatchers won't be any easier for children than it is for adult beginners. Seek out a nearby lake or marsh where children can see large waterbirds like egrets and herons, or gatherings of waterfowl. Nesting birds are also engaging for children to observe. You can return to the nest site to watch the nestlings being fed by the adults and later getting ready for their first flight. On your excursions, talk about bird behavior: how waterbirds and ducks forage and what they eat, and how and with what materials birds build their nests. This will help children understand the differences between families and species.

Wetlands and lakes (above) inhabited by large, easily spotted birds such as waterfowl are ideal places to take children. Young birders can also join field trips (below).

A visitor to Big Bend National Park in Texas (opposite) observes a bird in distant shrubbery, then raises her binos for a closer look.

Your local bird club may offer field trips or classes for children. Organizations that sponsor censuses, such as Christmas bird counts, often welcome children accompanied by adults. Counting birds for a day is a great way to spend time together for a good cause and introduce children to other enthusiastic birders.

than a fascination with birds.

The trick, if it can be called that, is to spend time in the field, and lots of it. In birding, practice really does make perfect. If you're just starting out, however, you can equip yourself with some basic information and techniques to make your search more productive.

Nature's Timetable

It won't take you long to tune into the seasons at your favorite local birding spots. But when planning a trip to a faraway region, it's wise to do some research on the best time to go. Birding is productive year-round in many locations, but is truly spectacular at certain seasonal peaks: spring migration for songbirds along the Gulf Coast of Texas; summer for nesting species at Pawnee National Grassland in Colorado; raptor migration in fall at Hawk Mountain Sanctuary in Pennsylvania; January and February for wintering eagles at Klamath Basin on the Oregon-California border. Though you can't count on nature to obey a schedule, you want to plan to be at your destination during prime time.

A little more effort will clue you in on which birds you'll see. Virtually every national park and wildlife refuge can provide you with a checklist of birds known to occur in the various seasons. The checklist tells you which birds are year-round residents, which are summer or winter visitors, which are migrants, and which are rare sightings. Note the birds likely to be present during your visit, and review their diagnostic marks and behavior in your field guide.

You can refine your strategy by knowing the best time of day to bird the area you'll be visiting. Birds are generally most active at dawn (the "dawn chorus" as birders call it) – not good news for late sleepers – and again at dusk. But once you've witnessed several dozen eagles rising into the dawn from their night roost in Klamath Basin, or thrilled to a dozen or so species of migrating warblers at Point Pelee, you'll never doubt the rewards of tumbling out of bed before first light. If you intend to bird tidal marshes, estuaries, and shorelines, determine how the tides will affect what you can expect to see. Incoming tides often force herons and other waterbirds to high ground, making them more visible.

When the tide recedes, exposed shorelines and mudflats attract crowds of feeding shorebirds.

Rapid Response

The magic of flight is one big reason birds are so compelling – and why they can be so difficult to identify. Only rarely can you study a species as it appears in your field guide, motionless, as if frozen on a perch. Even birds that seldom fly fast or over long distances, like meadowlarks and killdeer, can suddenly flush from a grassy field and disappear into vegetation just yards away. How can you possibly observe field marks such as barring, streaking, wing bars, or tail bands when the bird was a blur?

One answer is to speed up your viewing technique and gain just enough time to

note a particular behavior or pick out an essential field mark. The first step is to practice using your optical equipment until it feels like an extension of your body. When you spot what you think may be a warbler darting about a tree canopy, don't look down at your binoculars before bringing them up to your eyes. By then, the bird will have moved. Instead, keep your eyes on the bird as you lift your binos. Your binos should be easy to find – at the end of a strap looped around your neck. Because you've been tracking the bird with your eyes, it will be right there in your binos' field of view. You'll still need to focus your binos for sharpness. You can gain seconds here, too, by knowing which way to turn the focusing wheel.

But what should you do

diagonal course rather than straight on, avoiding sudden movements. Keep the sun at your back, if possible. This helps reduce glare, which makes birds look flat and tends to wash out detail.

Bird Talk

We'd all see more birds if we had an extra set of eyes or could swivel our head like an owl through 270 degrees. The alternative is to bird with friends and family or join a field trip. All those eyes looking in every direction will bring you more species and greater opportunities to study their behavior. Each observer may see different field characters, allowing everyone to compare sightings and solve vexing identification problems.

The biggest challenge of birding in a group is how to communicate a sighting specifically and accurately. The first temptation is to point. "There!" you enthuse at your companions, thrusting an index finger in the direction of a clapper rail that has just slipped out from dense marsh grass. Confronted with a sudden gesture from

when a whole flock of birds is foraging in foliage or clustered on a mudflat? Don't worry about individual birds at first. Take in the entire scene with your binos, then very slowly scan the area until you get a good view of a bird and its field marks. Never assume that the flock is homogeneous. Try to observe as many individuals as possible and be alert for those that stand out. You'll be glad you did when you discover a pair of Eurasian wigeons foraging among dozens of American wigeons, or a little gull drifting within a flock of Bonaparte's gulls.

Birds have one mission in life – survival – and once you enter their environment,

you don't want to appear threatening or overly conspicuous. In general, nature's palette is a subtle one, so dress in subdued or neutral shades. Since birds are concentrated where different habitats meet – such as the transition between woodlands and meadow, or dense marsh grass and open water – landscape features can act as a natural blind. Sneaking up behind trees or vegetation can help break up your silhouette while you survey the activity around you. Birds can be surprisingly slow to flee if you stalk them quietly, on a

Birders at Cape May, New Jersey (above), scan trees full of migrating warblers and songbirds.

A flock (right) that initially seems homogeneous may harbor more than one species.

A sign at Jamaica Bay National Wildlife Refuge in New York (opposite) makes a handy perch for a belted kingfisher.

a seemingly menacing large mammal, the shy wader disappears before anyone else sees it. Not only can pointing spook birds – especially those seen at close range – but it is an imprecise way to share a sighting with fellow birders.

Instead, you want to describe nearby landmarks that can lead your companions to the bird's location. "Clapper rail moving right of the bare ground in front of the dried marsh grass." In the absence of easily discernible landmarks, pick out objects in the distance or at the horizon to convey a bird's position. "Dickcissel, right up on a bush! See the green barn out there to our left? Follow it about a third of the way directly toward us."

The clock method used by the trio of experts earlier works well for both land and pelagic birding. Imagine, as they did, a clock face suspended vertically between you and that streamside willow thicket. Pinpointing birds is as simple as telling time: "Black-and-white warbler at four o'clock." "Indigo bunting at nine o'clock." On pelagic trips, the common practice is to shift the clock face so that it's horizontal, with noon at the bow and six o'clock at the stern.

When on land, you will often hear birds – shuffling in leaf litter or calling from dense brush – without seeing them. There are various ways to coax them into making an appearance, all of which should be used discreetly to avoid stressing your quarry. First, try the *pshhhing* employed by our three advanced birders. No one knows exactly why *pshhhing* attracts birds. One theory is that it mimics the scolding of a small bird, such as a wren, and nearby birds converge on the area to see what the fuss is about.

You can experiment by slowing down the *pshhhing* sequence or speeding it up, or by building to a crescendo. Once you've *pshhhed* a few rounds, wait for the bird to respond, then try again. Or add other enticements to your repertoire. Repeated *tsks*, made with the tongue against the roof of the mouth, or squeaks, produced by kissing the back of the hand, can persuade a sparrow or towhee to fly out from hiding.

There are no guarantees. Birds will sometimes reject even the most earnest *pshhhing*, *tsks*, or squeaking. And when birds do come into view, the fun lasts only about 10 minutes. Then, their attention span being what is it, they drift off and go about their other business.

AREA
BEYOND
THIS
SIGN
CLOSED
All public entry prohibited

Birding Etiquette

Respecting birds and their environment is an integral part of birding. Here are some of the guidelines issued by the American Birding Association (see Resource Directory) for protecting wildlife as well as ensuring that others enjoy their birding experience.

● Never chase birds or approach them too closely. It's especially important to keep your distance when observing or photographing nesting sites, roosting areas, and feeding locations. When feasible, watch from a blind or take advantage of natural cover.

● Avoid stressing birds by overusing methods of attracting them. Rare birds or those classified as threatened or endangered should never be lured by playing tapes or imitating their calls.

● Watch where you drive and walk. Staying on established roads and trails is the best way to protect wildlife habitats. When birding in areas without paths, work out the approach with the least impact on vegetation. Always respect private property and enter only with the owner's permission.

● Restrict the size of your birding group. Limiting the number of participants lessens the chance of disturbing birds and harming their environment.

● Share observations and knowledge. Even experienced birders can learn from the insights of others, and beginning birders especially appreciate helpful tips and suggestions.

Since the dawn of time, we humans have been honing our field skills to make swift, accurate identifications of the flora and fauna around us. Our earliest ancestors, crossing some vast African savanna, had to know which plants were edible and which were toxic, which creatures would sustain them and which might do them in. Size, shape, color, peculiar markings, sound, behavior, and even distribution were all essential clues.   ◆   Modern field guides make distinctions between birds by pointing out the most precise field marks or diagnostic characters such as eye rings, wing bars, and leg color. This method is especially useful for identifying members of such difficult groups as gulls, small flycatchers, and fall warblers, though some birds may also be identified by their characteristic behaviors.   ◆   You'll be surprised at how much you already know. Take, for example, the American robin. Everybody knows what that bird looks like. What characteristics make it so recognizable?

When you encounter a new species, you become a detective examining the subtlest clues of appearance and behavior.

The red breast, of course, but this is only the most obvious feature. You're undoubtedly also familiar with the robin's shape and its tendency to hop around the lawn pulling up earthworms or flock into *Pyrocantha* bushes to devour autumn berries. If you've lived in a place where robins breed (most of North America), you may even recognize the measured triplet notes of the evening song that heralds spring.   ◆   If you recognize the robin, you can see its similarity to other members of the thrush family – largish eye, rather sharp bill, deep chest, medium-length tail, and flutelike song. Such family characteristics help observers organize species into family

Males and females of a species may display different coloration. Female northern cardinals, as well as juvenile cardinals, seem brownish with yellow and red overtones, in contrast to the males' brilliant red.

Birding by Ear

The godfather of North American field identification, Roger Tory Peterson, was known to say that the most experienced birders did 90 percent of their work by ear. Indeed, for species that are difficult to see like the hermit thrush, the veery, and other forest thrushes, vocalizations may be the most important clue to their identity. For groups that are very similar in appearance – such as the small flycatchers of the genus *Empidonax*, as well as some grassland sparrows – sound may be the only reliable way to tell closely related species apart.

There are two main types of vocalization. Song is usually an elaborate and emphatic series of notes arranged in a complex pattern, sung most often by the male in order to proclaim his presence, attract a mate, or defend a territory. Call notes, usually uttered by both sexes, tend to be single notes or a series of similar notes emitted more frequently than songs. They are used to communicate location or a warning to mates or other members of the flock. While songs are heard mostly during the breeding season, call notes are uttered year-round. Whether it's the clucking of a California quail, the catlike mew note of an eastern towhee, or the four-note "potato-chip" call of the American goldfinch, the call notes can be just as characteristic, and identifiable, as the song.

Be attuned to nonvocal sounds as well. A rustling in the undergrowth may alert you to a towhee or fox sparrow double-scratching in the leaf litter. Drumming on wood is undoubtedly a woodpecker; each species has a characteristic "tattoo." A booming of wings in the shadows of the forest may indicate a ruffed grouse, or a loud whiffling heard at twilight over a marsh or swale may signal the careening flight display of common snipe.

The eastern meadowlark (above) has a melancholy, whistlelike song. Its range overlaps that of the similar western meadowlark, whose song is a gurgling, flutelike melody.

American robins (opposite, top), members of the thrush family, are found across North America. Familiarity with the robin's general shape and proportions helps identify other thrushes, such as the hermit (opposite, bottom).

groups and, for identification purposes, narrow the choices down to fewer and fewer possibilities.

One morning you see a thrushlike bird appear at the edge of some shrubbery. It has a robin's general shape but seems smaller, more delicate. There is no red breast but rather a speckling across the chest. You've studied the bird checklist for your area and know that both hermit thrush and Swainson's thrush, close cousins of the robin, are fairly common. It's probably one of those. You watch the bird forage on the ground and notice its more obvious signals – the rufous tail contrasting with the olive back, and especially the way the bird flicks its wings every few seconds. You didn't observe some of the finer distinctions (like whether the eye ring was whitish or buff), but because you watched the bird instead of immediately turning to your field guide, you did notice its distinctive behavior.

After the bird disappears into the bush, you pull out your guide and recognize the hermit thrush. The next time you encounter this species, it may be backlighted, and the contrasting tail and back color may not be visible, but if you watch the bird for a few moments, you'll notice the wing-flicking behavior. You may even see the whitish eye ring and recognize the thrush's distinctive *chuck* call note.

Just as the ubiquitous robin is a good reference point for thrushes, so your familiarity with other birds will give you a head start on their families. No one will have to tell you where to start looking in your field guide when a goose or duck flies by. Everybody knows what an adult bald eagle looks like, and that's a good benchmark against which to start judging the various large soaring eagles and hawks. You may not be familiar with any specific sparrow, but you'll know one when you see it feeding on the ground and you'll go to the right place in the guide to start narrowing down the possibilities.

With their high metabolic rate, birds are highly active creatures, always flying, feinting, flushing. Although larger species like waterfowl and hawks are easier to observe, rarely does a songbird provide an ideal view to a phlegmatic birder wrestling with binoculars or a spotting scope. Instead, you might see a fanning tail or get a fleeting glimpse of the face through the foliage, or you might hear a chip note in the undergrowth or the sibilant whispers of a flock overhead. Distinguishing between species depends on paying attention to as many of these clues as possible.

The Big Picture

As you progress, the whole bird will start to speak to you. Gestalt, jizz, gist – these various terms for the overall impression projected by a species are common parlance among birders.

Interestingly, there is a regional component to the use of these terms: *jizz* is popular in Europe, *gist* is heard more often in the eastern United States, and *gestalt*, a term originally used in psychology, is heard (where else?) in California.

Just as you can identify friends or family by body language or the sound of their voices, the attentive observer soon picks up on the jizz of a bird and can recognize a familiar species by the subtlest clues without seeing any of the definitive field marks. This ability of highly experienced observers seems uncanny to the uninitiated. It's as if the seasoned birder has a sixth sense and can identify the bird before it jumps out of the

bush. In reality, experienced birders are so familiar with the possibilities, through a knowledge of the distribution and seasonality of many species, and their potential for occurring in a given habitat, that the slightest clue – a chip note or a flash of tail feathers – alerts them to the bird's presence.

Ease of identification is the result of familiarity. It won't take long, for example, to identify the mockingbird that wakes you up every morning at 4:30 with its

vocal imitation of screeching brakes. Or to recognize the four-note call and bouncing flight of the American goldfinches that are flushed from your bird feeder by the neighbor's cat day after day.

Lasting Impressions

Shape, movement, and behavior are the primary ingredients of jizz. The unique skeletal structure and ecological adaptations of each species determine how the bird moves, and this body language becomes familiar to the observant birder. Among shorebirds, for example, plovers are potbellied and short-billed, and have large eyes. They tend to search for their food visually and pick it off the surface of the shoreline. Long-legged waders such as yellowlegs and willets, also called tringids, are slender and tend to move with jerky motions. They may probe or pick their prey from shallow water. Small sandpipers, or calidrids, including least, semipalmated, and western sandpipers, tend to coalesce into large flocks and probe the sand and mud diligently for food. On close inspection, head and bill shape also contribute to a bird's overall jizz; each species has a characteristic profile, however subtle.

Many other species display habitual and diagnostic behaviors. Palm warblers wag their tails; American redstarts fan their tails; and spotted sandpipers bob their bodies up and down. American avocets, when foraging, swing their slender bills like scythes.

Birds change shape or hold uncharacteristic postures, especially when alarmed or cautious, and this might confuse the novice. Most shorebirds stretch their necks or turn their heads to the side when they perceive a raptor or an intruder in the vicinity; roosting shorebirds sometimes stand on one leg and tuck their bills beneath their scapular feathers. Killdeers may feign injury when the nest is threatened. Songbirds puff up their body feathers during territorial defense or when cold. Bitterns and long-eared owls elongate and freeze when they perceive a threat. But even these uncharacteristic postures are recognizable with experience.

Less species-specific behaviors give clues to broad family or generic associations. Flight patterns are used by birders to identify raptors by family: accipiters (sharp-shinned and Cooper's hawks) tend to flap and glide; buteos (red-tailed and broad-winged hawks) soar;

northern harriers fly low to flush their prey; most falcons fly with direct, deep, and rapid strokes. There are, of course, exceptions: the American kestrel, the smallest falcon, hovers on rapidly beating wings; the red-shouldered hawk, though a buteo, flaps and glides like an accipiter; the Swainson's hawk and the zone-tailed hawk mimic the turkey vulture's teetering flight.

Size can be deceptive. Backlighting tends to make objects seem larger. Dark objects seem smaller than light ones. A red-tailed hawk may appear much larger when alone than when roosting close to a

golden eagle. A raven may look much larger against the backdrop of a cloudless sky than when walking in a pasture amid a herd of holsteins. Despite these potential pitfalls, size, particularly the relative

size of species in flocks of mixed species, is a useful identification tool.

Tricks of Appearance

Fledgling naturalists may find it humorous when veteran birders tell them that certain

The semipalmated plover (opposite, left) is a small, stocky shorebird that forages along the shoreline. The buff-breasted sandpiper (opposite, center) is a medium-sized sandpiper that picks insects from fields. The willet (opposite, right), a much larger shorebird, often wades up to its belly in water.

Courting cedar waxwings (right) exchange berries, insects, and flower petals, foods that they also feed their young.

The male roadrunner (below) gives its courtship gift to the female after copulation.

Mating Displays

Most courtship, mating, and nesting behavior coincides with the lengthening days of the approaching summer equinox, when food is most plentiful for hungry nestlings. Insect-eating species such as swallows and flycatchers time their breeding to coincide with the larval hatch of aquatic insects. Species that are generally considered berry-eaters (frugivores), like thrushes and waxwings, may depend on insects to feed their nestlings as well.

Monogamy is the most common mating system, particularly for species whose young require intensive parental care. On the other hand, in habitats where resources are concentrated and abundant, many birds may be promiscuous. The most common form of promiscuity is polygyny, in which the male of the species mates with several females. These single moms incubate their eggs and raise their chicks unassisted by the male. This explains the excessive puffing and preening of male red-winged blackbirds or the incessant chattering of male marsh wrens in nutrient-rich freshwater marshes; these "wealthy" males expend all of their energy attracting females.

Ritualized courtship displays – some subtle, some extravagant – serve in pair bonding, mate selection, territorial advertisement, and sexual stimulation. In courtship feeding – a common display – the female begs for food, mimicking a chick's behavior by crouching, fluttering her wings, and issuing begging calls. Feeding behavior may precede copulation, as when waxwings exchange hawthorn berries; coincide with copulation, as happens with cuckoos; or follow it, as when the male roadrunner presents a lizard to his mate.

When the sexes differ in appearance – as red-winged blackbirds do – the male usually expends his efforts defending a territory, while the female, with her plainer plumage, attends to the nest. When both sexes are similar in appearance, the male and female share equally in mating activities. Male and female herons and egrets bow, stretch their necks, duel with their beaks, fluff their feathers, and preen in a ceremonial ritual that rivals a human wedding.

From Our House to Birdhaus

Compared with a mourning dove's haphazard platform of sticks resting precariously on a branch, a hummingbird's nest – woven with fine strands of animal hair, sheathed in lichen, mortared with spider webs, and lined with thistledown – seems a miniature Renaissance palace. The osprey's eyrie, as wide as a human's outstretched arms and perched upon a telephone pole, is conspicuous. The killdeer's scrape, a minor depression in sandy gravel, is easily overlooked. Cliff swallows build mud condominiums in densely packed colonies, and great gray owls find a hollow stump in a lonely lodgepole pine forest. In its astounding variety, avian architecture reflects the diversity of life strategies employed by birds.

The **Altamira oriole** (left), a year-round resident of the Lower Rio Grande Valley in Texas, builds a pouch made of woven plant fibers.

Wood duck chicks (below) leap to the ground or into the water when ready to leave their tree-hole nests.

Immature bald eagles (opposite) lack the white head, yellow bill, and white tail typical of adults. In some areas of North America, immature bald eagles may be mistaken for immature golden eagles.

The hummingbird requires camouflage from predators and insulation for its tiny eggs. The osprey, protected by its size and the inaccessibility of its site, chooses a view of open-water foraging grounds. The dove, a prodigious egg layer, can afford to treat its nest cavalierly. The owl, needing vast forest feeding habitat, cannot afford to share its property with competitors. Swallows find safety in numbers and forage cooperatively through insect-rich pockets of air.

Although most species are remarkably regimented in their nest building, some are equally variable. The limpkin, a marsh-dwelling wader, may build a floating raft, rest its nest on a cypress limb or in a hollow tree, or even use an abandoned osprey nest.

One of the main distinctions is between cavity nesters and open-cup nesters. Some cavity nesters, such as woodpeckers and nuthatches, excavate their own cavities; others, like tree swallows, wood ducks, saw-whet owls, and starlings, appropriate abandoned holes. Of those who construct nests from scratch, barn swallows, thrushes, and warblers make open cups, and cliff swallows, marsh wrens, and orioles construct closed ovenlike nests.

species can be recognized by their expression. But it's true. In a flock that contains the very similar herring and Thayer's gulls, you can distinguish between the fierce-looking faces of the herring gulls and the gentler expression of the Thayer's – an admittedly anthropocentric interpretation of the latter's rounder head. Although ruby-crowned kinglets and Hutton's vireos are quite similar, the kinglets have an innocent, almost childlike expression, perhaps resulting from the pattern of white around their eyes. The vireo, with a larger forehead and more distinct spectacles, appears more serious, almost studious.

Birds are among the most brilliantly colored vertebrates. While color may be a source of aesthetic pleasure, it is not always a reliable indication of a bird's identity. Color changes with age, feather wear, and season, and males and females of the same species may have very different coloration.

Adult birds tend to molt all or most of their feathers at least once a year, usually just after the breeding season. New plumage is brighter than worn plumage, so the intensity and crispness of coloration and pattern vary according to the season. Many species go through several plumages before adulthood, and these may change seasonally. Some of the larger gulls molt eight times before they achieve what is called "adult summer," or "fourth-summer," plumage. For species that molt seasonally, the winter, or basic, plumage may differ dramatically from the summer, or alternate, plumage. This transition from one plumage to another presents its own set of identification problems because the birds pass through intermediary plumages during the molt.

Sexual differences, called dimorphism, add to the confusion. The young males of many species of perching birds, such as purple finches and some of the wood warblers, resemble adult females, then change into brilliant plumage when they reach adulthood. Likewise, male waterfowl, such as cinnamon teal and mallards, may molt into femalelike plumages, known as eclipse, in autumn.

Expect the Expected

Most field guides provide maps showing the broad distribution of each species. Color coding on the maps indicates the seasons when the species is likely to be found in the different regions of its range. While birds can show up early or late, most species are fairly consistent in the timing of their movements. Therefore, it is highly unlikely to see a Swainson's thrush after October 15 or before April 15 in Northern California, or an eastern kingbird after mid-October in New England, or a Swainson's hawk anywhere in North America during the winter.

When you encounter a perplexing species, consult the maps in your field guide or the checklist for the area. Which species might be considered likely on that date? In what habitats might you encounter the various possibilities? Of the choices available, the species you're looking at is probably the one most likely to be there at that season.

With all the plumage variation offered by age, sex, molt, feather wear, and geographical variation, identifying the more than 900 species of North American birds can be intimidating. For the novice, the array of possibilities seems positively overwhelming, but after a while, the beginning birder sees it for what it really is – the source of a lifelong pursuit.

CHAPTER 4

Migration

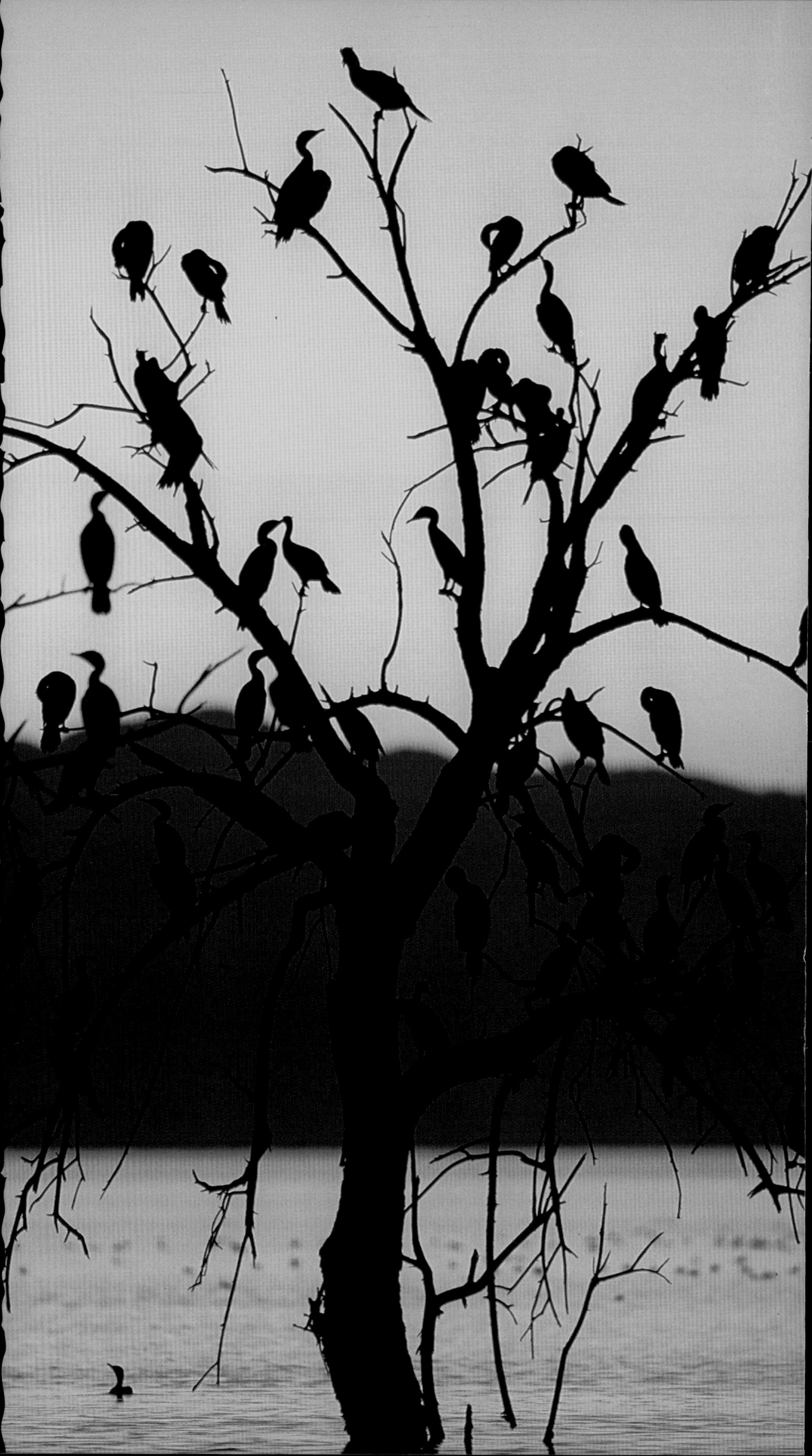

magine growing up in a village in the eastern Canadian forests. As a child you don't travel, always staying within a mile or so of home. Then, as an adolescent, you take a trip, an epoch journey south to a whole new world in the tropics. Imagine making this trip without parental guidance and without road maps. Envision, further, having no idea where to find food or supplies, or hostels where you can sleep safe and sound. Finally, imagine making this journey with no idea of precisely where your final destination may be and making it entirely at night. ◆ This journey would be difficult enough for humans, but picture a juvenile warbler making its first autumn migration south, needing to find safe habitats and sustenance to fuel its journey. Consider that a blackpoll warbler, weighing all of half an ounce, about as much as **The seasons that are the most** a ballpoint pen, flies 3,500 miles from the **challenging and perilous** northern temperate forests to the tropical **for birds are also the most** forests of South America – 2,000 miles of which **exciting for birders.** are over the open Atlantic – and you will realize that bird migration is one of the true miracles of the natural world. ◆ Migration is by far the most stressful and dangerous time of a bird's life cycle. Finding food can be difficult enough for a bird in its home range, but finding it in unfamiliar habitats during migration, all the while avoiding predators, can be a herculean task and a critical threat to the bird's survival. ◆ Migration is generally defined as seasonal movement between two areas in response to changing environmental conditions. Owing to their magnificent powers of flight, birds migrate farther and in greater numbers than any other land animals. Some migration is altitudinal, with birds coming down to lower and more

Double-crested cormorants that breed at northern latitudes winter in wetlands such as the Salton Sea in Southern California, as well as in coastal areas.

benign elevations in winter. But most avian migration is on a north-south axis, with mass movements away from northern climes in response to autumn's diminishing daylight, temperature, and food supply. In the spring, birds return north with an increase in these environmental factors.

Hemispheric Journeys

The origins and evolution of migratory behavior have long been debated. Some feel that bird migration had its beginnings in the Pleistocene, about one million years ago, and that the ice-age glaciers were what first pushed birds south. Through the selective pressures of evolution, those birds that moved survived. For some birds, only a short migration proved sufficient, while others developed into true world travelers.

The arctic tern, which nests along arctic rivers and migrates to antarctic waters in winter, travels more than 20,000 miles round-trip each year and is generally considered to be the migrant that travels the longest distances. Other birds come close. Peregrine falcons banded at arctic eyries have been recovered at Tierra del Fuego on the southernmost tip of South America. Swainson's hawks nesting in the Yukon spend the winter on the Argentine pampas. The buff-breasted sandpiper, another long-distance champion, nests in the high arctic and winters in the southern region of South America. Red knots, breeding on the tundra north of Hudson Bay, winter in Patagonia. On their return flight in spring, spurred by the nesting urge, knots are known to cover 4,000 miles nonstop from South America to Delaware Bay, where they

Accidentals, Vagrants, and Irruptives

Collectors dote on rarities – a one-of-a-kind antique or a long-forgotten stamp – and collectors of bird sightings are no exception. Finding an avian rarity is among the most exciting parts of birding. Though birds such as the nonmigratory California condor may be rare because of their minuscule population, "rarity" generally refers to a bird out of its customary range. A black-throated gray warbler, not known to migrate east of the Mississippi, always generates excitement when found in Massachusetts, as does a blue-winged warbler, an East Coast breeder, when it accidentally turns up in California.

Weather fronts and winds play a huge role in causing birds to wander from their normal migration paths. Hurricanes are legendary for transporting tropical species far to the north of their usual range. After a hurricane's passage, seabirds such as petrels and shearwaters may be found on lakes or reservoirs far inland. Simple navigational error is another major factor in vagrancy. A Townsend's solitaire migrating south out of central Alaska need be only 15 or 20 degrees off course to miss the Rocky Mountains, its normal wintering grounds, and end up on the New Jersey coast. Most of these birds are young and inexperienced, but adults can have their internal compasses go out of whack and turn into wrong-way migrants as well.

Some species are "irruptive," abandoning their normal home only when the food supply dwindles. Crossbills appear far south of their range when the cone crop is poor. And snowy owls, those magnificent denizens of the arctic tundra, have been known to stage an invasion of the Lower 48 when the lemming population crashes. The owls and other irruptives may come south only once or twice in a decade, and their numbers vary widely.

Snowy owls (above) sometimes range far south of their tundra habitat in search of food.

A researcher (opposite, top) examines a Wilson's warbler, a species that breeds in Alaska and winters in Mexico and Central America.

Red knots and ruddy turnstones (opposite, bottom) feed in Delaware Bay on their migration north.

The Arctic tern (below) travels more than 20,000 miles during its round-trip migration between the northern and southern hemispheres.

stop to feed at this major "staging area."

Since some long-distance migrants take two months to get from summer to winter quarters, and vice versa, they spend as long in migration each year as they do on their breeding or wintering grounds. Actual flight time may be far less, but birds need considerable time to rest and refuel en route. Migratory stopovers are crucial links in the chain that stretches from summer to winter homes. Some species feed so heavily that they double their body weight in preparation for the next

stage of their journey.

Whereas some species travel more or less solo, many birds form flocks during migration. Flocking helps ensure safe navigation and provides a certain amount of protection from predators. Geese also derive an aerodynamic advantage from their V formation, each bird, except the leader, flying in the slipstream of others. Broad-winged hawks travel in large flocks that spread out over the sky in a quest for thermals – rising columns of warmer air. When one bird finds a thermal, others quickly join it, gaining

valuable altitude on these unseen elevators. Altitude is then converted to miles as the hawks glide from the top of the thermal. For all birds, flocking assists individuals in finding food.

Navigation during

migration is a remarkable aspect of bird behavior. Diurnal migrants (those that fly during the day) orient themselves to the sun, but also use wind, topography, and landmarks to guide their flight. Nocturnal migrants, primarily songbirds, navigate using the stars and will compensate for the daily and seasonal movement of stars across the sky. Many birds, though, can migrate during cloudy or foggy nights, and it is now known that some songbird species can orient themselves to the Earth's magnetic fields.

Changes in the daylight hours stimulate the urge to migrate. Decreasing daylight triggers heavy feeding in autumn, and lengthening daylight triggers migratory restlessness in spring. Weather, specifically the passage of a front, is an "on" switch for migration. Cold fronts, with dropping temperatures and north or northwesterly tailwinds, spur heavy flights in fall, while the surging southerly winds of warm fronts promote north-bound migration in spring.

Opportunities for Birders

Few would dispute the notion that the migration seasons are the most exciting times of the birder's year. Spring and fall provide opportunities to see great numbers of birds and a wide variety of species, as well as the "rarities" that are such an integral part of the enjoyment of birding. During the migratory season, birds come to you, and you can study those that you don't normally see, species that may nest and winter thousands of miles away.

Often, because they are out of their native or normal habitats, and because they need to feed constantly to replenish their fat reserves, they are easily observed.

During migration, birds often concentrate in prime habitat. They tend to converge along "leading lines" such as mountain ridges, river valleys, lakeshores, and seacoasts, many of which are top birding sites. Raptors seek out mountain ridges where updrafts are prevalent. Hawk Mountain, Pennsylvania, is the most famous hawk-watch site, but the phenomenon occurs throughout the continent. Birds gather at lakeshore points such as Lake Superior near Duluth, Minnesota, and Lake Ontario near Braddock Bay, New York, because they prefer to avoid water crossings whenever possible.

Add a peninsula, and the concentrations are even greater. Sites such as Point Pelee, Ontario, and Whitefish Point, Minnesota, are famous for their spring bonanzas. At Cape May, New Jersey, prevailing northwesterly winds and peninsular topography create legendary gatherings of migrants in autumn as birds pause to rest and feed before crossing Delaware Bay on their way south. South Florida is the last stop for many southbound songbirds in the fall and the first stop for many spring migrants crossing the Gulf of Mexico. As such, Everglades National Park is of inestimable importance to migratory birds.

While the old "flyway theory" is now largely discounted (we now know that migration routes are much more varied and complex), some areas are far more crucial than others. For example, many spring migrant songbirds make their first landfall, exhausted and hungry, on the Texas coast after crossing the Gulf of Mexico from the Yucatán peninsula. Sites such as High Island, near Galveston, sometimes see spectacular "fall-outs" of migrants as birds drop into the first greenery they see. Imagine seeing 60 indigo buntings in one tree or a veritable blanket of summer and scarlet tanagers. Santa Ana National Wildlife Refuge in the Rio Grande Valley and nearby Bentsen-Rio Grande Valley State Park are well-known migrant traps in spring and fall. Here, you see an oasis effect, where birds pack into the only available habitat in an otherwise barren agricultural area.

Because migration is such a crucial time in a bird's life, these staging areas and stopover points are perhaps the most important habitats in North America and must be protected at all costs. At Cape May, for example, birds from all over the Northeast are compressed into less than a thousand acres. The need for conservation of such an area cannot be overstated.

The upside of such gatherings is that they create some of the greatest excitement in all of birding, and there will come a time when you will want to migrate to these legendary crossroads. For many species, you may see more individuals in a day or two than you would in a lifetime otherwise. Migration can create the most hectic birding you will ever experience, but also the most memorable.

Sandhill cranes (above) start arriving at Bosque del Apache National Wildlife Refuge in New Mexico in fall. Nearly 17,000 cranes winter at the refuge.

Flocks of American white pelicans (opposite) leave their Canadian nesting grounds for the U.S. Gulf Coast and both coasts of Mexico, where they spend the winter.

Red-winged blackbirds (below) winter in large flocks, a strategy that helps them find food and ensure protection from predators.

Chapter 5

Birding on the Road

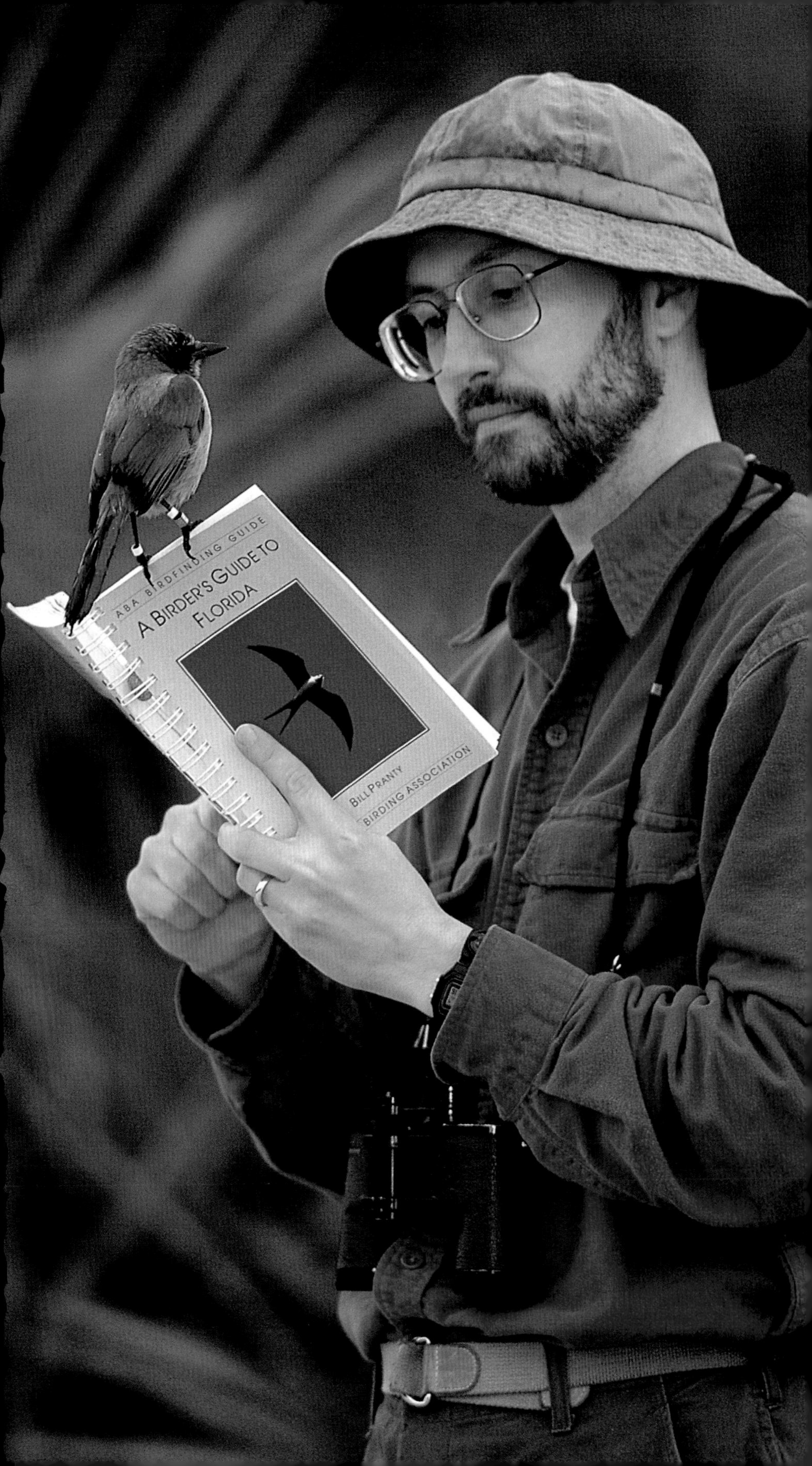

t happens to just about every birder. The first time you start seriously looking through a field guide covering all of North America, you're seduced. Drawn in, flipping pages with abandon, scanning the range maps, you realize how much there is to experience. Sure, local birding is great and provides wonderful opportunities to become familiar with birds close to home, but there are so many others to discover and enjoy. You fantasize about species you can never hope to see in your backyard. Once you start to travel, you'll be hooked. The entire world becomes your birding patch.   ◆   The logistics of planning a birding trip to a distant location can be overwhelming. Knowing the best places to visit and when to go, and especially the locations of the species you want to see, are just some of the pieces of the puzzle that need to be **As you plan a trip,** assembled to make your trip as enjoyable **consider attending a festival,** and successful as possible.   ◆   One good **joining a "bird-a-thon,"** place to start your planning is right at home. If **or going on a tour.** you join a National Audubon Society chapter or independent birding club, you're likely to meet well-traveled members who can provide a wealth of information and advice. Just listening to them talk about where they've been and what they saw is enough to make you want to hit the road.   ◆   As you plan your trip, you will want to contact the American Birding Association (see Resource Directory). The hefty catalog published by this national organization, available to both members and nonmembers, carries innumerable bird-finding guides rarely, if ever, found on the shelves of ordinary bookstores. Covering many of the best birding areas in North America, the guides give precise directions for various routes and trails,

Regional guidebooks called "bird finders" give directions to birding hot spots. This Florida scrub-jay, a threatened species found only in Florida's oak scrub, doesn't hesitate to approach a birder.

often accompanied by detailed maps, which make birding on your own easy and highly productive.

There are bird finders for almost every state in the country, as well as those that specialize in particular locales, including parts of Canada and Mexico. Is Alaska in summer your destination? There's a bird finder for top spots in the state and also a guide devoted to the Kenai Peninsula. Or will you be doing some birding along the Atlantic Coast in fall? Every state on the East Coast from Maine to Florida has a bird-finding guide that will help you plot an itinerary.

If you've chatted with other birders or skimmed through birding magazines, you've probably heard of something called the rare bird alert (RBA). Each state in the United States and each province in Canada has a telephone number that anyone can call to hear a recording of unusual avian sightings. Some states and provinces also have local bird alerts. If you called an RBA on the West Coast in the spring of 1998, for instance, you may have heard reports of the bristle-thighed curlews that surprised even seasoned birders by stopping in Northern California, Oregon, and Washington on their

way south from Alaska, rather than migrating across the Pacific Ocean. If you have Internet access, it's easy to find the RBA that applies to the areas you'll be birding. Have the appropriate numbers handy so you can call them when you're on the road.

Field Trips and Festivals

Chances are that your birding destination will be a national wildlife refuge, national or state park, or other sanctuary. Most of them sponsor free bird walks or field trips, led by park staff or refuge naturalists, which you can usually join without first making reservations.

Nonprofit natural-history associations affiliated with national parks offer their own schedule of field trips that often include birding. The associations usually charge a modest fee, and it is best to reserve a place before you arrive for your visit.

Another way to enhance your experience is to plan your trip around one of the ever-increasing number of birding festivals. Chambers of commerce, among other organizations, have discovered that birding is the fastest-growing recreational activity in the United States. Something like 60 million Americans enjoy feeding and watching birds, and the overall economic impact of birding is estimated at around $25 billion per year. As a result, birding festivals have grown from 12 in 1993 to about 140 in 1999. You can now find a festival celebrating everything from hummingbirds to vultures and godwits to eagles in every corner of North America. The profits from these festivals are generally used for a conservation project such as acquiring land for habitat protection, protecting an endangered species, or building a nature trail.

A festival can be a one-day affair or it can run to a week's worth of field trips, lectures, demonstrations, and slide shows. Local experts as well as nationally known birding celebrities serve as speakers and tour guides. Many festivals are held when birding in the area is at a seasonal peak. The Salton Sea International Bird Festival occurs in mid-February, when visitors can find nearly 100 species in a day spent birding around this inland sea in Southern California. Virginia's Chincoteague National Wildlife Refuge sponsors a week of bird walks and other programs in mid-October, during the fall migration of songbirds, shorebirds, and raptors. The National Fish and Wildlife Foundation (see Resource Directory) publishes a

schedule of events organized by state and province.

If you're traveling in late December, you may want to join a Christmas Bird Count. At the end of each year, the National Audubon Society organizes on the order of 2,000 Christmas counts to census bird populations throughout North America. Not only do these counts provide a wealth of scientific

Fall is a prime time to visit Cape May, New Jersey (above), where the Cape May Bird Observatory sponsors a hawk watch, workshops, and field trips.

Birders headed for Alaska's Kenai Peninsula will want to schedule a pelagic trip to view nesting seabirds on the Chiswell Islands (opposite).

Birding festivals like this one in Minnesota (left) offer art displays, equipment demonstrations, and field trips.

To List or Not To List

Keeping a "life list," a record of every species observed, is analogous to other hobbies that involve collecting. The difference is that birders don't collect avian specimens; they collect images in their minds. Listing expresses numerically what they've seen and turns record keeping into a game among fellow birders. Who has viewed the most species in one year? In their backyard? In their state?

Beyond simply listing species, recording field characters, behavior, vocalizations, and habitat, along with location and time of year, is an excellent way to hone your birding skills. Reviewing your observations helps prepare you for returning to the same place or finding the same species in another area of its geographic range.

Listing can have a downside, however, particularly when each species becomes just a check mark in a field guide. Once a bird is seen and noted, there's no reason to linger and appreciate it. The most famous birder of the 20th century, Roger Tory Peterson, was a lister. Yet it was not the only way he experienced birds, and it never diminished his passion for observing them. He knew that enjoying birds was the goal, and listing simply added to the rewards.

Some birders are habitual listers (left) who enjoy recording species seen for the first time, birds observed on a trip, and even birds spotted in their backyard.

Recording birds for scientific purposes (opposite, top) or joining a count to raise conservation funds can be a rewarding part of a trip.

Educational events such as hawk-banding demonstrations (opposite, bottom) are held at top birding sites.

and financially successful, attracting teams of birders from around the world.

Joining a Tour

If you prefer to bird with a group on a trip that is entirely organized by someone else, you have a multitude of choices with a range of costs. Local clubs, National Audubon Society chapters, and seed/feeder stores sometimes sponsor long-distance trips, in addition to their local offerings. Usually there are one or more experienced guides who organize the trip; participants pay their own expenses and share in the group costs. It's a wonderful way to make long-lasting friendships with other birders in your community.

Birding tour companies offer the opportunity to observe what seems like every species in the world. A few companies have been around for many years and have strong followings and reputations. Many more have started up over the past decade as the birding boom has accelerated. Most tours

data, they are also great fun and frequently end with a group dinner to tally the numbers of species and individuals seen. There's bound to be a count at or near your destination, and another pair of eyes is always welcome. You don't have to be an expert, and you won't be on your own; the CBC compilers divide their troops into teams captained by experienced local birders.

Nor do you have to be an ace to participate in many other bird counts held during the year, usually during spring migration.

Among the most popular are the bird-a-thons that serve as fund-raisers for conservation, education, and other worthy causes. Teams of birders set out to identify as many birds as possible in a given area over, say, a 24-hour period. Sponsors pledge a lump sum or a certain amount of money – from a dime to a few dollars or more – for each species seen. The World Series of Birding, organized by the Cape May Bird Observatory in New Jersey, and the bird-a-thon held by the Point Reyes Bird Observatory in California have become very competitive are excellent, and the guides are knowledgeable about the birds and proficient at finding them. If you don't want to worry about anything except seeing birds, then commercial tours are for you. Length of tours, group sizes, prices, and services vary widely.

Before selecting a company or a tour, obtain references from other birders who have experience with the company and have traveled with the tour guides; personality can make all the difference between a wonderful experience and an unpleasant one. For international birding in many areas, a commercial tour is highly recommended, since in-country logistics can be very difficult to arrange in advance, and language,

currency, and local travel often present insurmountable obstacles.

Birding on the road is a never-ending voyage of discovery, delight, and enlightenment. The bugle of a whooping crane, the hoarse hooting of a

flammulated owl, the roar of thousands of snow geese erupting in flight, the low cawing of an elegant trogon, or the twitter of a violet-crowned hummingbird hovering over a cardinal flower will forever enrich your life.

Birding Destinations

*With superlative birding found across the continent, your
greatest challenge is deciding where to go. You can
observe waves of migrating raptors, waterfowl, and
songbirds, thrill to close-up views of seabird islands,
or marvel at iridescent hummingbirds flashing in the light.*

Bonaventure Island

Quebec

Talk about an assault on the senses. You can't possibly imagine the noise, the smell, the chaos of a jam-packed seabird colony until you've experienced one firsthand – until you've stood on the brim of a dizzying cliff and looked down on thousands of birds streaming to and from their fishing grounds. Their mates, tending eggs or chicks on eroded ledges, converse in a gargling roar, and the salt-laced wind is ripe with the odors of death, defecation, and regurgitated fish.   ◆   Along Canada's Atlantic Coast, seabirds such as gannets, murres, puffins, razorbills, and kittiwakes typically breed on the most inaccessible slabs of rock where distance, smashing waves, and nonexistent beaches discourage a boat landing even by intrepid researchers, let alone casual observers. Thus **Bonaventure Island** in the Gulf of St. Lawrence, within view and easy reach of the village of Percé at the tip of Quebec's **Gaspé Peninsula**,

Settling on cliffs and tucking into crevices, seabirds take over an island in the Gulf of St. Lawrence.

has become a mecca for ecotourists and serious birders who want a close-up look at North America's largest gannet colony in all its social complexity.   ◆   From the waterfront at **Percé**, where visitors board ferries for a trip around the island or a direct two-mile crossing, Bonaventure resembles an immense whale that has surfaced to breathe. It's a small, roughly circular island of 1,800 acres covered with spruce-fir forest and abandoned fields well on their way to being reclaimed by nature. Bonaventure's seabird cliffs have been a federal migratory bird sanctuary since 1919, and in 1971 the Quebec government expropriated the entire island, creating a conservation park that also includes one of eastern

Northern gannets take up to four years to attain their creamy white adult plumage. It is believed that they mate for life.

Previous pages: A green heron stalks its prey in the Everglades.

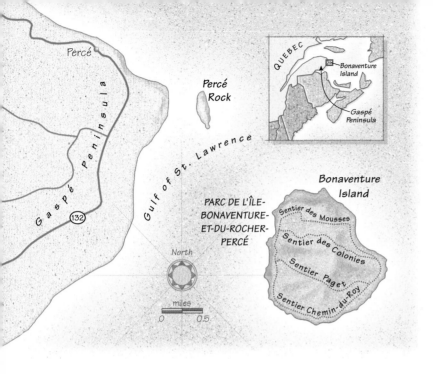

Percé

Percé
Rock

Gaspé Peninsula

Gulf of St. Lawrence

QUEBEC

Bonaventure
Island

Gaspé
Peninsula

132

PARC DE L'ÎLE-
BONAVENTURE-
ET-DU-ROCHER-
PERCÉ

Bonaventure
Island

Sentier des Mousses

Sentier des Colonies

Sentier Paget

Sentier Chemin-du-Roy

North

miles
0   0.5

Canada's most famous landmarks, the
monolithic **Percé Rock** with its 80-foot-high,
wave-cut archway.

Human and Avian Settlements

At an interpretive center on a wooded bluff
above Percé, visitors learn that Bonaventure
brims with history as well as seabirds.
The great Gallic navigator Jacques Cartier,
who discovered the St. Lawrence River and
claimed the Gaspé Peninsula for France,
anchored near the island on Saint
Bonaventure's Day in 1534, which explains
the island's name. News of teeming cod
stocks on nearby shoals lured French

fishermen, who used
Bonaventure as a
seasonal base.

A permanent French
settlement was established
in 1672, only to be aban-
doned a few years later
when English privateers
drove the settlers from
the island. But after the
French bastions of Quebec
and Montreal fell to the
British in 1759–60 and
Paris ceded its Canadian
possessions, colonists
arrived from Ireland and
the Channel Islands to
build a thriving cod
export industry. By 1831,
Bonaventure was home
to 35 families, whose number dwindled in
the next century as the fish stocks were
depleted. The last year-round residents left
in 1963, although a few weathered houses
and a rustic inn continued to be used in
summer until their owners were evicted.

A checklist of the birds of **Parc de l'Île-
Bonaventure-et-du-Rocher-Percé** flags 81
species, including 65 passerines, that nest
or are presumed to breed on the island.
Also on the list are a number of northern-
forest inhabitants like the boreal chickadee,
red-breasted nuthatch, ruby-crowned kinglet,
hermit thrush, bay-breasted warbler, white-
winged crossbill, and pine grosbeak, usually
encountered only on migration or during
uncommon winter irruptions. But the action
birders want to see first is concentrated on
ragged cliffs that rise more than 250 feet on
Bonaventure's southeast side. That's where
an estimated 27,000 pairs of northern gannets
breed, along with like-sized colonies of
common murres and black-legged kittiwakes,
a small contingent of razorbills, and maybe
a dozen pairs of Atlantic puffins.

Islands of Birds

The murres and kittiwakes cling to narrow,
wind-worn ledges on the crumbly
Bonaventure cliff face. But the gannets

assemble on wider, sloping terraces as well as the top of the island. There, movable rail fences separate human visitors from acres of dazzling white, goose-size birds whose nests – pedestals of seaweed, grass, and flotsam – are spaced an average of 32 inches apart. That's just beyond reach of a temperamental neighbor's sharp bill and ensures that every suitable circle of ground gets used by a breeding pair.

Your first and most spectacular view of the gannetry will probably be from the sea. A ticket bought on the village pier guarantees a trip to and from Bonaventure and a swing by Percé Rock, usually on a converted fishing boat with a guide whose seabird spiel in French and English is more or less accurate. To see the cliffs in favorable morning light and make the most of your time on the island, take the earliest possible boat and plan to stay until the last departure at five o'clock.

Percé Rock itself is awesome. A wedge of limestone nearly 300 feet high and 1,500 feet long, the massive formation, which can be reached on foot at low tide, was once attached to the shore and was pierced by two archways in Cartier's time. Double-crested cormorants, great cormorants, razorbills, and herring gulls nest on its flat, turf-covered top. But Percé Rock doesn't prepare you for the grand theater when the boat rounds Bonaventure's sharp eastern point and the gannetry – looming 25 stories high – comes into view. The birds mass together by the hundreds and thousands along immense slashes in the red sandstone, protesting the intrusion with an unabated chorus of primordial cries or by flinging themselves into the air in a clumsy, careless rush that can knock eggs and chicks over the edge.

Once airborne, however, a gannet, with its six-foot wingspan and streamlined body tapered at both ends, is the archetype of avian grace. The birds ride the sea wind like cross-shaped kites, soaring effortlessly, gliding past their nesting ledges, plunging into the ocean from a height of 30 to 100 feet to seize a herring, capelin, or mackerel. "Just before entry," writes British seabird authority Bryan Nelson, "the wings are extended backward, close to the body, wing tips beyond the tail, and the bird penetrates the water like an arrow… A gannet may be traveling at more than 60 miles per hour when it hits the water, often with a leaden thump that resounds for

Herring gulls (above) nesting on Percé Rock are opportunists that feed on dead gannet chicks.

Small gulls called black-legged kittiwakes (opposite) build their cliff-side nests of seaweed, grass, and mud.

Percé Rock (below), reached on foot at low tide, is embedded with fossils nearly 400 million years old.

hundreds of yards on a calm day and speaks volumes for the efficacy of the bird's cushioning of air-sacs."

View from the Top

Your captain will then head for the Bonaventure quay and the park's service area. Four connected trails ranging from one-and-a-half to three miles lead to the gannetry. The shortest is **Sentier des Colonies**, and before the island was depopulated by the government, visitors had the option of a one-hour hike to the cliff top or a ride in the innkeeper's horse-drawn wagon. Now it's shanks' mare only, but the trail is wide

and well maintained with places to catch your breath during a moderate climb from the shore to a high point of 440 feet before the path gently descends to the colony. Do leave time for a leisurely return to experience the botanical riches of the boreal forest and perhaps pick up a life bird or two. In particular, listen for the sweet, bubbling trill of the elusive Lincoln's sparrow in alder thickets.

You'll hear and perhaps smell the gannetry before the trail breaks out of the woods onto a breathtaking view: restless ranks of birds that spill over the precipice onto shelves that tilt precariously toward the sea. Warning: The effect of looking *down* on gannets hurtling into space, circling, diving, is hypnotic. At some point, you may think about spreading your arms and joining them. Perish the thought. A safer idea is to follow the trail that leads along the edge of the colony to an observation tower, paying special attention to an extraordinary series of displays that cement the gannet pair bond during the long breeding season, which begins with the birds' arrival on the cliffs in April and ends with the fledging

Birds in Black

The northern gannet is the superstar among Bonaventure cliff dwellers, but sharp eyes may spot four of the six species of auks that breed in the North Atlantic: common murres, black guillemots, razorbills, and Atlantic puffins. The murres are, well, common – though their numbers in the Gulf of St. Lawrence are nothing like the half-million pairs that occupy Funk Island off the Newfoundland coast. A few hundred pairs of razorbills burrow into Bonaventure's turfed ledges, guillemots are scattered along the rocky shore, and the comical-looking puffins are too few to be considered a colony.

The black-draped auks are the northern hemisphere's answer to the Antarctic's penguins. The two groups are unrelated but have developed similar lifestyles at opposite ends of the oceans – a textbook example of what scientists call convergent evolution. One big difference: Penguins lost the power of aerial flight. So did the great auk, an evolutionary misstep that led to its extinction by 1844. Both auks and penguins, however, are powerful underwater swimmers, using their stubby wings for propulsion. Murres, for example, can dive as deep as 600 feet to forage on schools of small fish.

For centuries, the isolation of their secret islands protected auks (and gannets) from such land predators as foxes. But seabirds, especially the abundant murres and puffins, were a handy source of food, bait, and lamp oil for fishermen who ravaged bird colonies from Maine to Labrador. By the late 1880s, there were precious few survivors, and many local populations were extinct. Populations of murres and puffins began to recover in the 1950s, thanks largely to government protection. Still, there are some former seabird outposts where the silence on summer days is unbearably sad.

of the last young in October.

Not all of the nests succeed, of course. Unhatched eggs, dead chicks, and bodies broken in crash landings bake in the sun despite cleanup efforts by the herring gull patrol. Down the way, a gannet is impaled on a high branch of a skeletal spruce, the victim of a gust of wind at the worst possible moment. Death is routine at any seabird colony. But in a healthy gannetry, upward of 80 percent of the pairs will fledge young.

For a decade, beginning around 1966, the Bonaventure gannet colony was in trouble. Productivity of fledged young dropped below 40 percent, and a breeding population that had grown steadily for more than a century took a nosedive. Scientists found high levels of DDT residue and other toxic chemicals in gannet eggs, adults, and their fish prey, and they documented the same problem with eggshell thinning that decimated numbers of bald eagles, peregrine falcons, and other top-of-the-food-chain birds before use of the poisons was strictly controlled.

The waters of the Gulf of St. Lawrence are cleaner today. And according to David Nettleship, the Canadian Wildlife Service's seabird authority, there is a surplus of food for seabirds because overfishing has depleted the top predatory fish. The Bonaventure gannet population, as a result, has reached record-high numbers and shows no sign of leveling off. "There's plenty of room for expansion," Nettleship adds, which explains those odd cliff-top fences. This island belongs not to birders but to the birds.

TRAVEL TIPS

DETAILS

When to Go

May to June is the best time to see nesting seabirds on Bonaventure Island. Parc de l'Île-Bonaventure-et-du-Rocher-Percé, including both Bonaventure Island and Percé Rock, is reached by boat from May through mid-October. Spring temperatures are in the 60s and 70s during the day and the 50s at night. Expect brief periods of rain in May and June.

How to Get There

Commercial airlines serve Montreal, 560 miles from Percé, and Quebec City, 420 miles away. Smaller airlines fly to Bonaventure, 120 miles from Percé, and to Gaspé, 40 miles away. VIA Rail Canada travels to Percé three times a week; call 800-361-5390 for information.

Getting Around

Rental cars are available at all airports.

Handicapped Access

Boat tours around Percé Rock and Bonaventure Island, including disembarkation at Bonaventure Island, are accessible. The park's Interpretation Center is also accessible.

INFORMATION

Parc de l'Île-Bonaventure-et-du-Rocher-Percé

4 rue du Quai, Percé, PQ G0C 2L0, Canada; tel: 418-782-2240.

Association touristique de la Gaspésie

357 Route de la Mer, Sainte-Flavie, PQ G0J 2L0, Canada; tel: 800-463-0323 or 418-775-2223.

Percé Tourism Bureau

142 Highway 132 Ouest, P.O. Box 99, Percé, PQ G0C 2L0, Canada; tel: 418-782-5448; www.gaspesie.qc.ca/perce.

Rare Bird Alert

Eastern Quebec (in French); tel: 418-660-9089. Montreal (in English); tel: 514-989-5076.

Tourisme Quebec

P.O. Box 979, Montreal, PQ H3C 2W3, Canada; tel: 800-363-7777 or 514-873-2015.

CAMPING

Forillon National Park

122 De Gaspé Boulevard, Gaspé, PQ G4X 1A9, Canada; tel: 418-368-5505.

Sixty miles from Percé, at the northeastern tip of the Gaspé Peninsula, the park has some 360 campsites, a group campground, and three wilderness campsites. Half of the sites are available on a first-come, first-served basis. The remaining sites can be reserved by mail. Reservations are also accepted by phone from mid-May to mid-August; call 418-368-6050.

Reserve Faunique de Port-Daniel

P.O. Box 38, Port-Daniel, PQ G0C 2N0, Canada; tel: 418-396-2789.

This wildlife preserve, about 50 miles southwest of Percé, has 38 campsites available on a first-come, first-served basis.

LODGING

Chalets La Plage

31 Rue Mont-Joli, Percé, PQ G0C 2L0, Canada; tel: 418-782-2311.

Six cottages are available, each with a private bath and kitchen. $

Hotel la Normandie

P.O. Box 129, Percé, PQ G0C 2L0, Canada; tel: 418-782-2112.

This hotel has 45 rooms with panoramic views of Bonaventure Island and Percé Rock. A garden, sauna, and restaurant (open for breakfast and dinner) are on the premises. $$–$$$

L'Auberge a Percé Lieu dit au Pirate

P.O. Box 10, Percé, PQ G0C 2L0, Canada; tel: 418-782-5055.

This bed-and-breakfast is part of an 18th-century house on Percé's waterfront. Five guest rooms and a restaurant are available. $$–$$$

Le Pic de l'Aurore

P.O. Box 339, Percé, PQ G0C 2L0, Canada; tel: 418-782-2166 or 800-463-4212.

Perched on a hill overlooking the sea, Le Pic de l'Aurore has 33 hotel rooms, nine with kitchens. Rustic cabins with fireplaces are also available. $$–$$$

Motel Bellevue

P.O. Box 171, Percé, PQ G0C 2L0, Canada; tel: 418-782-2182.

The motel's 14 rooms have views of Bonaventure Island and Percé Rock. $$

Motel le Mirage

Box 420, Percé, PQ G0C 2L0, Canada; tel: 418-782-5151.

Views of Bonaventure Island are available from the balconies and terraces of this motel's 60 rooms, many of which have refrigerators. Price includes breakfast. A swimming pool is on the premises. $$–$$$

Pavillon Côte Surprise

P.O. Box 339, Percé, PQ G0C 2L0, Canada; tel: 800-463-4212 or 418-782-2166.

This two-story hotel has 36 rooms with refrigerators. A restaurant is on the premises. $$

Pavillon Village

P.O. Box 339, Percé, PQ G0C 2L0, Canada; tel: 800-463-4212 or 418-782-2166.

Many of Pavillon Village's 90 rooms have balconies with seaside views. Some rooms have kitchenettes. $$

Rainbow Cottages

509 Route 132 Ouest, Percé, Québec PQ G0C 2L0, Canada; tel: 418-782-2254.

Guests stay in six cottages, with private baths and kitchens. $$

TOURS AND OUTFITTERS

Ecomertours Nord-Sud

606 des Ardennes, Rimouski, PQ G5L 3M3, Canada; tel: 888-724-8687 or 418-724-6227.

Multiday boat tours depart from Rimouski on the St. Lawrence River. Passengers visit a number of excellent birding spots, including Anticosti Island, Bonaventure Island, and Percé Rock. Additional tours stop at Forillon and other national parks.

Les Bateliers de Percé

162 Route 132 Est, Percé, PQ G0C 2L0, Canada; tel: 418-782-2974.

Boats depart daily for trips to the seabird colonies on Bonaventure Island. Available from May 15 to October 15.

Les Croisieres Duval

155 Place du Quai, Percé, PQ G0C 2L0, Canada; tel: 418-782-5355.

The operation, open from June 1 to October 25, runs two boats from Percé to Bonaventure Island.

MUSEUMS

Interpretation Center

Parc de l'Île-Bonaventure-et-du-Rocher-Percé, Rang de l'Irelande, Percé, PQ G0C 2L0, Canada; tel: 418-782-2721.

Exhibits cover the birds and mammals of the Gulf of St. Lawrence. A film examines the gannets that colonize offshore islands.

Excursions

Cape Breton Highlands National Park

Ingonish Beach, Nova Scotia B0C 1L0, Canada; tel: 902-285-2691 or 902-285-2270.

Stretching across the northern end of Cape Breton Island in Nova Scotia, this 235,000-acre park looks west onto the Gulf of St. Lawrence and east onto the Atlantic Ocean. Birders see black guillemots, dovekies, razorbills, northern gannets, and black-legged kittiwakes. Notable land birds include blackpoll warblers, Bicknell's thrushes, fox sparrows, and various birds of prey – peregrine falcons, northern hawk owls, boreal owls, and a large population of bald eagles. Numerous hiking trails wind through the park.

Forillon National Park

122 de Gaspé Boulevard, Gaspé, Québec PQ G4X 1A9, Canada; tel: 418-368-5505.

The Appalachian Mountains end at this national park, where Cap Gaspé juts into the Gulf of St. Lawrence. Boats leave the mainland to view cliff-side colonies of nesting common murres, double-crested cormorants, razorbills, black-legged kittiwakes, and herring and greater black-backed gulls. Harlequin ducks may also be seen, especially in spring. Birding in the park's woodlands, open fields, and salt marshes is equally rewarding, and whales can be spotted offshore.

Fundy National Park

P.O. Box 40, Alma, New Brunswick E0A 1B0, Canada; tel: 506-887-6000.

The unequaled tide at the Bay of Fundy's head can reach nearly 70 feet. The surge ebbs to reveal an expanse of mudflat, a crustacean banquet for sandpipers and other shorebirds, especially during migration. The park's dense forest is laced with streams and punctuated by waterfalls and bogs. The combination of hardwoods and conifers attracts boreal species commonly seen farther north, as well as numerous eastern warblers. Peregrine falcons, reintroduced nearly 20 years ago, breed in the park.

Acadia
National Park
Maine

CHAPTER **7**

As the setting sun threw a diffused glow of orange and pink into the western sky, two birders watched the wavelets of **Pretty Marsh Harbor** shatter the early-spring sunset into thousands of illuminated facets. Perhaps this is the way a dragonfly, with its compound eye, might experience the scene, one of the birders mused. Venus, well above the horizon, was gaining strength in the cobalt-blue sky. Then the pair heard the sound of northern music as a common loon yodeled far in the distance, toward the junction of bay and ocean. As small skeins of oldsquaw flew past the spruce-studded peninsula on the west side of the harbor, the birders could make out a lone black guillemot surfacing in the inky water formed by the shadow of the trees. Another day of birding **Acadia National Park** had drawn to a close. ◆ Situated for the most part on Mount Desert Island, itself snuggled into a protective pocket of Maine's rocky coastline, Acadia National Park is a stunningly beautiful place.

Mountaintop vistas and coastal overlooks yield close-up views of 325 species, from shorebirds and seabirds to raptors and warblers.

There are cool conifer forests to stroll through and low mountain peaks that afford breathtaking views of the island. Pink granite ledges along the coast form tidal pools with a bounty of marine life. Numerous lakes, ponds, and streams provide visual contrast to the park's woodlands. And there's **Somes Sound**, the only fjord in eastern North America, which nearly splits the island in half. ◆ Then there are the birds. Some 325 species have been found on Mount Desert Island or in the surrounding waters, and about 150 species, including 21 warblers, nest on the island. The diverse habitats and wide variety of species make the park a prime

Common loons seek out secluded nest sites along the shores of lakes and ponds. Their unmistakable calls, often described as yodels, are haunting.

and off-limits to birders without special permission. A thousand acres of the park, well worth a birder's attention, lie off the main island, at Schoodic Peninsula and several small islands, including Isle au Haut. A good starting point for birding the park is one of the three visitor centers. The nature center, on the one-way loop road that circles Acadia's eastern half, has exhibits of the park's flora and fauna. You can also learn about recent sightings of rare or interesting birds and obtain a bird checklist.

While at the nature center, be sure to explore **Sieur de Monts Spring**, a small spring surrounded by deciduous forest. Songbirds forage in the tree canopy and shrub layer and along the forest floor in spring migration, and defend their territories during the nesting season. Depending on the time of year, watch for rose-breasted grosbeaks, scarlet tanagers, yellow-billed and black-billed cuckoos, black-and-white warblers, ovenbirds, American redstarts, and red-eyed vireos. Veeries and wood thrush both breed here. The redstart, the most animated of the group, is a joy to watch as it flits about, garbed in the colors of Halloween, snaring aerial insects in a fashion more typical of flycatchers. Songbirds are also attracted to the **Wild Gardens of Acadia**, adjacent to the spring. The gardens, maintained by the Bar Harbor Garden Club, reflect the park's major natural habitats, with displays of representative trees and shrubs all handily labeled.

Cadillac Mountain, rising to an elevation of 1,530 feet, is the dominant feature of the island and on clear days offers outstanding

birding destination all year long: in spring and summer for songbirds, in fall for raptors and migratory songbirds, and in winter for waterfowl, winter finches such as evening and pine grosbeaks, and murres and other alcids.

From Warblers to Hawks

To many, Acadia National Park is synonomous with Mount Desert Island. In actuality, about 50 percent of the island, mostly in the western section, is in private ownership

A female scarlet tanager (right) builds a saucer-shaped nest from grasses, weeds, and twigs after being courted by a male.

Penobscot Mountain (opposite) rises above Long Pond, where birders can spot waterfowl and wading birds.

Red-tailed hawks (below, upper) are one of the common species tallied during the park's hawk watch.

Pileated woodpeckers (below, lower), the largest North American woodpeckers, rival the size of an American crow.

panoramic views. Although it is often too windy for much bird life, autumn raptor migration is a welcome exception. A highly popular hawk watch, initiated in 1995, has counted 2,500 to 3,500 hawks each season. From the **North Ridge Trail**, you are treated to close-up views of the birds as they pass by the peak. All three accipiters – Cooper's and sharp-shinned hawks and northern goshawks – and broad-winged and red-tailed hawks, American kestrels, merlins, peregrine falcons, ospreys, and bald eagles stream past the summit, buffeted this way and that by the winds deflected up the mountain's slope. Not all the peregrines are migratory. Two pairs breed on the island. They typically lay eggs in late April, the chicks hatch in late May, and the young birds are flying by July. One pair prefers the east face of **Champlain Mountain**, the island's easternmost peak. The other favors the cliffs overlooking **Jordan Pond**.

Bog Life

Birders head to the **Wonderland Trail** and **Ship Harbor Nature Trail**, in close proximity to each other in the southwestern corner of the island near Bass Harbor, to see migratory and nesting warblers – including the heavenly blackburnian and black-throated green –

as well as red-breasted nuthatches, and olive-sided and yellow-bellied flycatchers. Both trails offer encounters with the absurdly tame spruce grouse, also known by the derogatory alternate name of "fool hen." From late winter through early spring, American woodcocks engage in mating displays in the shrubby forests surrounding the Ship Harbor Trail parking lot. Beginning at twilight, the male struts on territory and emits his *peent*ing call. He then lifts off, ascending in spiral flight, continuing to *peent* as he rises. At the apex of his flight, he sings his bubbly song and comets to earth with a delightful twittering sound from the air rushing through three stiff primary wing feathers. Once earthbound, he starts his strutting anew.

Across from these trails is the **Big Heath**, a bog that is one of the most ecologically important areas in the park.

Not quite land or water, quaking bog environments are flush with life. Wetlands-loving shrubs like leatherleaf and sheep laurel grow out of a lush, spongy blanket of sphagnum moss. So, too, does black spruce, the common tree here. During early summer, you can find rare plants indigenous to northern bogs: calapogon and arethusa orchids, and carnivorous pitcher plants and sundews, which consume a variety of insects. Palm warblers, yellow-bellied flycatchers, winter wrens, and furtive Lincoln's sparrows nest in the bog, drawn to the abundant insect life and the added protection from predators that the soggy environment provides. When birding the area, stay on the trails, though narrow, to avoid damaging the extremely fragile vegetation.

View from the Summit

The 2,000-acre **Schoodic Peninsula**, about an hour east of the island, is the only part of Acadia National Park attached to the mainland. The gorgeous scenery and significantly reduced crowds make it a worthwhile destination, birds or no birds. Fortunately, birds abound, and a stroll along the rocky coast or a hike to the top of Schoodic Head can be highly productive.

As you cross **Mosquito Harbor**, scan the coastal waters for winter waterfowl such as bufflehead, American goldeneye (be ever vigilant for the coveted Barrow's goldeneye, which turns up once in a while), and the ubiquitous common eider, a large black-and-white duck with an elegantly sloping forehead. Common and red-throated loons are regular sights.

A little more than two miles after entering the park, you will come upon a gated gravel road leading to a parking area just shy of the summit of **Schoodic Head**, a modest 440 feet above sea level. A trail leads to the top, then descends through the **Anvil** to the paved perimeter road. During your hike, watch for red and white-winged crossbills singing from the tops of the spruce trees. Spruce grouse feed on the spruce buds or can be seen working their way through the

forest understory. Pileated and black-backed wood-peckers attack the dead and dying trees, and bore-al chickadees dart about in search of insects. During the nesting season, look for warblers – bay-breasted, blackburn-ian, blackpoll, yellow-rumped, black-throat-ed green, black-throated blue, Cape May, Tennessee – searching the needle-filled branches for caterpillars.

As you continue around the one-way loop road and gain the eastern side of the peninsula, stop at a nondescript pulloff, marked with a sign that states "Do not remove rocks," providing access to a cobble-filled beach. From this vantage point, **Rolling Island**, a small, forested island of several acres, is in front of you, several hundred feet away. Look near the center of the island and you'll be rewarded with a view of a bald eagle nest, a massive accumulation of material usually visible with binoculars and quite easily spotted with a scope. Up to 12 pairs of eagles nest in the park – a number that has slowly increased over the decades as the species benefited from federal protec-tion and reduction in pesticide use. From the park's mainland and island lookouts, you can see eagles, both these and others in the area, plying the skies. Moments like this are the essence of Acadia's compelling combination of outstanding coastal scenery and great birding opportunities.

Remembering Rachel

Rachel Carson is best known for her highly influential 1962 book *Silent Spring*, focusing on the impact of indiscriminate pesticide use on ecosystem food chains, of which birds are an integral part. If the spraying of poisons continued, she feared, we would one day see a spring without birds and their song.

Carson, who died in 1964, is less well remembered for an earlier trilogy devoted to the bounty of the marine environment: *Under the Sea Wind*, *The Sea Around Us*, and *The Edge of the Sea*. Much of the inspiration for these works came from her explorations of Maine's scenic coastline, launched from her summer home in West Southport. The 5,000-acre **Rachel Carson National Wildlife Refuge**, consisting of 10 divisions along a 50-mile stretch of southern coast, honors her memory and preserves the habitats that so entranced her.

At **Upper Wells**, the refuge's only developed part, the self-guided, mile-long **Carson Trail** meanders through a coastal forest of white pine overlooking the **Merriland River** tidal marsh. Kinglets, numerous warblers, and fly-catchers frequent the woodlands. The marshes support belted kingfishers and wading birds. Black ducks breed here, and in fall and winter the number and diversity of waterfowl increase significantly. Rough-legged hawks course over the open areas during winter. About 15 miles north is the **Biddeford Pool** division, marshland fringing a shallow tidal basin, one of the most productive locations in coastal Maine for shorebirds in spring and fall. In summer, it supports as many as nine species of wading birds.

With the warbling of songbirds, the rattle of kingfishers, the plaintive whistles of shorebirds, and the quacking of ducks, spring is never silent at this refuge. Nor, for that matter, are the other seasons.

Rachel Carson (above) is regarded as one of the founders of the modern environmental movement.

American redstarts (top) glean caterpillars from foliage and nab flying insects.

Barrow's goldeneyes (opposite, top) are winter visitors to the park, sometimes spotted among flocks of common goldeneyes.

Atlantic puffins (opposite, bottom) and other seabirds are often sighted in the waters around Mount Desert Island.

TRAVEL TIPS

DETAILS

When to Go

Birding is productive year-round. Migratory songbirds and other species are seen in spring, as well as in fall, when raptors pass through the area. Over 150 species nest in the park in late spring and summer. Waterfowl and seabirds can be observed in the park's lakes and ponds and in the waters surrounding Mount Desert Island in winter. Spring is foggy, with temperatures ranging from 30°F to 70°F. Summer daytime temperatures vary widely, from 45°F to 90°F, and nights can be in the 40s or below. Autumn highs are in the low 70s, and nights can reach freezing. In winter, daytime temperatures are in the mid-30s, and nights are often below zero. Annual rainfall averages 48 inches; annual snowfall, 61 inches.

How to Get There

Bangor International Airport is about 50 miles from the park.

Getting Around

There is no public transportation within the park. Cars may be rented at the airport.

Handicapped Access

Thompson Island and Hulls Cove Visitors Centers, Blackwoods and Seawall campgrounds, and most picnic areas are accessible.

INFORMATION

Acadia National Park

P.O. Box 177, Bar Harbor, ME 04609; tel: 207-288-3338.

Bar Harbor Chamber of Commerce

P.O. Box 158, Bar Harbor, ME 04609; tel: 800-288-5103 or 207-288-5103.

Rachel Carson National Wildlife Refuge

321 Port Road, Wells, ME 04090; tel: 207-646-9226.

Schoodic Peninsula Chamber of Commerce

P.O. Box 381, Winter Harbor, ME 04693; tel: 800-231-3008 or 207-963-7658.

Southwest Harbor-Tremont Chamber of Commerce

P.O. Box 1143, Southwest Harbor, ME 04679; tel: 800-423-9264 or 207-244-9264.

Rare Bird Alert

Tel: 207-781-2332.

CAMPING

Mount Desert Island's two campgrounds offer a combined 550 campsites. Seawall sites are available on a first-come, first-served basis. To reserve Blackwoods sites, write up to four months in advance to the National Park Reservation Service, P.O. Box 1600, Cumberland, MD 21502, or phone 800-365-2267. Five lean-tos are available on Isle de Haut from May 15 to October 15. Campers must pay a fee and obtain a permit; for information, call 207-288-3338.

LODGING

PRICE GUIDE – double occupancy

$ = up to $49 $$ = $50–$99
$$$ = $100–$149 $$$$ = $150+

Coach Stop Inn

Bar Harbor Road, Route 3, P.O. Box 266, Bar Harbor, ME 04609; tel: 207-288-9886.

Originally a coach stop and tavern, the 200-year-old building is located on three acres about five miles from the town of Bar Harbor and two miles from the park. The inn's five units have private porches or patios; some have fireplaces and sitting rooms. A full breakfast is served. $$–$$$

Graycote Inn

40 Holland Avenue, Bar Harbor, ME 04609; tel: 207-288-3044.

Surrounded by an acre of landscaped grounds, this 1881 Victorian offers 12 guest rooms with private baths and fireplaces. A full breakfast is served. $$–$$$$

Harbor View Motel and Cottages

P.O. Box 701, Southwest Harbor, ME 04679; tel: 800-538-6463 or 207-244-5031.

The motel has 28 units, most with decks overlooking the harbor. Three of the units have a bedroom, living area, and full kitchen. Seven one- and two-bedroom cottages, rented on a weekly basis, have full kitchens. $–$$$

Hearthside Bed-and-Breakfast

7 High Street, Bar Harbor, ME 04609; tel: 207-288-4533.

Ten rooms in a restored 1907 shingle house each have private baths; some have porches, fireplaces, and whirlpools. Guests are served a full breakfast in the dining room or on the porch in warm weather. Afternoon tea welcomes birders back to the inn after a day spent in the park. $$–$$$

Inn at Canoe Point

P.O. Box 216B, Bar Harbor, ME 04609; tel: 207-288-9511.

The large Tudor house, built in 1889, is surrounded by a pine forest directly across from the park. Ocean views are available from the inn's two suites and three guest rooms. A common room has a granite fireplace and views of the sea and mountains. Breakfast is served on a large deck overlooking Frenchman's Bay. $$–$$$$

Mira Monte Inn

69 Mount Desert Street, Bar Harbor, ME 04609; tel: 207-288-4263

Built in the 1860s, this elegant inn occupies two acres with formal gardens, and is a five-minute walk to town. Sixteen rooms, all with private baths, are furnished in period style. Three multiroom suites are good options for groups or families. Open in summer only $$$–$$$$

Pointy Head Inn
HC 33, Box 2A, Bass Harbor, ME 04653; tel: 207-244-7261.

This three-story inn fronts Bass Harbor at the southeast corner of Mount Desert Island, just outside the national park boundaries. Birders staying at the inn are close to Bass Harbor Marsh and nature trails leading to coastal overlooks. A full breakfast is served. $$$

TOURS AND OUTFITTERS

Acadia National Park
P.O. Box 177, Bar Harbor, ME 04609; tel: 207-288-3338.

Rangers lead a variety of field trips, including boat cruises around Mount Desert Island and a peregrine-falcon watch at Champlain Mountain. During Hawkwatch (September 1 through mid-October), an interpreter identifies raptors at Cadillac Mountain.

Bay Ferries, Ltd.
Tel: 888-249-7245.

A high-speed catamaran provides daily service between Bar Harbor, Maine, and Yarmouth, Nova Scotia. Passengers see a number of seabirds and marine mammals during the trip.

Maine Audubon Society
P.O. Box 6009, Falmouth, ME 04105; tel: 207-781-2330.

In mid-September, the 111-foot catamaran *Friendship V* travels from Bar Harbor to Mount Desert Rock and Grand Manan Banks, where passengers observe a variety of seabirds. Reservations are required and a fee is charged. Maine Audubon also sponsors field trips to Mount Desert Island and nearby locations.

Excursions

Baxter State Park
64 Balsam Drive, Millinocket, ME 04462; tel: 207-723-5140.

This rugged and remote park includes Mount Katahdin, the highest point in Maine, and a portion of the Appalachian Trail. Baxter's 204,000-plus acres support many breeding birds: common loons, mergansers, and other waterfowl inhabit the lakes and ponds; boreal species such as gray jays, northern goshawks, and woodpeckers tenant the forests; and American bitterns and other wading birds dwell in the marshes.

Parker River National Wildlife Refuge
261 Northern Boulevard, Plum Island, Newburyport, MA 01950; tel: 978-465-5753.

Though less than 5,000 acres, this refuge is a year-round birder's delight, with habitats ranging from shoreline and salt marsh to freshwater enclaves and a patchwork of woodlands. Beginning in late summer, swallows, waterfowl, and shorebirds, including sandpipers and godwits, can be seen migrating south. Common eiders and other sea ducks, as well as loons and pelagic birds, winter in the area. Spring brings a parade of northbound migrants and nesting species, such as Wilson's phalaropes, sharp-tailed sparrows, and the threatened piping plover.

Green Mountain National Forest
231 North Main Street, Rutland, VT 05701; tel: 802-747-6700.

Divided into two sections, the 350,000-acre forest offers a fine sampler of New England hardwood, with birches and maples interspersed among conifers, bogs, streams, waterfalls, and some of Vermont's highest mountains. American black ducks, wood ducks, and other waterfowl breed in beaver ponds and marshy areas. Songbirds and warblers nest in the forests, which are also inhabited by northern goshawks, Cooper's hawks, barred owls, and northern saw-whet owls.

Central Park
New York

CHAPTER 8

More than 140 years ago, when Frederick Law Olmsted and Calvert Vaux set out to create **Central Park** from desolate pig farms and general wasteland, the desire to provide a mecca for birders almost certainly wasn't on their minds. The monumental landscaping effort they supervised – planting some four million trees and shrubs, bringing in five million cubic yards of soil, and forming numerous bodies of water – was designed to offer a sylvan setting for city dwellers to enjoy. The unintended effect was the creation of a landscape highly attractive to birds. Over the arc of time, more than 250 species have been recorded in the park, and this bounty has drawn countless birders. ◆ The park is especially active in spring, when it becomes a magnet for migrating songbirds. For a hungry and tired northbound warbler or thrush flying over the metropolitan area, the soft, green landscape of the 843-acre park stands out in alluring

In the heart of America's largest city lies an oasis for urban birders.

contrast to the surrounding spires of inhospitable concrete and steel. On a "big day" in spring, it's hard to keep up with the stream of sightings as they are passed from one group of birders to the next: "A hooded warbler is flitting around a shrub next to Azalea Pond." "Did you get the blackburnian in the willows by Willow Rock?" On such a day, tallying two dozen species of wood warblers is not out of the question. ◆ For spring birders, the **Ramble**, a 40-acre section in the middle of the park, is a prime destination. Heavily wooded and dotted with outcroppings of metamorphic schist estimated to be half a billion years old, the area is crisscrossed by so many paved paths that the colorful orioles, tanagers, grosbeaks, and – crème de la crème – the wood warblers are never far from view as they forage about

Manhattan's famous park has a wealth of bird-friendly features, including willow-rimmed lakes and dense woodlands with a rambling stream.

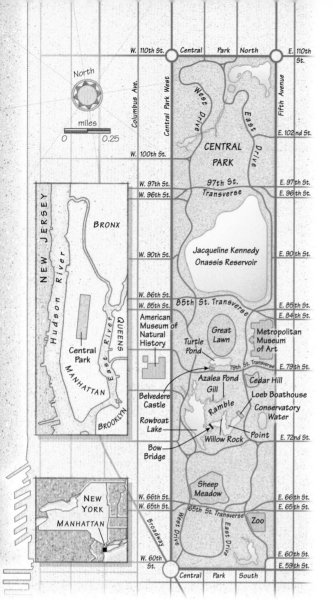

in the canopy. Two especially good places within the Ramble are around **Azalea Pond** and on the **Point**. Azalea Pond and its associated stream, the **Gill**, can be excellent locations to view birds drawn to water, such as northern and Louisiana waterthrushes.

You'll likely encounter a bounty of other warbler species in the Ramble: black-and-white, black-throated green, black-throated blue, yellow, yellow-rumped, palm, prairie, northern parula, Cape May, bay-breasted, and magnolia warblers, plus American redstart, common yellowthroat, and ovenbird. The much sought-after mourning, worm-eating, Wilson's, Canada, prothonotary, cerulean, Kentucky, golden-winged, hooded, and blackburnian warblers also make an appearance each spring. The six species of eastern thrushes, the six eastern vireos, yellow-billed and black-billed cuckoos, blue-gray gnatcatchers, brown creepers, and indigo buntings also frequent this productive area.

The Point, a high-ridged peninsula along the southern edge of the Ramble, juts out into **Rowboat Lake**, the park's second-largest body of water. Looking west from the ridge provides a great vantage point across the little cove near **Willow Rock**, where songbirds nab insects in the foliage of the graceful willows. In addition to the many canopy-flitting warbler species, you can reliably see orchard and northern orioles, rose-breasted grosbeaks, scarlet tanagers, and ruby-crowned and golden-crowned kinglets. Solitary and spotted sandpipers and American woodcocks sometimes forage along the edges of the cove.

To the east, **Loeb Boathouse** has the Central Park Bird Register and Nature Notes. The loose-leaf notebook is filled with recent observations. Some entries are crisply anecdotal: "Turkey vulture over Belvedere Castle at 11 A.M." Others are full-page descriptions, with detailed notes on behavior. If you are uncertain where to begin your Central Park birding experience, the register should be your first destination.

Stroll south from the Ramble and you'll cross **Bow Bridge** over a narrow section of **Rowboat Lake**. From here, you can scan for wading birds, such as great blue herons, great egrets, and green herons (which have nested in the park). Keep an eye out for the several swallow species reliably seen here, including tree, barn, bank, and northern rough-winged, as they zoom over the lake. Swamp sparrows are sometimes encountered in the marshy vegetation along the water's edge.

Raptor Season

A relatively recent birding phenomenon is the Central Park Hawk Watch, which runs from August 15 to December 15. To join other hawk aficionados, climb to the top of **Belvedere Castle**, north of the Ramble. If

you spend an entire season, you may see as many as 16 species of birds of prey, including owls. The broad-winged hawk is the most numerous, and it may surprise you to learn that the season record of 10,605 broad-wings rivals some of the better annual tallies at the famous Hawk Mountain Sanctuary in Pennsylvania. The highest seasonal total for bald eagles to date is 62.

Dominating the middle of the park is the 106-acre **reservoir**, recently renamed in memory of Jacqueline Kennedy Onassis. The oldest existing reservoir in the city (excavation began in 1858), it once supplied much of the water for lower Manhattan. Nowadays, it provides habitat for overwintering waterfowl, including such diving species as ruddy ducks, buffle-heads, lesser scaups, ring-necked ducks, red-heads, canvasbacks, and hooded mergansers, which disappear several times a minute as they dive for bottom-dwelling plants and other food. Also crowding the water are mallards, black ducks, wigeons, and

Wintering waterfowl (above) take up residence in the park's lakes and reservoir.

Red-tailed hawks (right), American kestrels, and peregrine falcons are the raptors known to breed in New York City.

gadwalls, and the two eastern teals – blue-winged and green-winged – all of which tip up to feed just beneath the surface. Look, too, for northern shovelers straining plankton and small insects from the surface with their spatulate bills.

Gulls occur here, too – the common species such as ring-billed, herring, and great black-backed gulls – and, once in a while, glaucous and Iceland gulls. These two northern species with frosted wings, rather than black wing tips, can be distinguished from the more common gulls by their paler appearance and from each other by size: The glaucous is slightly smaller than the great black-backed, while the Iceland is slightly smaller than the herring gull.

Winter is the time to make a special effort to look for owls in the park, especially saw-whet and long-eared owls, which take advantage of the ample rat and mouse population. The conifers on **Cedar Hill**, northeast of the Boathouse, have been known to conceal as many as three long-eared owls – another reason that Central Park is an urban paradise for both the birds and the birders who pursue them.

Nesting in the Urban Jungle

Central Park birders aren't easily awed. After all, the park has served as a backdrop for some compelling human dramas, and birds new to the park come along all the time. But the decision by a pair of red-tailed hawks to set up housekeeping on busy Fifth Avenue, across the street from the park, took even seasoned observers by surprise.

The saga began in the mid-1990s when a pair of these large hawks began building a nest in a tree overlooking the Great Lawn, one of the park's most popular sections. Within a couple of weeks, the effort failed. Moving 10 blocks south and a bit east, they tried again, but the female and then the male were so mobbed by crows that they both flew into buildings and were injured. The male, released back into the park, found a new mate, and the two selected the highly visible and now famous 12th-story ornate window arch at 74th Street and Fifth Avenue.

The hawks' first two years at the site brought additional failures and an illegal nest removal during a cleaning operation. In the third year, young were fledged, and similar success has occurred in subsequent years. Benches on the western side of the park's model boat pond provide an excellent vantage for viewing the nest.

TRAVEL TIPS

DETAILS

When to Go

The park hosts migratory warblers and other birds in spring and fall and nesting species in summer. Raptors migrate through from late August to December. Wintering species include waterfowl, found at the park's reservoir. Spring temperatures vary from 40°F to the upper 70s. Summer is hot and humid, with highs in excess of 90°F. Autumn is cool; winter temperatures average in the low to high 30s. Rain rarely exceeds two inches in most months; expect several inches of snow in winter.

How to Get There

New York City is served by three major airports: La Guardia, in Queens, eight miles east of Manhattan; JFK, also in Queens, 14 miles southeast of Manhattan; and Newark, in New Jersey, 15 miles southwest of Manhattan. Manhattan is also served by long-distance bus and train service.

Getting Around

Rental cars are available at the airports and in the city, but parking in Manhattan is limited and expensive and traffic can be horrendous. Visitors can take buses, shuttles, and taxis from the airports to Manhattan, where subways, buses, and cabs provide easy access to Central Park.

Handicapped Access

Most paths in Central Park are paved and fully accessible.

INFORMATION

Central Park Conservancy

The conservancy operates three visitor centers in the park, at Belvedere Castle, 212-772-0210; the Charles A. Dana Discovery Center, 212-860-1370; and the Dairy, 212-794-6564.

New York City Audubon Society

71 West 23rd Street, Suite 606, New York, NY 10010; tel: 212-691-7483.

New York Convention and Visitors Bureau

810 Seventh Avenue, Third Floor, New York, NY 10019; tel: 212-484-1200.

Rare Bird Alert

Tel: 212-979-3070.

LODGING

PRICE GUIDE – double occupancy

$ = up to $49 $$ = $50–$99

$$$ = $100–$149 $$$$ = $150+

Beacon Hotel

2130 Broadway, New York, NY 10023; tel: 212-787-1100.

The Beacon, located three blocks west of Central Park, offers 100 rooms with kitchenettes. $$$

Bed-and-Breakfast Bureau

306 Eighth Avenue, Suite 111, New York, NY 10001; tel: 212-645-4555.

This service, owned by birders, helps visitors find accommodations in bed-and-breakfasts and private apartments. Prices vary.

Bed-and-Breakfast Network of New York

130 Barrow Street, Suite 508, New York, NY 10014; tel: 212-645-8134.

More than 200 accommodations are available through this booking agency. Prices vary.

Excelsior Hotel

45 West 81st Street, New York, NY 10024; tel: 212-362-9200.

This hotel has 150 rooms and suites, many with kitchens.

Accommodations at the front of the hotel overlook Central Park. A restaurant is on the premises. $$$

Lucerne Hotel

201 West 79th Street, New York, NY 10023; tel: 800-492-8122 or 212-875-1000.

The hotel offers more than 200 basic rooms and 41 suites, the larger of which contain kitchenettes. The Lucerne has its own restaurant. $$$$

Mayflower Hotel

15 Central Park West, New York, NY 10023; tel: 265-0060.

Overlooking Central Park, the Mayflower has about 370 rooms with kitchenettes. Rooms on the upper floors, though more expensive, have excellent views. $$$$

Milburn Hotel

242 West 76th Street, New York, NY 10023; tel: 212-362-1006.

Two-room suites with kitchens are available at this hotel, which also offers basic accommodations. $$$

Pickwick Arms

230 East 51st Street, New York, NY 10022; tel: 212-355-0300.

Pickwick Arms has 400 guest rooms, a café, and a restaurant. Some rooms have private baths. $$–$$$

TOURS AND OUTFITTERS

New York City Audubon Society

71 West 23rd Street, Suite 606, New York, NY 10010; tel: 212-691-7483.

The society offers bird walks in Central Park and in the metropolitan area.

Urban Park Rangers

City of New York, Parks and Recreation, The Arsenal, Central Park, 830 Fifth Avenue; New York, NY 10021; tel: 888-697-2757 or 212-628-2345.

Rangers lead birding trips in Central Park and other public

areas year-round. They also conduct the Central Park Hawk Watch from August 15 to December 15, Wednesday through Sunday, at Belvedere Castle. A ranger/biologist helps birders identify passing raptors.

Excursions

Cape Cod National Seashore

99 Marconi Site Road, Wellfleet, MA 02667; tel: 508-349-3785.

This seashore, an arm of land extending into the Atlantic Ocean, is a major stopover for migratory birds before and after the summer tourist season. Songbirds seek out Cape Cod's uplands in spring and fall. Large numbers of shorebirds are seen along the 40 miles of beach and in the marshes and salt ponds. Jaegers, murres, guillemots, and shearwaters may be observed from shore or via pelagic trips.

SPECIAL EVENTS

Birdathon

New York City Audubon Society, 71 West 23rd Street, Suite 606, New York, NY 10010; tel: 212-691-7483.

This mid-May marathon count, in which teams compete to identify the most bird species, covers all five boroughs of New York City. Funds raised during the event support the Audubon Society's ecology projects and teacher scholarships.

MUSEUMS

American Museum of Natural History

Central Park West at 79th Street, New York, NY 10024; tel: 212-769-5100.

The museum houses extensive ornithology exhibits and displays concerning the evolutionary connection between dinosaurs and modern birds.

Belvedere Castle

79th Street Mid-Park; tel: 212-772-0210.

Exhibits at this Central Park facility, just north of the Ramble and 79th Street Transverse, highlight the park's natural history and bird life.

White Memorial Foundation and Conservation Center

71 Whitehall Road, Litchfield, CT 06759; tel: 860-567-0857.

The Bantam River flows through this 4,000-acre sanctuary, forming an extensive marsh inhabited by rails, bitterns, soras, and other wetland species. May is the prime month for seeing migratory birds, including more than 20 species of warblers. About 100 birds nest in the center's various habitats, and waterfowl such as mergansers, teals, canvasbacks, and gadwalls winter on Bantam Lake, along with several bald eagles. A one-mile boardwalk skirts a pond, and 35 miles of trails lead through the property.

Jamaica Bay Wildlife Refuge

Gateway National Recreation Area, Floyd Bennett Field, Building 69, Brooklyn, NY 11234; tel: 718-318-4340.

This area and the adjacent waters south of Queens and Brooklyn were once bereft of wildlife. Thanks to a massive cleanup and restoration, Jamaica Bay again teems with birds. More than 320 species have been seen in the refuge's salt marshes, ponds, and uplands. These birds include an abundance of hawks, owls, waterfowl, songbirds, wading birds, and shorebirds such as American oystercatchers, ruddy turnstones, and red knots. The refuge has numerous trails, and the birding is good year-round.

Cape May
New Jersey

CHAPTER 9

Packed into a living room, a crowd of adults and several children gathers around a coffee table piled high with chips and dip, beer and soft drinks. All eyes are glued to the television, and as the drama unfolds, conversations become muted. "Come on, you gotta come through," says one fan, reverently. Minutes later, when the announcer declares "yes, it's now assured," everyone erupts in cheers. "Yesssss," rejoices one young woman. Two guys in back high-five, and the celebration begins in earnest. ◆ The Super Bowl? The Final Four? The Daytona 500? No, the scene is a late September evening in Cape May, New Jersey, and these folks are watching the Weather Channel. The meteorologist has just announced that a "Bermuda" high-pressure area off the Atlantic Coast, which had brought a week of Indian summer, is finally moving east. A huge cold front barreling across the country will push offshore the following day. This is the condition for which birders lust: the timing is perfect for a major migratory movement at

A strategic peninsula draws kettles of hawks, fallouts of songbirds, thousands of shorebirds – and birders from around the world.

the cape. ◆ Autumn migration in North America can precipitate some of the finest birding anyone will ever experience, and **Cape May** is one of the finest places to enjoy it. Alexander Wilson, the father of American ornithology, once joked that if birds are good judges of climate, then Cape May must have the best climate in North America, because it has the most birds. ◆ The town of **Cape May** and nearby **Cape May Point** are situated at the southern tip of the first major peninsula leading south down the East Coast. Because most land birds prefer not to fly over

Migrating northern flickers are frequent autumn sightings at Cape May. On one legendary day, 5,000 were counted.

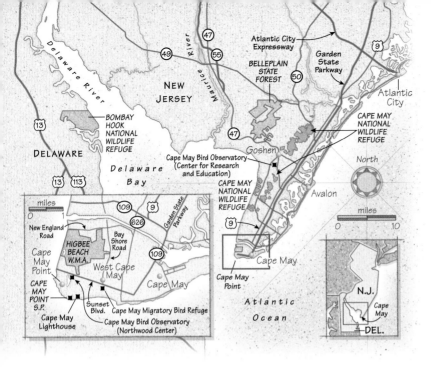

As the winds of the cold front abate, generally after two or three days, the birds, having rested and refueled, continue their flight south. Many will cross the now calm waters of the bay, but others – including up to 50 percent of the raptors – elect to fly around Delaware Bay, creating good birding along the entire bayshore to the north and west of Cape May. There is inevitably a lull before the next cold front, and once again birders are glued to the tube, watching the Weather Channel and excitedly awaiting the next flight. Veterans who have been visiting the cape for decades usually plan to stay a week or 10 days. This will almost always assure one or two good fronts and exceptional fallouts of migrants.

water, the coastlines of Delaware Bay to the west and the Atlantic Ocean to the east funnel birds to land's end at Cape May Point. Think of the cape as a geographical hourglass with birds pouring like sand through the waist of the glass.

Historic Migrations

On gentle winds, many birds cross the 13-mile stretch of water from Cape May to the Delaware coastline. But when the blustery northwesterlies of a cold front threaten to push them to their doom over the open ocean, most birds put down to feed and rest. At times you can actually witness the confusion and indecision of flocks upon reaching the lighthouse as they assess whether to go or stay.

Legendary single-day flights of 300,000 American robins, 2,500 eastern bluebirds, and 5,000 northern flickers have occurred. Yellow-rumped warblers numbering 150,000 were once estimated around the cape. At least 17 species of raptors are recorded each fall. The official count conducted by the Cape May Bird Observatory averages about 60,000 raptors each autumn, and record flights have included 89,000 for the season and 21,000 in one day. Accipiters and falcons predominate, with merlins and peregrines relatively common in late September and early October. Cape May is one of the premier places in the world to watch peregrines – more than 1,000 have been recorded by the hawk count in recent autumns.

Cape May is also one of the major vagrant traps in North America. Such western rarities as sandhill crane, white pelican, Swainson's hawk, rufous hummingbird, and ash-throated flycatcher are sighted annually. The real rarities are birds from other continents: whiskered tern (the first North

American record), brown-chested martin (second North American record), mongolian plover (first East Coast record), and Eurasian kestrel. More than 400 avian species have been recorded at Cape May, one of the highest totals anywhere in North America. Alexander Wilson had it exactly right.

Autumn Hot Spots

Thanks to the numbers and variety of birds routinely found here, more than 100,000 birders visit each year, including many from Great Britain and the Continent. Because Cape May is a seashore resort, and because of its Victorian history and architecture, the town itself can be crowded during early fall, when the

A prairie warbler (above) flicks its tail from side to side as it pursues insects in shrubs and trees.

Hawk-banding demonstrations (opposite) and raptor-identification clinics are regular fall programs at Cape May Point State Park.

An American oystercatcher's nest (right) is a shallow depression in the sand above the high tidemark.

climate is still mild. Birding areas, however, are packed only on weekends at peak season, and numerous conservation areas easily absorb the visitors.

In autumn, many birders begin their day at **Higbee Beach Wildlife Management Area**, just north of Cape May Point. Spreading over 1,000 acres managed by the state's Endangered and Nongame Species Program, "Higbee's" is prime habitat for songbird fallout, with many trails through fields, woods, and dunes. Mornings in early fall find eastern kingbirds, orchard and Baltimore orioles, and waves of warblers streaming over at first, then dropping in to treetops and thickets, where they are easily observed as they hungrily begin to forage. Later in the fall, blue jays, American robins, and northern flickers noisily vie for perches, all the while watching out for patrolling Cooper's hawks.

By mid-morning, many folks gravitate to the 180-acre **Cape May Point State Park**, usually the best place to witness the hawk migration. The park has fine trails and good views of ponds, ocean, and the entrance to Delaware Bay. Flocks of cormorants and skeins of geese, crossing through kettles of

turkey vultures and broad-winged and sharp-shinned hawks can make one wonder if an air-traffic controller might not be needed. Later in the day, when the hawk flight slows, many birders scan the "rips," an area of strong currents where bay meets ocean, for northern gannets, cormorants, scoters, gulls, terns, and the occasional brown pelican or parasitic jaeger.

Another popular stop is the **Cape May Migratory Bird Refuge**, about 200 acres protected by the Nature Conservancy. There, freshwater wetlands behind the coastal dunes attract shorebirds, waders, waterfowl, and rails. Birders often find a buff-breasted sandpiper, sedge wren, or least bittern, or a real goody such as ful-

vous whistling-duck, cave swallow, or black rail. There are many more spots in addition to these key areas, and one observer was heard to say, "I've birded Cape May for three days now and hardly made a dent!"

Becoming increasingly popular is the Avalon Seawatch, where the Cape May Bird Observatory maintains a full-time seabird migration watch and has recorded more than a million seabirds heading south in fall. The town of **Avalon**, 14 miles north of Cape May, is better for sea watching than Cape May itself because of geography. Avalon juts more than a mile out to sea. Over-ocean migrants such as red-throated loons, northern gannets, scoters, cormorants, and jaegers are suddenly almost on the beach at Avalon, affording watchers wonderfully close views by telescope. Almost daily there is something unusual – eiders, razorbills, black-legged kittiwakes, perhaps even a shearwater. Start looking early in the morning; easterly or southerly winds are best.

The magic of Cape May is that anything can happen at anytime, anywhere. A favorite story tells of a waitress serving tables at an outdoor café in the center of town. An avid bird-bander, she recognized what customers thought was a mouse

Feeding Frenzy

The greatest spectacle of all in the Cape May region occurs in May, when more than 1½ million shorebirds gather on Delaware Bay beaches to feast on the eggs of the horseshoe crab. Indeed, this is the second largest gathering of shorebirds in North America, second only to the fall staging on the Copper River Delta in Alaska.

Horseshoe crabs, *Limulus polyphemus*, are not true crabs but ancient arthropods more closely related to spiders. The Delaware Bay shores are by far the world's largest spawning grounds for the creatures. In the middle of May, when the full or new moon creates the highest tides, thousands upon thousands of these armored marvels mate at the high-tide mark. Females then lay 4,000 pinhead-sized eggs in a shallow scrape, coming ashore as many as 20 times over the next month or two to mate and lay a total of 80,000 eggs each. Every new tide of egg-laying females unearths some of the previously laid egg masses, which results in a slurry of food for armies of shorebirds joined by a blizzard of gulls in a true avian feeding frenzy.

Shorebirds depend on this egg resource to fuel their annual migration to breeding grounds in the arctic tundra. Five species of sandpipers concentrate on bay beaches: sanderling, ruddy turnstone, red knot, semipalmated sandpiper, and dunlin. More than 80 percent of the New World population of red knots, perhaps 250,000 birds, may be using Delaware Bay beaches – an occurrence of immense conservation significance. The knots arrive, hungry and exhausted, following a 60-hour nonstop flight from South America – a trip of up to 4,000 miles. In a two-week stay, they may double their body weight by eating some 9,000 eggs per day.

This fragile link in a chain stretching from Tierra del Fuego to the high arctic is increasingly imperiled by the overharvesting of horseshoe crabs, which are used as bait by fishermen. Conservation groups are imploring the state to formulate a management plan that will curtail the exploitation of the crabs and assure healthy shorebird populations.

Female horseshoe crabs (left) each lay thousands of eggs that provide a banquet for laughing gulls (below) and migrating shorebirds.

A black-bellied plover (opposite, top) gaining its breeding plumage pulls a worm from a Delaware Bay beach.

Snow buntings (opposite, bottom) arrive in late fall. They return to their arctic breeding grounds in winter.

scurrying under the table. She scooped up the wayward migrant black rail and popped it into the pocket of her apron. Later that night, when she finished work, she released it into a nearby marsh.

Shifting Seasons

The birding dictum that seasons overlap is nowhere truer than at a migratory crossroads like Cape May. There isn't a month of the year when some avian migrants aren't moving. Cold weather to the north may continue to send birds south as late as February, yet a warm January can see returning waterfowl and red-throated loons. The last of the shorebirds depart for the Arctic the first week of June, while the first southbound shorebirds, returning from the tundra, arrive the last few days of June. Because the arctic summer is so brief, July and August are by far the best months for "fall" shorebirds on Cape May marshes and mudflats.

Autumn migration may have put Cape

May on the map, but ongoing ornithological studies prove that it is a place for all seasons. Summer marshes are host to the largest laughing gull colony in the world, and protected beaches have breeding piping plovers, American oystercatchers, least and common terns, and black skimmers. Numerous rookeries hold abundant herons, egrets, and glossy ibis. The **Cape May National Wildlife Refuge**, about 9,000 acres of woodlands, fields, and wetlands along the Delaware Bay side of the peninsula, and the **Belleplain State Forest**, nearly 15,000 acres north of Cape May, abound with breeding songbirds, including many near the northern limit of their breeding range, such as prothonotary warbler, yellow-throated warbler, and summer tanager.

In winter, the coastal marshes hold untold thousands of brant, and the waters of Delaware Bay are major feeding grounds for common and red-throated loons, scoters, scaup, and oldsquaw. Raptors are numerous in winter, particularly along the Delaware bayshore. Bald eagles are fairly common, and rough-legged hawks and short-eared owls can usually be found. The northern harrier, the consummate "marsh hawk," is a hallmark of the vast winter wetlands, and snow geese bring a blizzard of white to the somber brown marshes.

Cape May in springtime is one of the great secrets of birding. It's no coincidence that the World Series of Birding, sponsored by the New Jersey Audubon Society, is held in Cape May in mid-May. During this major fund-raiser for conservation groups, teams of birders from across the country scour all of New Jersey. The record tops 220 species, but more than 200 have been recorded in a day by a single team in Cape May County alone. Songbirds and shorebirds are the prime spring targets, but anything can show up, be it a swallow-tailed kite, anhinga, white-faced ibis, or scissor-tailed flycatcher. In recent years, as many rarities have been found in spring as in fall. A south-facing peninsula can act as a migrant and vagrant trap in spring as well – either by serving as a barrier for reverse migrants (overshoots returning south) or by acting as the nearest landfall for birds heading north. Some local birders prefer spring in Cape May. It's far less crowded than in the fall, and the birding can be just as hot.

Butterfly Migration

Butterflies concentrate at Cape May for the same reasons as birds. The foremost species is the monarch, on its journey south to winter on Mexican mountaintops. Tens of thousands are tallied each season. Migrating buckeyes, red admirals, question marks, and mourning cloaks also vie for attention, creating a pageant of color against seaside goldenrod on roadsides, marsh edges, and dunes.

Some species of butterflies travel north in late summer and early autumn in a curious process known as emigration, a one-way movement not fully understood by scientists. Most years, the large and brilliant cloudless sulphur arrives in Cape May from the south in large numbers, and the sachem may be abundant. Other species, such as the long-tailed skipper, fiery skipper, and ocola skipper, are true "vagrants" and actively sought by butterfly watchers. In 1995, Cape May County's first record of a gulf fritillary emptied the Cape May Hawkwatch Platform as eager naturalists rushed to see this striking orange butterfly feeding in a nearby garden.

Combine birds and butterflies, add clouds of migratory dragonflies, mix in a migrating red bat or two and daily sightings of bottlenosed dolphins beyond the surf, and you'll see why Cape May is one of America's most dramatic windows on the pageant of migration.

Thousands of monarch butterflies (left) have been tagged by Cape May researchers. The first ones found at their Mexican winter roost were discovered in 1999.

Migrating Baltimore orioles (opposite) pass through Cape May in spring and fall. Some birds breed in the area.

TRAVEL TIPS

DETAILS

When to Go

Peak migration, including great numbers of raptors, occurs in September and October. Horseshoe crabs come ashore to lay eggs in May and early June, followed by thousands of ravenous shorebirds. Spring temperatures are mild, with lows in the 50s and highs in the 70s. Summer temperatures are in the mid-80s, with lows in the 60s. In fall, days are in the 60s, nights in the 40s.

How to Get There

Atlantic City International Airport is 48 miles from Cape May; Philadelphia International Airport, 87.

Getting Around

Car rentals are available at the airports. New Jersey Transit, 800-582-5946, operates daily bus service between Atlantic City and Cape May.

Handicapped Access

The boardwalk trail, hawk-watch platform, and visitor center at Cape May Point State Park are accessible.

INFORMATION

Cape May Bird Observatory

600 Route 47 North, Cape May Court House, NJ 08210; tel: 609-861-0700.

Cape May Point State Park

P.O. Box 107, Cape May Point, NJ 08212; tel: 609-884-2159.

Belleplain State Forest

County Route 550, P.O. Box 450, Woodbine, NJ 08270; tel: 609-861-2404.

Chamber of Commerce of Greater Cape May

513 Washington Street Mall, P.O. Box 556, Cape May, NJ 08204; tel: 609-884-5508.

Rare Bird Alerts

Tel: 609-861-0466 (Cape May) or 908-766-2661 (statewide).

CAMPING

Belleplain State Forest

County Route 550, P.O. Box 450, Woodbine, NJ 08270; tel: 609-861-2404.

The state forest's 200 campsites and 15 lean-tos are available on a first-come, first-served basis. Reservations are accepted for minimum stays of two nights.

Cold Spring Campground

541 New England Road, Cape May, NJ 08204, tel: 800-772-8530 or 609-884-8717.

This wooded campground, open from early May to mid-October, has 100 sites. Reservations are recommended during peak birding periods.

LODGING

PRICE GUIDE – double occupancy
$ = up to $49 $$ = $50–$99
$$$ = $100–$149 $$$$ = $150+

Cape Harbor Motor Inn

715 Pittsburgh Avenue, Cape May, NJ 08204; tel: 609-884-0018.

Accommodations include both simple rooms with refrigerators and suites with full kitchens and living rooms. The 28-room motel, open April through November, is centrally located. $–$$$

Henry Ludlam Inn

1336 Route 47 North, Woodbine, NJ 08270; tel: 609-861-5847.

This 18th-century house sits off Ludlam Pond, near Belleplain State Forest. Each of the five guest rooms has a private bath; three

have a fireplace. Watch birds from the lakeside gazebo or from one of the inn's canoes. Cape May is a 30-minute drive away. $$–$$$

Jetty Motel

Second and Beach Avenues, Cape May, NJ 08204; tel: 609-884-4640.

The Jetty's 32 accommodations range from basic motel rooms with refrigerators to large suites. South of Cape May, near the lighthouse, the oceanfront motel is open from mid-April through mid-October. $$–$$$$

Off Shore Motel

1801 Route 47 South, Rio Grande, NJ 08242; tel: 609-886-6400.

This motel, four miles from Cape May, has 50 units. All rooms have refrigerators; some have microwaves. $–$$$

Sea Breeze Motel

204 Pittsburgh Avenue, Cape May, NJ 08204; tel: 609-884-3352.

The Sea Breeze offers 12 rooms, each with a small refrigerator. The motel is open from April to the end of October. $$–$$$

Victorian Guest Accommodations

P.O. Box 18, Cape May, NJ 08204; tel: 609-884-9199.

This service books lodging in area bed-and-breakfasts.

TOURS AND OUTFITTERS

Cape May Bird Observatory

600 Route 47 North, Cape May Court House, NJ 08210; tel: 609-861-0700.

The observatory leads scheduled nature walks and field trips to destinations throughout the Cape May area. The two-hour to day-long activities are available for a modest fee. Birders may also arrange to attend three-, four-, or five-day workshops on various topics, such as raptor migration and wintering waterfowl.

Focus on Nature Tours

P.O. Box 9021, Wilmington, DE

19809; tel: 302-529-1876.

All-day pelagic excursions depart from Cape May and Brielle, New Jersey, to view seabirds and marine mammals in New Jersey and Delaware waters. Tours departing from Lewes, Delaware, head for the tips and edges of deepwater canyons off Delaware and Maryland.

Wildlife Unlimited

10 Wahl Avenue, Dias Creek, NJ 08210; tel: 609-884-3100.

Passengers view wildlife in area salt marshes and explore bays and beaches where osprey, herons, egrets, laughing gulls, and various seabirds nest. The focus of the tour changes with the season: raptors in fall, waterfowl and shorebirds in winter, waves of migrants in spring. The 40-foot-long *Skimmer* departs from Cape May.

SPECIAL EVENTS

Cape May Autumn Weekend and Bird Show

Hawk, songbird, and butterfly migrations are the focus of field trips, boat trips, workshops, and lectures held the first weekend in November. The Bird Show features vendors, exhibits, and activities for children. For information, call 609-861-0700 or 609-884-2736.

Cape May Spring Weekend

During three days in mid-May, birders join field trips to Cape May or offshore trips to observe seabirds and marine mammals. Other programs sponsored by the Cape May Bird Observatory cover migration, bird identification, nature photography, and optical equipment. For information, call 609-861-0700 or 609-884-2736.

World Series of Birding

This fund-raiser, which benefits conservation organizations, pits teams of birders against each other in a contest to see the most species. Sponsored by the New Jersey Audubon Society, the event is held the second or third Saturday in May. For information, call 609-861-0700 or 609-884-2736.

Excursions

Blackwater National Wildlife Refuge

2145 Key Wallace Drive, Cambridge, MD 21613; tel: 410-228-2677.

In this refuge east of the Chesapeake Bay, thousands of ducks and geese winter in the company of about a thousand tundra swans. Blackwater also has a healthy population of predatory birds: great horned and short-eared owls, northern harriers, and red-tailed and rough-legged hawks. Nearly 200 bald eagles winter here, some of which remain to nest. Fall and spring are good times to look for eastern warbler species.

Great Dismal Swamp National Wildlife Refuge

3100 Desert Road, P.O. Box 349, Suffolk, VA 23439; tel: 757-986-3705.

Wading birds are a prime attraction at this densely wooded swamp overlapping the Virginia-North Carolina border. Snowy, great, and cattle egrets, great blue, little, and green herons, and black-crowned night-herons stalk fish and other prey in the refuge. Birders may also see glossy ibises, soras, and American bitterns. Wood ducks and pileated woodpeckers nest in the swamp. Freshwater Lake Drummund is host to geese, ducks, and tundra swans in fall. Bobcats, black bears, beavers, and river otters are occasionally seen.

Bombay Hook National Wildlife Refuge

2591 Whitehall Neck Road, Smyrna, DE 19977; tel: 302-653-9345.

Bombay Hook consists largely of tidal salt marsh, along with freshwater ponds and forested swamps. A 12-mile auto tour connects these habitats, providing views of the 150,000 geese, ducks, and swans that migrate through or winter in the refuge. Birders can also survey the area from three 30-foot-high observation towers. Shorebirds arrive in May and June, and summer is the best time to see herons, egrets, and glossy ibises. The annual Delaware Birding Festival is held here and in the nearby Prime Hook refuge in late May.

Hawk Mountain Sanctuary

Pennsylvania

CHAPTER 10

t's a battle against the cold to a degree you hadn't expected. You're glad for the second sweater below your parka, yet long for a third. Thankful now for the thermos of hot chocolate you lugged up the mountain, you hunker down a little deeper, trying to find that certain spot among the jumble of rocks out of the biting northwest gale. ◆ The flight is slow at first, but by late morning, patches of sun begin to break through the leaden clouds and the wind thankfully begins to drop. Distant specks materialize, specks that slowly grow closer. A binocular-shaken speck becomes a bird, then the bird becomes a hawk, then a buteo, and finally an adult red-tailed hawk, wings folded, rocketing by on the autumn updrafts, passing mere yards off the promontory. ◆ You become adept at picking out the red-tails, most appearing up ridge over peak Number Four, coming one after another on their annual journey south. Someone calls out, "Big bird over Number Two. It looks good." You pick

Birds of prey migrate along a legendary ridge where raptor conservation began.

up the bird and agree, yes, this one is different. The dark, flat wings are rock steady despite the wind as it approaches. A senior staff naturalist, today's official counter, takes a long look at the bird. A patch of sunlight strikes the still-distant shape and reveals a brilliant gold head. Several watchers turn toward the naturalist, who flashes a small but satisfied smile before announcing loudly and enthusiastically what all the assembled are hoping for, "Golden eagle coming in." ◆ The young eagle sails in, riding the updrafts with insouciance, its long glide interrupted by only a few correcting half flaps. On set wings, it drifts past the lookout, close, the gleaming gold of the head and neck offsetting burnt umber and the brilliant

Hawk Mountain, where hunters once killed thousands of raptors, now welcomes visitors armed only with binoculars.

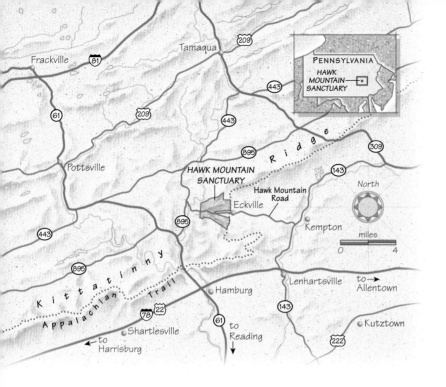

Golden eagles (opposite, top) are an impressive sight; their wingspan exceeds six feet.

Red-tailed hawks (below) in flight show a dark belly band and long, dark marks along the leading edge of the underwings.

Forest hawks like the northern goshawk (opposite, bottom) are agile fliers capable of threading through dense woodlands.

white in the tail and wings. Then, as quickly as you read these words, it is gone, autumn gold, south with the fall. You're shaking, but not from the cold. What cold? All of that is forgotten as the naturalist announces, "Three more birds coming. Get on these." Overhead a common raven croaks its approval of the fine November day.

Conservation Victories

For many visitors, **Hawk Mountain Sanctuary** is Indian summer, watching lazy kettles of broad-winged hawks high overhead in hazy September skies, with autumn leaves just beginning to turn the rolling mountains to orange and gold. For others, the greatest excitement comes later, when the somber tones of the bare trees presage the coming winter. In November, the winds may have pulled the color from the trees and the warmth from the rocks, but the colors are on the birds: the rich tones of an adult red-shouldered hawk soaring below eye level, the tawny hues of a young goshawk, the gunmetal blue back of an adult Cooper's hawk weaving

through the trees.

Whatever the season, Hawk Mountain is one of those places to which every hawk watcher, indeed every environmentalist, must eventually journey. It is a pilgrimage, for Hawk Mountain is where it all began, not only hawk migration counts but raptor conservation as well. Author and hawk expert Pete Dunne has aptly called Hawk Mountain "the Godfather site." Here you can feel the tradition and sit on the same rocks that have been host to some of the bravest and most committed conservationists of all time.

Situated on the **Kittatinny Ridge** in eastern Pennsylvania, north of **Reading**, this 2,400-acre site was the world's first refuge for birds of prey and the first place where raptor migration counts were ever conducted.

The story of Hawk Mountain Sanctuary is a triumph of conservation. In 1932, a young ornithologist, Richard Pough, came to the mountain to witness the annual slaughter of hawks, shot for both sport and bounty. His grim photographs of hundreds of dead raptors came to the attention of a New Yorker named Rosalie Edge. In September 1934, with help from a few friends, she purchased an option on 1,393 acres, including the rocky outcropping

where the shooting occurred, and founded Hawk Mountain Sanctuary.

She hired Maurice Broun, a young Cape Cod ornithologist, and his wife Irma as caretakers and wardens, and after many angry confrontations, the guns of autumn were silenced. A hawk count done that year became an annual effort to monitor populations of raptors. The rest is not only history but legend, a conservation odyssey delightfully captured in Maurice Broun's classic book, *Hawks Aloft*.

Just as many of the titans of conservation once mounted the trail up the mountain, so do today's environmentalists. The staff members at Hawk Mountain are at the forefront of raptor protection on an international scale, organizing and supporting research and education efforts worldwide. Their model intern program has trained dozens of young conservationists now working in key positions in many foreign lands. It was Hawk Mountain's raptor counts that, in part, alerted the world to the plight of bald eagles and peregrine falcons due to the ravages of DDT. Today, the staff coordinates, reviews, and analyzes data from many sites throughout the country and hemisphere, ever alert for emerging threats to raptors.

Catching the Updrafts

The autumn migration begins at Hawk Mountain in mid-August, with the first movement of American kestrels, ospreys, and bald eagles. The wave builds through September, cresting with broad-wings in mid-September and sharp-shinned hawks in late September and early October. October brings the greatest variety of raptors; November sees the drama of rolling cold fronts and snow flurries, and waves of red-tails and red-shouldereds bolting south. The flow ends about mid-December with the passage of the last red-tails, goshawks, eagles, and a rough-legged hawk or two. While any strong cold front will produce a good flight, veteran watchers talk of two magic dates at the sanctuary. Most years, the big broad-winged hawk push will occur one or two days either side of September 17, and the peak for golden eagles is often a few days either side of November 1, depending on frontal passage. Because peak season – early September to mid-October – brings thousands of weekend visitors, many birders prefer mid-week or early or late season.

Hawk Mountain averages about 20,000 birds of prey each fall, sometimes several thousand in a day. The totals can be higher if the main broad-winged hawk flight passes directly over the sanctuary, or lower if the flocks are dispersed or displaced by weather conditions. Broad-wings, mainly using thermals for migration, are less dependent on ridges and updrafts than other raptors.

Updrafts are the reason for the raptor concentrations at Hawk Mountain. In fall, raptors follow ridge lines south, getting a free ride on winds deflected up and over the mountain by a northwest flow. Kittatinny Mountain, essentially the front range of the Appalachians, runs northeast-southwest and offers the final set of ridges in the region. Hawk Mountain's lookout sits atop the last ridge of the system, which is in effect the final opportunity for hawks to use updrafts. If they lose the ridge, the birds are forced to use the slower travel mode of thermals, or energy-inefficient direct flapping flight, to travel over the flat-lands of the Piedmont.

A Predatory Lifestyle

Raptors have many special attributes that support their predatory nature, among them powerful beaks, long curved talons, and extraordinary vision thought to be eight times more acute than that of humans.

Specialized powers of flight also allow for successful hunting. Buteos, such as the red-tailed hawk, circle high on broad wings and spread tails, sometimes hovering in place before dropping on prey. Accipiters like the Cooper's hawk generally live in forests and use short wings and a long, rudderlike tail to maneuver while chasing prey, principally smaller birds. Falcons, birds of open country, use rapid direct flight far more than other hawks. The peregrine is one of the fastest birds in the world, stooping (diving) on prey from above at speeds up to 150 miles per hour.

No single feature defines eagles, essentially very large, strong hawks. The golden takes a wide variety of prey, including birds caught on the wing. The magnificent stoop of a golden eagle rivals that of the peregrine. The bald eagle, more of an opportunistic feeder, is not above scavenging if necessary or convenient. Because balds take many fish, they are usually associated with water. Unlike ospreys, which dive into the water feet first, eagles pluck fish from the surface, without diving in.

Vultures are true scavengers, playing an important role as nature's cleanup crew. The turkey vulture hunts with both sight and smell. The black vulture hunts by sight alone, often soaring higher than the turkey vulture for a better view.

While most birds of prey feed during migration, some flocking species such as Swainson's hawks and broad-winged hawks may cover vast distances without food, relying instead on body fat. A soaring hawk, riding thermals and updrafts on set wings, expends little more energy than a perched bird uses to hold on to a branch.

Up and Down the Ridge

Many birders are surprised to learn that fall is not the only season to enjoy Hawk Mountain. The sanctuary visitor center and its exceptional displays are open

Peregrine falcons (left) are consummate hunters with a wide-ranging diet: seabirds, ducks, shorebirds, and even other raptors.

American kestrels (opposite, top) bear the dark mustache marks seen also on peregrine and prairie falcons.

Bald eagles (opposite, center) do not develop white head plumage until they are four years old.

Ridge lines (opposite, bottom) are like highways for raptors exploiting updrafts as they migrate.

year-round. Excellent hiking trails are particularly popular in spring, and although raptors are not nearly as geographically concentrated as in fall, there is a small but steady spring hawk flight. In late spring and summer, sanctuary trails offer looks at rose-breasted grosbeaks, scarlet tanagers, indigo buntings, and red-eyed vireos. Warblers nesting on the mountain include ovenbirds and worm-eating, black-and-white, and black-throated green warblers. Finally, winter at the lookout can bring peaceful vistas of snowy landscapes, as well as hiking or even cross-country skiing on the **Appalachian Trail**, which runs along the border of the sanctuary.

Hawk Mountain will always be the premier hawk-watch in the region, but other nearby sites also offer a pageant of autumn migration. Farther up ridge, **Raccoon Ridge** in **New Jersey** and **Bake Oven Knob** in **Pennsylvania**, east of Hawk Mountain, provide great views of the flight, with counts rivaling Hawk Mountain's. Farther south (down ridge), **Second Mountain** lookout near **Harrisburg** sees substantial flights, and **Waggoner's Gap** near **Carlisle** always has a good autumn flight – particularly for red-tails and golden eagles. The draw of these watch sites is different, yet similarly pleasing views, and vastly fewer people during peak season.

Going to Hawk Mountain is like going to the well, the well from which so much has sprung. Many feel the need to return, to drink again and again – to feel and respect the history and tradition, to sit among the sacred rocks and scan down-ridge, waiting. Waiting for first the speck, then the shape, then the flutter in your chest when you realize the identity, and the naturalist pronouncing to the multitude, "Golden eagle coming in."

TRAVEL TIPS

DETAILS

When to Go

Fall raptor migration begins in mid-August and winds down in mid-December. The migration peaks from early September to mid-October, when broad-winged hawks and sharp-shinned hawks pass through. Thousands of birders arrive during this time; consider weekday visits. A smaller concentration of raptors appears during the spring migration. Late spring through summer is a good time to view nesting songbirds. Daytime temperatures reach 80°F in mid-August, but drop into the low 40s and 50s by the end of October. Expect blustery conditions on the mountain.

How to Get There

Philadelphia International Airport is a two-hour drive from the sanctuary.

Getting Around

Automobiles, necessary for travel to the sanctuary, are available for rent at the airport.

Handicapped Access

The main floor of the visitor center, the self-guided trail to the sanctuary's habitat garden, and the garden's observation deck are accessible. The trail to South Lookout and the lookout platform are also accessible.

INFORMATION

Hawk Mountain Sanctuary

1700 Hawk Mountain Road, Kempton, PA 19529; tel: 610-756-6000.

Lehigh Valley Convention and

Visitors Bureau
2200 Avenue A, Bethlehem, PA 18017; tel: 800-747-0561.

Reading-Berks County Visitors Bureau

352 Penn Street, Reading, PA 19602; tel: 800-443-6610.

Schuylkill County Visitors Bureau

91 South Progress Avenue, Pottsville, PA 17901; tel: 800-765-7282.

Rare Bird Alert

Tel: 717-622-6013 in Schuylkill County, 610-376-6000 (ext. 2473) in Berks County.

CAMPING

Appalachian Campsites

P.O. Box 27, Shartlesville, PA 19554; tel: 800-424-5746.

The year-round facility has about 150 sites and a café.

Blue Rocks Campground

341 Sousley Road, Lenhartsville, PA 19534; tel: 610-756-6366.

Open from April 1 to November 1, this campground offers 200 sites on 125 wooded acres.

LODGING

PRICE GUIDE – double occupancy

$ = up to $49 $$ = $50–$99
$$$ = $100–$149 $$$$ = $150+

Around the World Bed-and-Breakfast

30 South Whiteoak Street, Kutztown, PA 19530; tel: 610-683-8885.

The bed-and-breakfast has two guest rooms and two suites, all with private baths. Guests begin their day with a country breakfast. $$–$$$

Campus Inn

15080 Kutztown Road, Kutztown, PA 19530; tel: 610-683-8721.

A continental breakfast is served at this 29-room hotel. $$

Gloria's Forget-Me-Not Guest House

33 Hawk Mountain Road, Kempton, PA 19529; tel: 610-756-3398.

The main guest house, a Victorian dating from the late 1800s, has two rooms with a shared bath. Also on the property is a cottage with private bath and refrigerator. All guests are served a full breakfast. $$–$$$

Hawk Mountain Bed-and-Breakfast

221 Stoney Run Valley Road, Kempton, PA 19529; tel: 610-756-4224.

Each of the inn's eight guest rooms has a private bath and separate entrance. Two large rooms have fireplaces and Jacuzzis. A full breakfast is served. $$$

Lincoln Motel

R.R. 4, Box 171, Kutztown, PA 19530; tel: 610-683-3456.

The Lincoln has 14 rooms, each with private bath. $–$$

Patchwork Bed-and-Breakfast

R.D. #2, Box 2135, Orwigsburg, PA 17961; tel: 570-943-2737.

Full breakfasts at the Patchwork include local specialties. Three guest rooms are available. $$

Reiff Farm Bed-and-Breakfast

495 Old State Road, Oley, PA 19547; tel: 610-987-6216.

This Pennsylvania Dutch homestead, dating from the early 1700s, overlooks the Oley Valley. Guests have access to foot and horse trails on surrounding land, where 50 bird species have been identified. Three guest rooms are available in the main house, two in a log cabin. A full breakfast is served. $$

River Inn

1476 Route 61 Highway South,

Pottsville, PA 17901; tel: 570-385-2407.

This inn on the Schuylkill River offers standard rooms of varying size. Refrigerators are supplied on request. $$

Serenity Farm and Milk House

R.D. 2, Box 2040, Orwigsburg, PA 17961; tel: 570-943-2919.

Two guest rooms share a bath in the large stone farmhouse. The Milk House, a stone cottage, has a sleeping loft, full kitchen, living area, and private bath. Guests in the farmhouse are served a full country breakfast; those in the cottage may order breakfast for a small additional charge. $$–$$$

Stone House

16 Dock Street, Schuylkill Haven, PA 17972; tel: 570-385-2115.

Ten minutes north of Hawk Mountain Sanctuary, the Stone House has four rooms, each with private bath. A full breakfast is served. $$

TOURS AND OUTFITTERS

Hawk Mountain Sanctuary

1700 Hawk Mountain Road, Kempton, PA 19529; tel: 610-756-6000.

Guides stationed at sanctuary lookouts answer questions and help visitors identify birds. From spring through fall, sanctuary staff and guest instructors offer workshops on raptor identification, raptor photography, and other subjects, and lead field trips to various sanctuary sites. Many programs are free; fees are charged for longer workshops. Scheduled classes and lectures on native flora and fauna are also available.

Excursions

Monongahela National Forest

200 Sycamore Street, Elkins, WV 26241; tel: 304-636-1800.

Birders at this 900,000-acre forest hike through dense hardwood, stands of red spruce at high elevations, and upland bogs laced with creeks. Four species of thrush – Swainson's, wood, hermit, and veery – nest in the forest. Scanning the canopy is the best way to spot eastern warblers such as Canada, blackpoll, magnolia, chestnut-sided, and black-throated blue and green. Hikers occasionally see wild turkeys foraging on the forest floor.

Niagara Reservation State Park

P.O. Box 1132, Niagara Falls, NY 14303; tel: 716-278-1770.

Iceland, Bonaparte's, ring-billed, Franklin's, great black-backed, herring, and 14 other species of gulls feed within view of the famous falls in autumn and winter. Also seen here are common goldeneyes, red-breasted and common mergansers, harlequin ducks, and other waterfowl. Birding is productive at various locations along the Niagara River, including Fort Niagara, where the waterway flows into Lake Ontario.

Shenandoah National Park

3655 U.S. 211 East, Luray, VA 22835; tel: 540-999-3500.

A scenic drive runs through this narrow park, whose 195,000 acres spread along 80 miles of the Blue Ridge Mountains. More than 200 bird species have been recorded in the park's abundant forests and at higher, less verdant elevations. Among Shenandoah's nesting birds are vireos, scarlet tanagers, and warblers, including Kentucky, black-throated blue, black-throated green, and hooded. High-elevation lookouts are good places to watch migrating raptors in fall.

Point Pelee National Park
Ontario

C H A P T E R **11**

When it comes to warblers, nothing is quite like **Point Pelee** in mid-May. On a good day, you'll find scores, hundreds of these feathered jewels – blackburnian, black-throated green, Cape May, yellow-rumped, and chestnut-sided warblers, just to name a handful – most returning from wintering grounds in the tropics. Overall, of the 55 species of North American wood warblers, 42 have been recorded in Point Pelee – 38 in a single season.   ◆   What makes the place so wonderful? Geography, geography, geography. Carved by glaciers during the Ice Age, this sharply pointed peninsula juts south into Lake Erie, giving northbound spring migrants their first sight of land after crossing the lake. Untold thousands of migrants funnel through this unique landmass. The funnel analogy is especially apt during the southbound return migration in autumn, as you can see when you look at a map or satellite image of the funnel-shaped wedge of land pointing toward the United States.   ◆   Point Pelee was designated a national park in 1918. Encompassing a mere six square miles, it is one of the smallest in the country – but enormously popular with birders. Aside from shape and location, Point Pelee enjoys a variety of habitats attractive to birds. Freshwater marshes make up the bulk of the park, but you'll also find wet and dry deciduous forest, sandy beaches, and cedar savannah, supporting many animal species and more than 750 kinds of plants. Another bonus is the climate, the mildest in Ontario. Situated at about the same latitude as Northern California, Point Pelee boasts a mean temperature in January of 27°F, practically balmy for Canada.

A small peninsula on Lake Erie welcomes dozens of warbler species on their long flights north and south.

A marsh wren strikes a characteristic pose, cocking its tail as it clings to a reed.

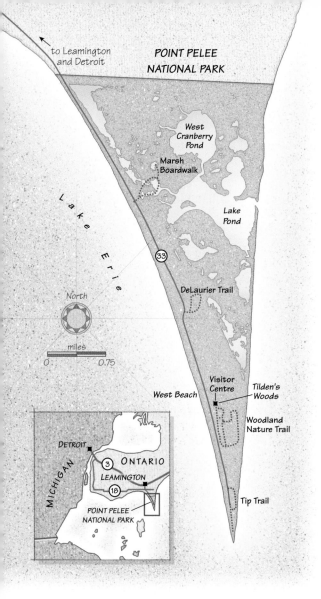

to Leamington
and Detroit

**POINT PELEE
NATIONAL PARK**

West
Cranberry
Pond

Marsh
Boardwalk

Lake
Pond

Lake Erie

(33)

DeLaurier Trail

North

miles
0   0.75

Visitor
Centre

West Beach

Tilden's
Woods

Woodland
Nature Trail

Tip Trail

DETROIT

ONTARIO
(3)
LEAMINGTON
(18)

MICHIGAN

POINT PELEE
NATIONAL PARK

Male common yellow-throats (right) can be distinguished from females by their prominent black mask. Their *wichity wichity wichity wich* call helps locate them in dense vegetation.

Warblers such as the Blackburnian, Nashville, and Cape May (opposite, top to bottom) often fly hundreds of miles at night before arriving at Point Pelee.

seven and a half miles of the park. An additional 7½ miles of seasonal trails are open during April and May.

You'll want to arrive at the Tip early in the morning. Songbirds migrate primarily at night, and many of them land here, exhausted, with the coming of dawn. The birds frequently rest on the beach for a time, regaining their strength before moving into trees and shrubbery. Birders are often surprised to find warblers and other wood-land birds feeding on insects right on the sand. For photographers, there's no better place to get close-ups of normally elusive chestnut-sided, blackburnian, and other brightly colored warblers. These birds often stay in the vicinity of Point Pelee for several days or longer before departing for breeding grounds farther north.

From the Tip you can stroll through the woods on the **Tip Trail** or walk along **West Beach**. In addition to songbirds, you'll find several species of shorebirds foraging at the water's edge, as well as red-breasted mergansers; Bonaparte's, ring-billed, herring, and possibly black-backed and little gulls; Caspian and common terns; and sometimes scoters.

A short distance north of the Tip, not far from the tram loop, is an open, grassy area nicknamed the "Sparrow Field." Savannah, chipping, white-crowned, field, and song sparrows all forage on the ground for seeds or sing their distinctive

Tip of the Funnel

Start your explorations at the Visitor Centre, four and a half miles south of the park entrance. You'll find up-to-date information on the progress of the bird migration as well as any rare sightings. Park naturalists give advice on which areas are best for seeing particular species, and they lead bird walks during spring migration. From the Visitor Centre, you can board a free tram for a 1½-mile ride to the **Tip**, the southernmost point of mainland Canada. A network of walking paths and interpretive trails, either boardwalk or crushed stone, covers some songs. Also look for the less common grasshopper, Le Conte's, Henslow's, and clay-colored sparrows.

Woodland Denizens

The **Woodland Nature Trail** winds its way back toward the **Visitor Centre**, taking you through hardwood forest and swamp and giving you good views of mourning and Kentucky warblers, as well as Lincoln's sparrows. The emphatic song of the ovenbird – *teacher, teacher, teacher* – punctuates the morning calm, in marked contrast to the ethereal, flutelike symphonies of wood thrushes. In the wetter areas, you should be able to find wood ducks, the most exquisite of North American waterfowl, and also northern shovelers and green herons. Listen for the distinctive song of the northern waterthrush, *twit twit twit sweet sweet sweet chew chew chew*. This secretive bird usually lurks on or near the ground, rapidly bobbing its tail as it walks through boggy areas.

Just across from the Visitor Centre is **Tilden's Woods**, an area of mature wet and dry woodland inhabited by white-eyed and yellow-throated vireos and Kentucky, golden-winged, hooded, and prothonotary warblers.

While at Point Pelee, you may want to visit the old homestead on the **DeLaurier Trail**. The DeLauriers, who arrived in 1832, were among the first European families to colonize the area, and the restored buildings offer a fascinating look at life in settlement days. The orchards and fields, abandoned nearly a century ago, are returning to a wild state. Savannah, chipping, field, white-throated, and white-crowned sparrows are found along the trail foraging on the ground or singing from low perches, while willow and alder flycatchers sally out from the trees to hawk flying insects. You'll also find bobolinks, singing their bubbly *bob-o-link* song, as well as eastern bluebirds, northern mockingbirds, and, of course, a variety of warblers.

Marsh Sightings

The **Marsh Boardwalk**, about a mile and a half south of the park entrance, leads

through the peninsula's wetland habitat, which covers approximately two-thirds of Point Pelee's overall area. Observation towers at the start and end of the board-walk, which extends a mile into the marsh, offer a fine view of the surrounding area with its cattails, water lilies, bladderwort,

pondweed, and other aquatic plants. Watch for common yellowthroats, swamp sparrows, and marsh wrens, as well as more retiring Virginia rails and soras. You may also see a beautiful hooded merganser – the male bearing conspicuous white patches on the head and breast. Be sure to keep an eye out for least and American bitterns blending into the vegetation. An early-morning visit to the marsh often yields sightings of other wildlife, such as muskrats, which are quite common, and snapping, Blanding's, and other turtles.

For shorebirds, gulls, and terns, head for the onion fields just outside the park boundaries. Sanderlings, ruddy turnstones, dunlins, American golden-plovers, and black-bellied plovers feed or rest here, giving your daily list a nice boost. It's not unusual for an experienced birder to find 100 different species in a single day during migration.

In spring, the birds arrive in waves, depending on weather fronts and other conditions. The migration doesn't truly get going until well into March, as flocks of red-winged blackbirds, American robins, mourning doves, and various waterfowl pass through. Warm periods in April bring the first insectivorous birds, but it really isn't until mid-May that the warblers arrive in force.

Fall migration has its own special appeal. Warblers are relatively quiet and drab, but hawks are numerous. Many raptors follow the Lake Erie shoreline, and they end up being funneled to the tip of Point Pelee. You're assured of seeing hundreds of American kestrels and sharp-shinned hawks passing overhead, and if you're lucky, you may spot a peregrine falcon or a golden eagle.

Riding the Wind

As remarkable as the power of flight itself is the diversity of structural design that enables different birds to fly in ways that work best for their particular needs.

Pheasants and grouse, for instance, have short, fast-moving wings that permit them to burst noisily from cover and fly short distances with great speed; by startling or confusing a predator, they have a chance to escape. The short, rounded wings and long tails of woodland hawks such as Cooper's hawks, goshawks, and sharp-shinned hawks allow these accipiters to thread their way quickly and easily through branches in surprise attacks on prey. Falcons such as peregrines and merlins, however, are open-country predators. They use their relatively short tails and long, pointed wings – and their phenomenally high speed and endurance – to outfly their prey.

The basics of flight are the same in most birds. Air moving across their wings produces an upward force, called lift, strong enough to overcome the force of gravity. The only exceptions are hummingbirds, which flap their tiny wings in a figure-eight pattern, moving so fast that you can barely see them. Like living helicopters, hummingbirds can move easily in any direction or hang in the air as they sip nectar from flowers. Yet they're also capable of migrating thousands of miles.

Birds also display an astounding range of adaptations. Both a wandering albatross and a red-tailed hawk are capable of soaring hundreds of miles with little effort. The albatross has enormously long, slender wings, perfect for taking advantage of ocean wind currents. The red-tailed hawk's wings are nowhere near as long in proportion to its body, but are very broad, enabling the hawk to use the updrafts of warm air that occur only over land.

The great blue heron (above), with its six-foot wingspan, flies with slow, steady wingbeats, tucking its head close to its shoulders.

The house wren (left) is equipped with strong pectoral muscles that enable fast, sustained flight.

Least bitterns (opposite, top), members of the heron family, nest in Point Pelee's wetlands.

The Marsh Boardwalk (opposite, bottom) loops for one mile through a seemingly infinite sea of cattails.

DETAILS

When to Go

Early to late May is the peak time to view shorebirds, migratory warblers, and other songbirds. Birders also come from late August through the fall to watch migrating hawks. Daytime temperatures in spring, usually in the 50s and 60s, reach the 70s by late season; lows are in the 40s. Fall highs are in the 60s and 70s, lows in the 40s and 50s. Expect occasional rainfall in spring and autumn.

How to Get There

Commercial airlines serve airports in Detroit, Michigan, about two hours from the park, and Windsor, Ontario, an hour away.

Getting Around

A car is essential; rentals are available at both airports.

Handicapped Access

The Visitor Centre, Marsh Boardwalk, DeLaurier Trail, and Tip area are accessible.

INFORMATION

Point Pelee National Park

1118 Point Pelee Drive, Leamington, ON N8H 3V4, Canada; tel: 519-322-2365.

Convention and Visitors Bureau of Windsor, Essex County, and Pelee Island

City Centre Mall, 333 Riverside Drive West, Windsor, ON N9A 5K4, Canada; tel: 800-265-3633 or 519-255-6530.

Leamington and District Chamber of Commerce

P.O. Box 321, Leamington, ON N8H 3W3, Canada; tel: 800-250-3336 or 519-326-2721.

Rare Bird Alerts

Tel: 519-322-2371 (spring and fall migrations in the park); www.erca.org. (fall hawk migration).

CAMPING

Point Pelee National Park

1118 Point Pelee Drive, Leamington, ON N8H 3V4, Canada; tel: 519-322-2365.

Campsites are available for organized groups by advanced arrangement.

Wheatley Provincial Park

P.O. Box 640, Wheatley, ON N0P 2P0, Canada; tel: 519-825-4659.

Wheatley, a 20-minute drive east of Point Pelee, has 220 campsites. Most sites may be reserved up to 11 months in advance; call 888-668-7275. The remaining sites are available on a first-come, first-served basis.

LODGING

PRICE GUIDE – double occupancy

$ = up to $49 $$ = $50–$99
$$$ = $100–$149 $$$$ = $150+

Marlborough House

49 Marlborough West, Leamington, ON N8H 1V9, Canada; tel: 519-322-1395.

Three guest rooms, one with a private bath, are available at this bed-and-breakfast, housed in an 1890s Victorian. A full breakfast is served. $$

Pelee Island Hotel

Westshore Road, Pelee Island, ON N0R 1M0, Canada; tel: 519-724-2912.

This hotel on Pelee Island, a short ferry ride from the mainland, has 14 rooms, some with views of Lake Erie. Guests are served a full breakfast. $$

Point Pelee Bed-and-Breakfast Reservation Service

115 Erie Street South, Leamington, ON N8H 3B5, Canada; tel: 888-339-0418 or 519-326-7169.

The service handles information and reservations for nearly 35 bed-and-breakfasts in the Point Pelee area. Visitors should book accommodations well in advance, especially when planning to visit the park in May.

Sun Parlour Motel

200 Talbot Street East, Leamington, ON N8H 1N2, Canada; tel: 519-326-6131.

Just outside the park, the motel has 17 rooms, three of which are equipped with full kitchens. $$

Sun Ridge Bed-and-Breakfast

RR 5, Leamington, ON N8H 3V6, Canada; tel: 519-326-2478.

This Victorian farmhouse has three rooms and a large attic loft that accommodates five guests. Visitors are served a full breakfast. $$

Westview Motel

West Dock, Pelee Island, ON N0R 1M0, Canada; tel: 519-724-2072.

This Pelee Island motel, a short ferry ride from the mainland, offers views of Lake Erie. In addition to five motel rooms, Westview has two cottages, each with a kitchen, living room, and bedroom. A restaurant is on the premises. $$–$$$

Wigle's Colonial Motel

133 Talbot Street East, Leamington, ON N8H 1L6, Canada; tel: 519-326-3265.

The motel offers basic comfort at a reasonable price. A few of the 22 rooms have refrigerators and stoves. $$

Wild Rose Guest House

RR 1, Wheatley, ON N0P 2P0, Canada; tel: 519-825-9169.

Operated by avid birders, the Wild Rose offers four-day/three-night packages in May and three-day/two-night packages in fall. Packages include accommodations, breakfast and lunch, and guiding services at the park and other birding spots. One hundred and fifty bird species have been identified on the Wild Rose's wooded grounds. $$$$

TOURS AND OUTFITTERS

Point Pelee Birding
RR 1, Leamington, ON N8H 3V4, Canada; tel: 519-326-0687.

Field trips are led year-round to Point Pelee National Park and other nearby birding areas.

SPECIAL EVENTS

Festival of Birds
Point Pelee National Park, 1118 Point Pelee Drive, Leamington, ON N8H 3V4, Canada; tel: 519-322-2365.

The entire month of May, the peak of spring migration, is declared a birding festival, with field trips and workshops on bird identification and other topics. The park also sponsors evening lectures at the Visitor Centre Theatre.

Festival of Hawks
Essex Region Conservation Authority, 360 Fairview Avenue West, Essex, ON N8M 1Y6, Canada; tel: 519-776-5209.

Daily totals of up to 96,000 raptors, including tens of thousands of broad-winged hawks, have been recorded at the Holiday Beach Conservation Area on Lake Erie between late August and December. During the last three weekends in December, birders attend the festival's guided walks, photography and identification workshops, and raptor banding demonstrations. Children's activities are available.

Excursions

Algonquin Provincial Park
P.O. Box 219, Whitney, ON K0J 2M0, Canada; tel: 613-637-2828.

The two-million-acre park teems with such boreal species as gray jays, boreal chickadees, black-backed woodpeckers, and spruce grouse. The deciduous and boreal forests, bogs, and marshes also attract warblers, thrushes, and various southern species. Algonquin's 260-bird checklist includes crossbills and redpolls, winter visitors sometimes seen in large numbers.

Hiawatha National Forest
2727 North Lincoln Road, Escanaba, MI 49829; tel: 906-786-4062.

Michigan's Upper Peninsula is a prime location for seeing northward migrations of songbirds. Nearly two dozen kinds of warblers pass through the forest in spring. Migratory shorebirds stop at the abundant wetlands. The forest grants splendid opportunities to see breeding species in summer, waterfowl in autumn, and owls in winter.

Horicon Marsh National Wildlife Refuge
4279 Headquarters Road, Mayville, WI 53050; tel: 920-387-2658.

The largest freshwater cattail marsh in the United States sustains large numbers of migratory ducks, geese, and sandhill cranes. Wading birds such as common moorhens and Virginia rails are supported by the refuge. Herons and egrets nest on an island in the refuge and forage in surrounding wetlands.

Ottawa National Wildlife Refuge Complex
14000 West State Route 2, Oak Harbor, OH 43449; tel: 419-898-0014.

Some of the state's few remaining wetlands are part of this three-refuge complex: Ottawa (open to visitors) and Cedar Point and West Sister Island (closed to protect nesting birds and other wildlife). The trio, on Lake Erie's south shore, are at a crossroads for birds of the eastern and central regions of the continent. Two-thirds of black ducks migrating through the area stop at these lakeside marshes.

Churchill
Manitoba

CHAPTER 12

Perched on the western rim of Hudson Bay, Churchill, Manitoba, is a drab little outpost in a vast wilderness of tundra, boreal forest, muskeg bogs, and lakes stretching for thousands of miles across northern Canada. For travelers who want to see arctic wildlife up close, however, it's a world-class destination. ◆ Though Churchill is a considerable distance south of the Arctic Circle, the frigid winds that blow across the ice-covered water have created a bayshore tundra like that found much farther north. Go a short distance inland and you enter a transition zone where tundra meets boreal forest, creating a rich mixture of plants and animals. This is a harsh land, with an extremely short "warm" season that draws migratory birds from as far as South America to feed on the clouds of mosquitoes and other insects. ◆ Here is where you can study shorebirds in the full splendor of their breeding plumage. Ordinarily dingy, gray short-billed dowitchers assume the stunning cinnamon colors of their nuptial garb, dunlins sport reddish backs and black bellies, and American golden-plovers ... well, they simply become one of the most beautiful shorebirds in the world. ◆ Many migrants arrive at or pass through the Churchill area in May, but June through early July is probably the best time for birders to visit. The birds arrive en masse. They mate, lay eggs, and raise young; then they depart. By mid-July, most male shorebirds have already left. During that brief window, you can find nesting dowitchers, dunlins, and golden-plovers, along with whimbrels, Hudsonian godwits, stilt sandpipers, Pacific loons, Bonaparte's gulls, Smith's longspurs, and

As icebergs recede and wildflowers emerge, the brief but spectacular breeding season begins for birds of the Canadian tundra.

The breeding plumage of the stilt sandpiper gives the bird protective camouflage on the tundra. The female usually lays four eggs, greenish orbs with brown speckles.

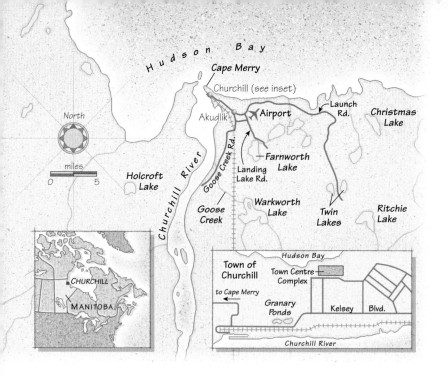

itchers, and Hudsonian godwits stride boldly past, poking at the mud and water with their oversized bills, while red-necked phalaropes spin in the shallows, stirring up food in their characteristic manner. This is also a great place to observe arctic terns, which have a nesting colony at the ponds (the birds will knock your hat off if you get too close), and various ducks – greater scaups, northern shovelers, gadwalls, American wigeons, northern pintails – that forage there. The ponds are also one of the best places to catch a glimpse of a Ross's gull.

Nearby **Cape Merry**, a picturesque promontory at the mouth of the Churchill River less than two miles farther up the road, offers numerous gulls and sea ducks – common eiders, oldsqaws, surf and white-winged scoters, common goldeneyes, and red-breasted mergansers – flying or sitting just offshore. You may also spot beluga whales swimming slowly among the icebergs.

Another productive location is **Goose Creek Road**, which runs in a southwesterly direction from Churchill for approximately 10 miles, taking you through spruce forests, willow thickets, marshes, ponds, and streams. Just before you get to the railroad

many more. With a bit of luck, you'll even see that Churchill specialty: the delicate, pink-breasted Ross's gull.

The change of seasons is amazingly compressed. You might get there in late June and find that the weather is uncomfortably cold and the Churchill River is choked with icebergs. A week or so later, the weather could be pleasant, with wildflowers blooming profusely all around you and the river free of ice.

Shorebird Paradise

Churchill is a bird photographer's dream as well. Less than a mile from the Churchill Motel, a short walk or drive northwest on Kelsey Boulevard, is a series of shallow pools known locally as the **Granary Ponds** right behind a huge grain elevator complex. Sitting at the water's edge, with or without a blind, you'll see stilt sandpipers, lesser yellowlegs, short-billed dow-

Lesser yellowlegs (above) are very vocal on their nesting grounds.

Churchill offers excellent opportunities to photograph wildlife (right).

Green-winged teals (opposite, top) are small dabbling ducks that feed close to the water's surface.

Hudsonian godwits (opposite, bottom) breed in the Churchill area.

crossing, check out the marshy area on both sides of the road for sharp-tailed sparrows, uncommon summer residents in the Churchill area. From there, you pass through several miles of stunted spruce forest, the place to spot woodland nesters such as gray jays, common and hoary redpolls, boreal chickadees, Bohemian waxwings, pine grosbeaks, white-winged crossbills, three-toed woodpeckers, Harris's sparrows, and northern shrikes. Lesser yellowlegs often perch on top of black spruces, calling loudly. In the ditches along Goose Creek Road, ducks such as green-winged teals, northern pintails, and American wigeons dabble for aquatic plants, seeds, and other nourishment.

Tundra Sightings

Taking a drive up **Landing Lake Road**, which runs south along the Churchill Airport runway and ends at Farnworth Lake, gives you a chance to explore some of the area's wet tundra habitat, where you can find breeding shorebirds. Larger birds such as whimbrels and Hudsonian godwits are easy to spot in the low-lying tundra vegetation. Get out of your car and walk along the road, scanning with binoculars for smaller, less noticeable shorebirds, such as short-billed dowitchers and dunlins. If you hear a strange winnowing sound, look up and you'll witness the spectacular courtship display of a pair of common snipe, with the wind whistling through the male's outermost tail feathers as he dives. Search for American golden-plovers in areas of dry tundra; the beautiful birds make no effort to conceal

themselves and are usually easy to spot.

While exploring the tundra, you may spot jaegers – usually parasitic, but sometimes long-tailed and even pomarine – cruising swift and low over land. These predatory seabirds are always searching for a luckless shorebird chick or some eggs to devour, so it's not a good idea to do much walking across the tundra. You may be helping the jaegers and other predators such as arctic foxes find their prey. In addition, it's all too easy to step on the cryptically marked shorebird eggs or chicks.

Keep an eye out for raptors while you're driving through open areas. It's not unusual to find short-eared owls cruising along in their wavering, mothlike flight. You may also see a hunting rough-legged hawk, hovering like a giant kestrel over a field, while it scans the ground. Merlins, a few of which nest in small trees in the area, sometimes rocket past, looking for small birds.

Farnworth Lake, which most of the local residents call Landing Lake, has nesting Pacific loons along its periphery. These lovely birds have ruby red eyes and heads that are light gray on top, with bold, black-and-white, diagonal lines on their necks and purplish throats. Watch them dive for fish or take off, running along the water to build up enough speed to become airborne. You can also find Bonaparte's gulls

Gull of the Arctic

Ross's gull is, without doubt, one of the world's most beautiful gulls. As an adult, this exquisite, almost ternlike denizen of the high arctic sports a stunning pink wash across its underparts and a thin necklace of black, arcing down from the back of its white head and across its throat. The adult's pink coloration actually comes from oil that the bird obtains from its preen gland and applies to its feathers. First-year Ross's gulls lack the distinctive black necklace and pink wash, but the bird's wedge-shaped tail is diagnostic at any age.

The gull was named after the Scottish explorer James Clark Ross, who, in 1823, served as navigator on one of the many futile attempts to locate the Northwest Passage. He did, however, succeed in collecting the first specimen of this gull, on Canada's Melville Peninsula.

Although the specimen was collected in North America, Ross's gull is primarily an Old World species that breeds almost exclusively in north-eastern Siberia. However, small colonies exist in Greenland and Norway, and in 1980 the gull was confirmed as nesting at Churchill. Since then, the gulls have nested – or attempted to nest – a number of times in the area.

Horned grebes (above) are named for their gold-tinted ear tufts, which they lose by winter.

The Ross's gull (left), a coveted sighting, is rarely seen south of Hudson Bay.

Dunlins (opposite, top), members of the sandpiper family, catch mosquitoes and forage for insect larvae when on the tundra.

Polar bears (opposite, bottom) head south toward Churchill when melting ice limits their access to seals, a mainstay of their diet.

(one of the few tree-nesting gulls), blackpoll warblers, and Harris's sparrows in the stunted trees around the lake.

Arctic Remoteness

The human history of Churchill and the surrounding area is also worthy of note. Native peoples, the Pre-Dorsets, hunted and fished here some 3,000 years ago. European explorers discovered Hudson Bay much later, in the early 1600s, searching for the elusive Northwest Passage.

More recently, in the early 1930s, Churchill became a seaport, the only one in subarctic Canada. Wheat from the southern prairies of Manitoba was – and still is – transported by train to the port, where ships carry the grain to Europe. But the shipping season is short – four months at the most – and then the bay and the river ice over and the port shuts down. Churchill has come to depend more and more on tourism to stay economically viable. People from all over the world come to see polar bears, which, along with birds, are the area's stellar attraction. Although Churchill has been dubbed the "Polar Bear Capital of the

World" by the local chamber of commerce, it's rare to see a bear during the peak birding season; the time for bears in numbers is September to mid-November.

Churchill is inaccessible by automobile. To get there, you must travel by airplane or train – a 38-hour ride from Winnipeg. One of the last great wilderness train rides in North America, it is a fascinating journey if you have the time and endurance to enjoy it. Some people opt to drive to Thompson, Manitoba, and take the train from there, though it's still a long haul. But you do have a chance of spotting some wonderful birds such as northern hawk owls and great gray owls perched in trees along the way.

DETAILS

When to Go

June through early July is the best time to see breeding shorebirds, songbirds, waterfowl, and seabirds. Weather is unpredictable, with temperatures ranging from the 40s to the 70s. Expect occasional rain, windy conditions, and mosquitoes.

How to Get There

Churchill is not accessible by automobile. Visitors drive or fly to Winnipeg, then take the 38-hour train ride to Churchill. VIA Rail Canada makes three trips per week; call 800-561-3949 (outside Canada) and 800-561-8630 (in Canada) for information. Visitors may also drive north of Winnipeg to Thompson, Manitoba, then travel overnight by Rail Canada to Churchill. Two carriers provide air service from Winnipeg to Churchill: Kivalliq Air, 877-855-1500, and Calm Air, 800-426-7000 (outside Canada) or 800-665-1177 (in Canada).

Getting Around

Car rentals are available in Churchill. Many visitors engage the services of guides and outfitters for birding in the area.

INFORMATION

Churchill Chamber of Commerce

P.O. Box 176, Churchill, MB R0B 0E0, Canada; tel: 888-389-2327 or 204-675-2022.

Travel Manitoba

155 Carlton Street, Winnipeg, MB R3C 3H8, Canada; tel: 800-665-0040.

CAMPING

There are no campgrounds in the Churchill area.

LODGING

PRICE GUIDE – double occupancy

$ = up to $49 $$ = $50–$99
$$$ = $100–$149 $$$$ = $150+

Aurora Inn

P.O. Box 1030, Churchill, MB R0B 0E0, Canada; tel: 800-265-8563 or 204-675-2071.

The inn offers 18 two-story suites and four guest rooms. Suites accommodate four to six people and have living rooms and fully-equipped kitchens. $$$

Bear Country Inn

P.O. Box 788, Churchill, MB R0B 0E0, Canada; tel: 204-675-8299.

The 27-room inn operates a free shuttle from the airport or train station. Guests are served a continental breakfast. $$

Churchill Motel

P.O. Box 218, Churchill, MB R0B 0E0, Canada; tel: 204-675-8853.

Recently renovated, the motel has 26 rooms with refrigerators. Visitors receive a discount for long stays. Free transportation is offered between the motel and the airport and train station. A restaurant is open during birder-friendly hours. $$

Northern Nights

P.O. Box 70, Churchill, MB R0B 0E0, Canada; tel: 204-675-2403.

Northern Nights has eight rooms with shared baths and 18 rooms with private baths. Free transportation is provided from the airport and train station. A restaurant, sauna, and hot tub are on the premises. $$

Polar Inn

P.O. Box 1031, Churchill, MB R0B 0E0, Canada; tel: 204-675-8878.

The inn has three types of accommodations: two one-bedroom apartments with living rooms and kitchens; two studios with kitchenettes; and 21 standard rooms with refrigerators. $$

Seaport Motel

P.O. Box 399, Churchill, MB R0B 0E0, Canada; tel: 204-675-8807.

The Seaport has 21 rooms with refrigerators. A restaurant and coffee shop are on the premises. The motel arranges free airport and train station pickup. $$

Tundra Inn

P.O. Box 999, Churchill, MB R0B 0E0, Canada; tel: 800-265-8563 or 204-675-8831.

The inn, which operates a restaurant across the street, has 31 rooms with refrigerators. $$

TOURS AND OUTFITTERS

Adventure Walking Tours

P.O. Box 1136, Churchill, MB R0J 0P0, Canada; tel: 204-675-2147.

Guides lead excursions to birding spots in the Churchill area and offer general wildlife tours, history tours, and guided hiking trips.

Churchill Nature Tours

P.O. Box 429, Erickson, MB R0J 0P0, Canada; tel: 204-636-2968.

Tours cover the Churchill area as well as other birding spots in Manitoba, including Riding Mountain National Park, Oak Hammock Marsh, and Delta Marsh.

Churchill Wilderness Encounter

P.O. Box 9, Churchill, MB R0B 0E0, Canada; tel: 800-265-9458 or 204-675-2248.

Bonnie Chartier, author of the American Birding Association's *A Birder's Guide to Churchill*, leads one- to six-day tours to see the birds of Manitoba from May through September. Off-season tours are available upon request. Birders see as many as 100 species during six-day trips.

North Star Tours

P.O. Box 520, Churchill, MB R0B 0E0, Canada; tel: 800-665-0690 or 204-675-2629.

North Star links visitors with local guides and assists with other travel arrangements, including accommodations and transportation.

Sea North Tours, Ltd.

P.O. Box 222, Churchill, MB R0B 0E0, Canada; tel: 204-675-2195.

From mid- to late June, the operator's 12-passenger Zodiacs transport birders to see gulls, jaegers, ducks, mergansers, loons, and other species found among the ice floes of Hudson Bay.

SPECIAL EVENTS

Delta Marsh Birding Festival

Box 38, RR 2, Portage la Prairie, MB R1N 3A2, Canada; tel: 204-857-8637 or 204-239-4287.

Situated in the Lake Manitoba basin northwest of Winnipeg, 52,000-acre Delta Marsh is a hot spot for birders in spring, when warblers and other migrants pass through. The four-day festival, held in mid-May, includes tours of the marsh and more than a dozen nearby sites, lectures by resident and visiting ornithologists, bird-banding demonstrations, and talks by notable photographers.

Excursions

Hecla/Grindstone Provincial Park

Department of Natural Resources, P.O. Box 70, Riverton, MB R0C 2R0, Canada; tel: 204-378-2261.

Between Hecla Island, the largest of several islands in Lake Winnipeg, and the mainland lies one of Manitoba's finest marshes, inhabited by yellow-headed blackbirds, five species of grebes – pied-billed, horned, red-necked, eared, western – and a host of waterfowl, including blue-winged and green-winged teals, buffleheads, and wood ducks. Birders on the lakeshore of the 267,000-acre island park see warblers, cormorants, gulls, and owls. Bald eagles nest on the island, which also supports a wolf pack.

Oak Hammock Marsh

P.O. Box 1160, Oak Hammock Marsh, MB R0C 2Z0, Canada; tel: 204-467-3300.

Remnants of the large bog that once linked southern Manitoba's lakes are preserved in this 8,900-acre marsh, where 275 bird species have been recorded. Thousands of

migratory waterfowl, such as Canada and snow geese, stop here, joined by godwits, sandpipers, plovers, and other shorebirds. Birders also see wading birds, songbirds, and warblers. Trails and boardwalks access the marsh. Canoe tours are available from spring through fall. Birders occasionally see snow buntings and snowy owls during winter snowshoe walks.

Riding Mountain National Park

Wasagaming, MB R0J 2H0, Canada; tel: 800-707-8480 or 204-848-7275.

Spreading eastward from the Manitoba escarpment, where visitors enjoy panoramic views, this 1,100-square-mile park contains boreal forest typical of the north country and deciduous woodlands similar to those farther east. This intermingling of habitats supports boreal species like three-toed woodpeckers, black-backed woodpeckers, great gray owls, and crossbills, and an array of nesting birds, including Nashville, Canada, and Connecticut warblers. The park's lakes attract nesting red-necked grebes, western grebes, and various waterfowl.

South Florida

CHAPTER 13

Driving south of Miami on Highway 1, you begin to sense the **Everglades** long before you get there. It's not just the heat and humidity but the beckoning skies to the south and west. Skies of crystal greet the early riser, but by mid-morning brilliant puffs of white dot the halcyon blue. Around noon, as convection draws moist sea air over the steaming grasslands and hammocks, the clouds become boiling masses of gray and white. They shed their burden in curtains of rain, linking the heavens and earth in an endless cycle. ◆ Convection means lift, and as the morning evolves, birds begin to fill the skies over the great sea of grass. Birders normally search bushes, trees, and ponds, but the best birding in the Everglades is often overhead, scanning for birds against the billowing clouds. ◆ The vultures are the first to rise on the morning thermals: turkey vultures on tilting, upswept wings, then black vultures, their hurried

Aquatic wonderlands, tropical prairies, and seabird colonies in the Gulf Stream create a mecca for birders.

flaps helping them gain essential lift. They are joined first by a red-shouldered hawk, its plaintive cries drifting down from on high, then by a sleek Swainson's hawk. Indeed, South Florida is the only place where Swainson's normally winter north of Argentina, though in very small numbers. ◆ A few great egrets are now circling on the growing warmth, but raptors predominate. An adult bald eagle gives brief chase to an osprey, hoping to pirate a fish. Close examination of a hovering buteo shows it to be a short-tailed hawk, a true Florida specialty, hanging in place, high, hunting. Low over the trees, two swallow-tailed kites appear, never flapping but swooping and gliding effortlessly over the pines, graceful

The large feet of the purple gallinule help it navigate lily pads and other swamp vegetation. This member of the rail family forages for snails and aquatic insects.

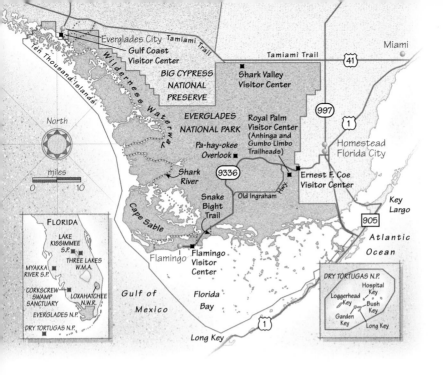

Everglades City · Tamiami Trail
Gulf Coast Visitor Center
Tamiami Trail · Miami
41
BIG CYPRESS NATIONAL PRESERVE
Shark Valley Visitor Center
Ten Thousand Islands
Wilderness Waterway
997
North
1
EVERGLADES NATIONAL PARK
Royal Palm Visitor Center (Anhinga and Gumbo Limbo Trailheads)
Pa-hay-okee Overlook
Homestead Florida City
miles
0   10
Shark River
9336
Old Ingraham Hwy.
Ernest F. Coe Visitor Center
Cape Sable
Snake Bight Trail
Key Largo
905
FLORIDA
LAKE KISSIMMEE S.P.
THREE LAKES W.M.A.
MYAKKA RIVER S.P.
CORKSCREW SWAMP SANCTUARY
LOXAHATCHEE N.W.R.
EVERGLADES N.P.
DRY TORTUGAS N.P.
Flamingo
Flamingo Visitor Center
Atlantic Ocean
Gulf of Mexico
Florida Bay
1
Long Key
DRY TORTUGAS N.P.
Hospital Key
Loggerhead Key
Bush Key
Garden Key
Long Key

pelicans. Next, a mixed flock forms overhead, prehistoric-looking anhingas joining four gangly wood storks. They rapidly gain altitude on a rising thermal, a valuable commodity the storks will convert to distance as they glide off in search of productive freshwater feeding areas.

Conservation Wins and Losses

Sadly, the storks' search has become harder and harder with each passing decade. In the 1940s, more than 4,000 pairs of wood storks nested in **Everglades National Park**. As few as 25 breeding pairs can be found today. Research has shown that nesting adult wood storks can range up to 60 miles from their nest sites daily in an attempt to find suitable water levels for feeding – and the water is vanishing.

The Everglades were once a river more than 50 miles wide and about six inches deep that flowed sluggishly but unimpeded through the saw grass from **Lake Okeechobee** south to **Florida Bay**, traversing some 2,000 square miles of wilderness. The Everglades have often been called timeless, but time has indeed caught up to them. Drainage to create agricultural lands, massive water withdrawals for irrigation, water diversions to Miami and other burgeoning coastal developments, and flood-control channelization and dikes have robbed the Everglades of their water source, their lifeline, and, as a result, much of their wildlife.

Complicated plans to restore the Everglades to a semblance of their former abundance include the removal of many constraining dikes and the addition of 108,000 acres to the park's current 1.5 million acres – an expansion designed to help replenish the natural flow of water. These plans may come to fruition, but there is still

masters of the springtime southern sky.

As you scan out toward **Florida Bay**, a flock of birds circles in unison, gleaming white as the sun catches them, then disappearing as they wheel away. They drift gradually closer, and black wing tips and chunky bodies identify them as white

a fundamental problem: There are too many competing interests and not enough precious water to go around.

The battle to protect the Everglades has been one of the great environmental struggles of American history. It gave birth to the National Audubon Society and forged such conservation titans as Marjory Stoneman Douglas, who wrote so eloquently about the area's ecology and wildlife in her 1947 classic *Everglades: River of Grass*. It has been a struggle in which the fights against plume hunting, poaching, and jetports have been won, only to have the park drained from outside its boundaries. In a perverse way, conservationists have won the battle but stand in danger of losing the war. To visit

the Everglades is an object lesson that saving a special place means having to save it again and again.

Florida Specialties

Nevertheless, the Everglades will always remain a definitive destination for the birder. It is a seminal spot, one of the places where bird-watching as we know it began. The

Burrowing owls (left), seen near their burrows by day, hunt rodents and large insects at night.

An anhinga (opposite) serves its chick regurgitated fish. Both the male and the female attend to the young.

White pelicans (below) feed cooperatively by herding fish into shallow water.

tram ride and observation tower at **Shark Valley Visitor Center** still present a vista that few would believe possible in modern Florida, with waves of white ibis undulating over endless sloughs of waving saw grass. The **Anhinga Trail** at Royal Palm still brings point-blank views of waterbirds, a photographer's dream, and the **Gumbo Limbo Trail** imparts the feel of a tropical paradise and offers exceptional land-birding during migration and winter.

During an evening walk along the **Old Ingraham Highway,** you are serenaded by chuck-will's-widows and dueting barred owls, and you may glimpse a bobcat beginning its evening

The crested caracara (above) is a falcon that consumes carrion. This scavenger also hunts small animals such as rodents and lizards.

Ospreys (right) catch fish in their talons, then carry their prey, always headfirst, to a perch or nest.

Great blue herons (opposite, top) often nest high in trees; a single tree may contain numerous nesting pairs.

Roseate spoonbills (opposite, bottom) find prey by touch rather than sight, sensing it with nerve endings inside their bills.

rounds. Near Flamingo, the **Snake Bight Trail**, popularly known to birders as "Mosquito Bite Trail" (be prepared!), may be arduous due to the heat and mud, as well as the insects, but ends with stunning views of Florida Bay. Here, immense flocks of shorebirds mingle with wading birds, many with a rosy hue – reddish egrets and roseate spoonbills. The sparkling shallows of Florida Bay may yield a distant view of the only naturally occurring flock of flamingos in all of the United States.

Part of the many charms of South Florida are the specialty birds. Of more than 300 species found in the Everglades, some are near the northern limit of their range and are rarely seen elsewhere in the continental United States. These include snail kites, short-tailed hawks, white-crowned pigeons, mangrove cuckoos, smooth-billed anis, gray kingbirds, and black-whiskered vireos.

While the clouds of hundreds of thousands of herons and egrets may be gone, possibly forever, there are still compelling reasons to visit the Everglades.

For the birder, South Florida is a package

deal, because after touring the national park, you've just begun to bird. **Loxahatchee National Wildlife Refuge**, north of the park, contains the only natural habitats remaining in the northern part of the Everglades system. At about 150,000 acres, Loxahatchee offers excellent birding on foot or by canoe, with limpkins, purple gallinules, and fulvous whistling-ducks easily seen.

The Florida prairie region north of Lake Okeechobee is a birding must. This is cattle country not unlike many parts of Texas, and some of the birds also have a western flavor. Visiting the excellent state parks and wildlife management areas in these palmetto prairies, such as **Myakka River State Park**, **Lake Kissimmee State Park**, and **Three Lakes Wildlife Management Area**, will produce crested caracaras, red-cockaded woodpeckers, and the endemic Florida scrub jay. Scan pastureland hillocks and fenceposts for burrowing owls, and lakeshores for water-

birds, perhaps a family of wild turkeys venturing out for a drink, or stately Florida sandhill cranes, an endemic nonmigratory subspecies found only in Florida.

Any tour should include a visit to the incomparable **Corkscrew Swamp**

Sanctuary, northwest of Everglades City. At this National Audubon Society preserve, a two-mile boardwalk winds through a variety of subtropical habitats, including the world's largest remaining old-growth bald cypress forest. Many birders have seen their "life" barred owl here, perched sleepily near the boardwalk, acclimated to the friendly foot traffic. Expect unparalleled photographic opportunities with close-up herons, egrets, ibis, and red-shouldered hawks.

Nesting Islands

South of the Everglades, the Florida Keys are the jump-off point for another adventure in American birding. At least once, every serious birder in North America should pay a spring visit to **Dry Tortugas National Park**, which consists of a cluster of small keys about 70 miles west of Key West, accessible by boat or seaplane. Much of 16-acre **Garden Key** is covered by the impressive 19th-century Fort Jefferson, but the planted palms and shrubs here and on nearby **Loggerhead Key** can provide some of the hottest birding on the continent.

During spring migration, the Tortugas are often the first landfall for weary neotropical migrants crossing the Gulf of Mexico. Early April to mid-May is the best time to visit, and if you're lucky enough to hit a weather-dependent major fallout, songbirds and raptors will be "dripping from the trees" wherever you turn. As a further draw, a number of West Indian vagrants, such as ruddy quail-dove, logger-head kingbird, and Bahama swallow, have shown up at Fort Jefferson over the years.

For many birders, the seabirds are the

major delight of the Tortugas. Though landing on the nesting islands is prohibited, a small boat will take you within viewing distance of a colony of 40,000 sooty terns and 2,000 brown noddies on **Bush Key**. The comings and goings of the ground-nesting terns and tree-nesting noddies are a stunning sight, and if you're on a tourboat, the *wideawake* calls of the sooties will lull you to sleep at night. Nearby, on **Long Key**, are about 100 pairs of magnificent frigatebirds, the only breeding colony in North America. Here, you can watch the courtship rituals of these huge birds, with their seven-foot wingspans, as the glossy black males inflate their bright red gular sacs, or throat pouches, to entice females. The only U.S. colony of masked boobies, numbering about 60 birds, is on **Hospital Key**. Brown boobies do not nest on the islands but are always present, and red-footed boobies, black noddies, and white-tailed tropicbirds are

Bush Key (opposite, top) in the Dry Tortugas, reached by boat, hosts thousands of sooty terns and brown noddies.

A great egret (left) displays graceful white plumes known as a nuptial train.

among the rarities seen most seasons.

Tour companies generally make the boat trip from Key West across the deep green waters of the Gulf Stream. This pelagic birding experience usually adds numbers of bridled terns, Audubon's shearwaters, and perhaps band-rumped storm-petrels to your trip list. The magic of the Tortugas, beyond the fascination of watching the intricate nesting behavior of the seabirds, is that these islets offer the only chance to see these species in North America and a rare opportunity to see them near land. As pelagic birds, they spend most of their lives out to sea, far from the view of birders' binoculars.

A grazing cow (opposite, bottom) stirs up insects and other prey for a cattle egret. These egrets, originally from Africa, first bred in Florida in the 1950s, then spread across the continent.

The snail kite (right) has one of the most specialized avian diets. It consumes only apple snails (below).

The Kite and the Snail

That Florida specialty, the snail kite, is a specialist itself, with an extremely discriminating palate. This bird of prey feeds exclusively on freshwater apple snails, and its range and population are forever entwined with the distribution and abundance of its only source of nourishment.

Identifying the snail kite can be a challenge. Though it has the general shape of a buteo, it courses over the wetlands much like a northern harrier. The adult male even shows white uppertail coverts, just like a harrier. It is related to the swallow-tailed kite, but its rounded wing tips are quite unlike the elegant falconlike shape of that bird. At close range, you will note the snail kite's distinctive bill – long, thin, and delicately decurved, evolution's perfect instrument for extracting "escargot" from their protective shells.

The snail kite is found in the United States only in shallow, freshwater wetlands from the central Everglades north to the headwaters of the St. Johns River. The population of this endangered species hit rock bottom in 1972 with 65 birds. The number has since grown to about 900, due mostly to intense protection and water-level restoration. The kite's constant search for its only prey can make it hard to find. Consult bird alerts and fellow birders for information about recent sightings.

DETAILS

When to Go

Birding in South Florida is best from November through April, when daytime temperatures average in the 70s and 80s. The rainy season, May through November, is hot and humid, with frequent thunderstorms and temperatures in the 80s and 90s. April through early May is the prime time to visit Dry Tortugas National Park.

How to Get There

Miami International Airport is about 50 miles from Everglades National Park, 125 miles from Corkscrew Swamp Sanctuary, and 160 miles from Key West, departure point to Dry Tortugas National Park.

Getting Around

An automobile is necessary for visiting mainland South Florida birding destinations. Car rentals are available at the airport. Dry Tortugas National Park is reached by boat or seaplane only; for a list of authorized carriers, call the park at 305-242-7700.

Handicapped Access

Visitor centers, tram tours, and most self-guided nature trails at Everglades National Park are accessible.

INFORMATION

Arthur R. Marshall Loxahatchee National Wildlife Refuge

10216 Lee Road, Boynton Beach, FL 33437; tel: 561-734-8303.

Corkscrew Swamp Sanctuary

375 Sanctuary Road, Naples, FL 34120; tel: 941-348-9151.

Dry Tortugas National Park

40001 State Road 9336, Homestead, FL 33034; tel: 305-242-7700.

Everglades Area Chamber of Commerce

P.O. Box 130, Everglades City, FL 34139; tel: 800-914-6355.

Everglades National Park

40001 State Road 9336, Homestead, FL 33034; tel: 305-242-7700.

Rare Bird Alert

Tel:561-340-0079

CAMPING

Everglades National Park has 362 campsites, available on a first-come, first-served basis from May through October, and by reservation from November through April. To reserve a site, call 800-365-2267. Campers at Dry Tortugas National Park must supply their own food and fresh water. Parties of more than 10 must reserve sites in advance by writing the park. For details, call 305-242-7700.

Backcountry Travel

Permits, required for backcountry travel in Everglades National Park, may be purchased at ranger stations and the visitor center no more than 24 hours in advance.

LODGING

PRICE GUIDE – double occupancy	
$ = up to $49	$$ = $50–$99
$$$ = $100–$149	$$$$ = $150+

Flamingo Lodge

1 Flamingo Lodge Highway, Flamingo, FL 33034; tel: 800-600-3813 or 941-695-3101.

This resort at the southern tip of the park has 103 motel rooms and 24 duplex cottages. In addition, six wood-frame cottages have full kitchens, two double beds, a sitting room, and a private bath.

The lodge offers canoe, kayak, and bicycle rentals. A restaurant is on the premises. $$–$$$

Ivey House

P.O. Box 5038, Everglades City, FL 34139; tel: 941-695-3299 or 860-739-0791.

A former boardinghouse for men working on the Tamiami Trail in the 1920s, the bed-and-breakfast has 11 guest rooms, most with shared bath. Free bicycles and a coin laundry are available. Ivey House is closed May through October. $–$$$.

Katy's Place

31850 Southwest 195th Avenue, Homestead, FL 33030; tel: 305-247-0201.

A tropical garden surrounds this two-story inn, which has three large guest rooms, one with king-sized bed and private bath, the others with queen-sized beds and shared bath. A pool, Jacuzzi, and a pond with tropical fish are on the premises. $$–$$$

On the Banks of the Everglades

P.O. Box 570, Everglades City, FL 34139; tel: 941-695-3151.

This bed-and-breakfast occupies a building originally used by the Bank of the Everglades in the 1920s. Several accommodations are available, including a variety of rooms with shared or private baths, and a suite with a living room, dining room, kitchen, and private bath. $$–$$$

Room at the Inn

15830 Southwest 240th Street, Homestead, FL 33031; tel: 305-246-0492.

Set on two rustic acres, this country ranch house has four guest rooms with period antiques and private baths. A stone fireplace crowns the sitting room. Amenities include a swimming pool, heated spa, sun deck, and wet bar. $$–$$$

TOURS AND OUTFITTERS

Everglades National Park

40001 State Road 9336,

Homestead, FL 33034; tel: 305-242-7700.

Park rangers lead tours that focus on wildlife, including birds.

Florida Nature Tours
P.O. Box 618572, Orlando, FL 32861; tel: 407-363-1360.

Tailored specifically to birders, these tours depart from Key West for three-day explorations of the Dry Tortugas. The 40-passenger boat lands on Garden Key and Loggerhead Key and approaches Hospital, Bush, and Long Keys. Birders eat and sleep on board. Florida Nature Tours arranges private charters and offers multi-day tours to prime birding spots on the South Florida mainland.

Sunny Days Catamarans
Greene and Elizabeth Streets, Key West, FL 33040; tel: 800-236-7937 or 305-296-5556.

Passengers depart from Key West aboard a high-speed catamaran for daylong trips to Garden Key in Dry Tortugas National Park. A guide, daytime meals, snorkel gear, and instruction are included.

Yankee Fleet
P.O. Box 5903, Key West, FL 33041; tel: 800-634-0939 or 305-294-7009.

Passengers travel on a high-speed catamaran from Key West to Garden Key in Dry Tortugas National Park and explore the island on their own. Yankee Fleet also arranges private charters.

SPECIAL EVENTS

Buteos on the Beach
Broward County Audubon Society, P.O. Box 9644, Ft. Lauderdale, FL 33310; tel: 954-776-5585.

One of the main attractions of this four-day festival, held in early October, is the opportunity to see southbound raptors. Guided field trips visit Everglades National Park, Corkscrew Swamp Sanctuary, and other nearby wildlife areas.

Excursions

Congaree Swamp National Monument
200 Caroline Sims Road, Hopkins, SC 29061; tel: 803-776-4396.

Protected within this 22,200-acre International Biosphere Reserve is the United States' last sizable area of southern bottomland hardwood forest. Within it flourish nearly 90 species of trees, including old-growth bald cypress and other giants. Warblers, woodpeckers, wading birds, raptors, and waterfowl nest in the swamp. Some of the park can be explored on foot, or, when flooded, by canoe.

Dauphin Island Audubon Sanctuary
P.O. Box 848, Dauphin Island, AL 36528; tel: 334-861-2120.

Migrating birds that winter in Central America – warblers, flycatchers, vireos, grosbeaks, buntings – find a number of hospitable spots along the Gulf Coast at the beginning and end of their journey across the Gulf of Mexico. The 164-acre Audubon sanctuary encompasses shoreline, salt marshes, and forest. Birders, who access the sanctuary by a system of trails, also come to see wading birds, shorebirds, and, in fall, abundant migrating waterfowl.

J. N. "Ding" Darling National Wildlife Refuge
1 Wildlife Drive, Sanibel, FL 33957; tel: 941-472-1100.

Set on Sanibel Island and reached by a causeway from mainland Florida, this refuge is an excellent place to see wading birds, 50 species of which inhabit the mudflats and adjacent mangrove forests. Waders include wood storks, white ibises, five species of herons, and reddish, great, and snowy egrets. The refuge is also home to nearly one-third of the roseate spoonbills found in the United States. Birders follow a wildlife drive or explore on foot and canoe trails.

Lower Rio Grande Valley

Texas

CHAPTER **14**

Only by virtue of a political boundary is the **Lower Rio Grande Valley** part of the United States. It's more like a slice of Mexico, with its subtropical environment and remarkable diversity of animal and plant life. Along the Rio Grande, known south of the border as the Río Bravo del Norte, is a riparian zone of willows, cattails, and retama. Just beyond grows a thorn forest dominated by cedar elm, spiny hackberry, and Texas ebony, often festooned with tassels of Spanish moss. Slightly higher and drier areas support thorn scrub, locally known as South Texas brush, dense with spiny plants such as acacias, brasil, lotewood, huisache, and honey mesquite. ◆ Within these communities are more avian specialties than anywhere else in North America. No fewer than 27 species rarely found outside Texas reside there year-round, though a few, such as the brown jay and Tamaulipas crow, are more numerous in winter. Other exciting

Birds with vibrant plumage suggesting their tropical origin lure birders to the southern tip of the Lone Star State.

specialties that birders come here to see include the brightly colored green jay, Altamira oriole, great kiskadee, hook-billed kite, and ringed kingfisher. ◆ What is simply called "the valley" in Texas extends southeast from Falcon Dam for about 120 miles to Boca Chica, where what remains of the river after irrigation flows into the Gulf of Mexico. Something like 95 percent of the valley's native habitat has been converted to citrus orchards, farmlands, malls, and urban sprawl, including hundreds of mobile-home communities built to accommodate 120,000 "winter Texans." Of the few scattered islands of native habitat that still exist within this sea of development, the 2,080-acre Santa Ana National Wildlife Refuge and the 588-acre Bentsen-Rio Grande Valley State Park are the best known and most

The least bittern is an elusive, small heron skilled at wending through dense marsh vegetation. Birders may hear its soft clucking during breeding season.

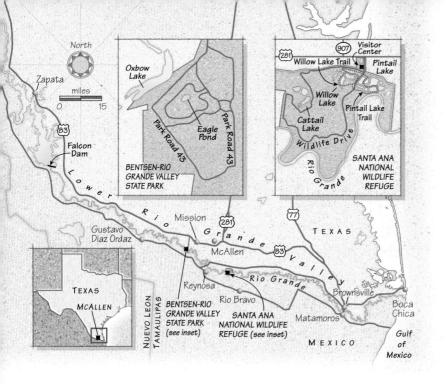

than the feeders at **Bentsen-Rio Grande Valley State Park**. Birdseed and fruit, set out by both campers and park personnel especially during winter and spring, lure such shy birds as chachalacas, white-tipped doves, golden-fronted woodpeckers, great kiskadees, green jays, and Altamira and Audubon's orioles. At dusk, pauraques, members of the nightjar family, tune up their hoarse whistle *go-weeeeer* or *guh, guh, guh, go-weeeeer*. You'll hear them when the birds leave their roosting places to feed on insects, and at dawn.

Aside from the specialties, four doves – white-winged, mourning, Inca, and common ground-doves – frequent the campground year-round. Look also for tufted titmice, white-eyed vireos, brown-headed and bronzed cowbirds, and northern cardinals and pyrrhuloxias. Cardinals – the male a brilliant red, the female a pale red-blushed brown – prefer scrubby sites. Their relatives, the pyrrhuloxias, have a bill that is curved and yellow rather than red, and prefer more open brushy areas.

Some birders visiting Bentsen spend their time simply walking the campground loop, checking out the birds that come in to feed. The more elusive birds require a bit more effort. Roaming the outer loop road and the short trail to **Eagle Pond**, a small artificial pond inside the campground loop, will give you a chance to find hook-billed kites, brown-crested

productive for birders. Both are situated along the Rio Grande, seven and a half miles and four miles, respectively, south of busy Highway 83 in the vicinity of McAllen.

The two sites support about the same bird species, but the strategies for birding them are very different. Most important, Santa Ana is open only during daylight hours, while Bentsen is accessible after dark (until 10 p.m.) and offers campers nighttime birding opportunities not available at Santa Ana. Before you begin birding these areas, you should check the wildlife logs maintained at the park headquarters and refuge visitor center to see which birds have recently been sighted and where. Certain much sought-after species such as red-billed pigeon, clay-colored robin, and tropical parula can be highly localized when they turn up.

Campground Bonanza

There is no better place to observe many of the valley's specialty birds at close hand

flycatchers, and Couch's kingbirds. The hook-billed kite is most often seen in flight, but if you are lucky, you may discover a kite (look for the heavily barred under-parts, long, banded tail, and long, yellow legs) sitting on a bare limb, devouring tree snails. Holding a snail in its talons, the kite uses its large hooked bill to extract its dinner.

Another must-see area at Bentsen is **Oxbow Lake** along the northwestern edge of the park. Herons, egrets, grebes, and kingfishers, as well as anhingas and neotropic cormorants, are usually found at this *resaca*, an old meander of the Rio Grande. Anhingas and neotropic cormorants look alike at first glance. Both warm up each morning by holding out their wings to absorb the sunlight; Anhingas possess a pointed bill for stabbing prey underwater, while the cormorant's heavier, hooked bill is designed to grasp fish and amphibians.

A peregrine falcon usually takes up winter residence at Oxbow Lake. American kestrels are common, and sharp-shinned,

Golden-fronted woodpeckers (left) excavate nesting cavities in trees and may return to the same site in subsequent years.

Chacalacas (opposite) announce their presence with a boisterous call that repeats their name.

Black-bellied whistling ducks (below) breed in the Lower Rio Grande Valley, often occupying holes in trees.

Cooper's, Harris's, and gray hawks are regularly encountered. The gray hawk, smaller than the more common red-tailed hawk, has grayish plumage and a banded tail; the adults are barred beneath. White-tailed kites are less dependable but hardly rare. In late spring and summer, elf owls, the smallest of all the owls, inhabit the area.

Listen for their loud, continuous *churps* soon after dark. Eastern screech-owls, abundant throughout the park, sing their mellow, quavering whistle-songs throughout the night.

Seeking the Green Jay

The strategy for birding **Santa Ana National Wildlife Refuge** is to work the trails that

radiate out from the refuge visitor center.

The one-mile **Willow Lake Trail** loop passes through both thorn scrub and thorn forest habitats, where you will be able to spot most of the refuge's land birds. One resident you certainly won't miss is the plain chachalaca, a long-tailed grouselike bird that spends most of its time in the trees and greets every dawn with a *cha-cha-la-ca, cha-cha-la-ca, cha-cha-la-ca*. You'll find both the golden-fronted woodpecker and the much smaller ladder-backed woodpecker along the trail. The great kiskadee, also named for its noisy call – *kis-ka-dee* – is a large, brightly colored flycatcher with a lemon-yellow belly and cinnamon back and wing linings. You'll see it launch from a perch after insects and drop to the water, like a kingfisher, to skim small fish from the surface. Other year-round residents include the long-billed thrasher, which closely resembles the brown thrasher but is much grayer above with a longer, more strongly curved bill, and the olive sparrow, a large though furtive sparrow with a brown stripe on each side of its crown. In spring and summer, brown-crested flycatchers, Couch's kingbirds, and painted buntings can be common here as well.

You will also find the green jay, not as readily as at the Bentsen feeders but still without much trouble if you make a few squeaking sounds with your lips on the back of your hand in brushy spots. Perhaps more than any of the other birds of the Lower Rio Grande, this lovely creature best represents the valley's connection with the tropics. Found in Central America and Mexico, the gaudy bird ranges no farther north than the woodlands and brush of south Texas. It even looks tropical, with its green-and-yellow tail, green back, and blue-and-black head. Like all jays, it is a lively and noisy bird, but it can also be shy and retiring.

Willow Lake, a series of ponds maintained by the pumping of water from the nearby Rio Grande, has two observation points, one with a photo blind. Here is where you will find one of Santa Ana's target birds: the least grebe, a dainty little waterbird with a thin bill, yellow eyes, and a blackish crown. The grebes favor the edges of the lake where they can disappear into cover in case a predator shows up. Black-bellied whistling-ducks and waders such as white-faced ibis and black-necked stilts feed and rest in the center of the lake or along the shallower edges. Also watch for all three North American kingfishers: the little green kingfisher, usually detected by its insectlike stutter-call; the midsized belted kingfisher;

The green jay (opposite, top) is an omnivore that consumes nuts and seeds, insects, lizards, and the fledglings of other species.

Anhingas (opposite, bottom) feed primarily on fish. They are often spotted perched in the sun drying their wings.

Birders eagerly look for Mexican species new to Texas. The masked tityra (right) was first recorded at Bentsen-Rio Grande State Park in February 1990.

Expect the Unexpected

The Lower Rio Grande Valley is an avian threshold where Mexican birds wander north in search of food and shelter. The refuges tend to concentrate new arrivals, and because so many people bird the valley hot spots, a surprisingly large number of "first-ever" species are found.

Since the early 1970s, a number of U.S. firsts have been recorded at Bentsen-Rio Grande Valley State Park and Santa Ana National Wildlife Refuge by the Texas Bird Records Committee of the Texas Ornithological Society. At Bentsen, the newcomers have included crimson-collared grosbeak, collared forest-falcon, mottled owl, masked tityra, and stygian owl. Crane hawk, ruddy ground-dove, and yellow-faced grassquit crossed the river at Santa Ana.

How many of these Mexican birds eventually will take up residence in the valley is unknown, but if the past is any indication, some undoubtedly will. The hook-billed kite first appeared in the United States at Santa Ana in May 1964. A pair of kites nested there that same year, but the species was found only occasionally for several years thereafter. By the 1970s, however, the kites were more numerous, and the species is now regularly found from Santa Ana to Falcon Dam. The first clay-colored robin, a paler cousin of the American robin, was found at Bentsen in May 1959. Appearing several times over the next two decades, the species finally nested at Bentsen in the early 1980s. Since then it has been recorded regularly in the area and, like the hook-billed kite, is considered a full-time resident of the valley.

Groove-billed anis
(right) are large cuckoos
that seem black overall
but may show green and
purple iridescence.

Male belted kingfishers
(below) are less colorful
than females, which
sport an obvious rust
band across their bellies.

The striking male
painted bunting (opposite)
is an aggressive bird that
fights with other males
in defense of its territory.

ridged bill and black plumage have given
rise to a nickname: the Black Witch. The
birds congregate in small flocks in brushy
areas but can be shy and difficult to see
despite their 12-inch size. Listen for their
distinct calls, a liquid *tee-ho*, with emphasis
on the first syllable.

The prime spot for hummingbirds is
the old site of the manager's house along
the seven-mile **Wildlife Drive**. The birds
dote on the bright red flowers of the
shrimp plants that grow in profusion there.
Rufous hummingbirds are usually present
in winter, and ruby-throated and black-
chinned hummingbirds come in spring
and fall. But the one that everybody
wants to see is the resident buff-bellied,
which rates as a Valley specialty though it
occasionally turns up along the Gulf Coast.
A series of sharp clicking notes signals the
buff-bellied's approach. When the hummer
appears, you'll be able to identify it by its
large size, reddish bill, deep green chest,
and buff-colored belly.

Refuge in the Making

These two choice birding sites, Bentsen
and Santa Ana, will someday be part of a
"wildlife corridor" within the Lower Rio
Grande Valley. Led by the U.S. Fish and
Wildlife Service, federal, state, and private
organizations intend to restore and protect
132,500 acres between the Gulf of Mexico
and Falcon Dam – from tidal flats and
coastal prairie to riparian woodlands,
thorn and Sabal palm forest in the Rio
Grande floodplain, and interior wetlands
and thorn scrub beyond the river.

Preserving these habitats holds the key
to the survival of 115 vertebrate species listed as endangered or threatened, or which
occur at the periphery of their range.
Besides the 27 avian specialties, this list
includes the ocelot and exceedingly rare
jaguarundi. The corridor will be called the
Lower Rio Grande Valley National Wildlife
Refuge, and when birders and wildlife
watchers visit the refuge, they will be able
to explore 123 units of habitat throughout
the valley.

and the larger ringed kingfisher, which has
a loud, harsh rattle-call. All three hunt
from above, diving into the water after
their prey, sometimes remaining submerged
for several seconds before emerging with
their catch tightly clasped in their
substantial bills. They then fly to a perch
before swallowing their prey head first or,
if the unfortunate creature is too large,
beating it to death.

Pintail Lake, reached by a one-mile
loop trail, is a more open environment and
the best place for shorebirds and
ducks. In spring and summer,
look for fulvous whistling-
ducks, least bitterns, and
purple gallinules. Along
the weedy edges in
winter, you'll
usually spot a variety
of sparrows, buntings, and
cowbirds. The taller thorn
scrub vegetation may add
groove-billed anis to your trip
list. A member of the
cuckoo family and closely
related to roadrunners, the
anis is one of the valley's most
interesting-looking birds. Its huge,

TRAVEL TIPS

DETAILS

When to Go

Fall through spring is the best time for birding the lower Rio Grande Valley and Texas Gulf Coast. Many birders visit in April and May for the spring migration. Temperatures range from the 50s to the 80s in fall and early spring, and often reach the mid-90s in late spring. Fall and winter are the rainy seasons, though precipitation rarely lasts for an extended period.

How to Get There

Major airlines serve airports at McAllen and Harlingen, less than 50 miles from Santa Ana National Wildlife Refuge and Bentsen-Rio Grande Valley State Park.

Getting Around

An automobile is necessary for birding the refuge and park. Car rentals are available at the airports. A seven-mile drive traverses the Santa Ana National Wildlife Refuge. From late November to early April, the drive is open only on Tuesday and Wednesday; at other times, visitors tour the refuge on a tram, which runs every two hours. Both Santa Ana and Bentsen have hiking trails.

Handicapped Access

Blacktop roads in Bentsen-Rio Grande Valley State Park are usually accessible. An accessible half-mile trail runs through Santa Ana National Wildlife Refuge.

INFORMATION

Bentsen-Rio Grande Valley State Park

P.O. Box 988, Mission, TX 78573; tel: 956-585-1107.

Santa Ana National Wildlife Refuge

Route 2, Box 202A, Alamo, TX 78516; tel: 956-787-3079.

Great Texas Coastal Birding Trail

Texas Parks and Wildlife, 4200 Smith School Road, Austin, TX 78744; tel: 512-389-4800.

Harlingen Area Chamber of Commerce

311 East Tyler Street, Harlingen, TX 78550; tel: 800-531-7346 or 956-423-5440.

McAllen Chamber of Commerce

P.O. Box 790, McAllen, TX 78505; tel: 877-622-5536.

Rare Bird Alerts

Tel: 956-969-2731 (Rio Grande Valley), 512-265-0377 (Corpus Christi), or 713-964-5867 (statewide).

CAMPING

Bentsen-Rio Grande Valley State Park, 956-585-1107, has a campground with more than 140 sites. Reserve sites well in advance during the high season, November through April. Santa Ana National Wildlife Refuge does not permit camping.

LODGING

PRICE GUIDE – double occupancy

$ = up to $49 $$ = $50–$99
$$$ = $100–$149 $$$$ = $150+

Hudson House Motel

500 Ed Carey Drive, Harlingen, TX 98550; tel: 800-784-8911 or 956-428-8911.

Hudson House has 37 guest rooms. Rooms with kitchenettes are available for rent on a weekly basis. $$

Inn at El Canelo

P.O. Box 487, Raymondville, TX 78580; tel: 956-689-5042.

Situated on a ranch north of the Lower Rio Grande, the inn has a main house with two guest rooms, each with private bath and balcony. A separate guest house has three rooms, each with living, dining, and kitchen areas. Rates include breakfast, lunch, and dinner. Ferruginous pygmy-owls nest on the property. $$$$

Paradise Motel

313 South 10th, McAllen, TX 78501; 956-682-2453.

This affordable motel offers basic comfort in 43 rooms and four suites with kitchenettes. $

Ross Haus

P.O. Box 2566, Harlingen, TX 78551; tel: 800-580-1717 or 956-425-1717.

Each of four suites has a living/dining room, fully equipped kitchen, bedroom, and bath. A continental breakfast is provided for a small extra fee. A laundry room is on the premises. $$

Sun Valley Motor Hotel

1900 South 77 Sunshine Strip, Harlingen, TX 78550; tel: 956-423-7222.

This hotel has 87 basic guest rooms and 10 rooms with kitchenettes. Also available are two suites with living rooms. A restaurant is on the premises. $$

Vali-Ho Motel

2100 East Business Highway 83, Weslaco, TX 78596; tel: 800-445-1993 or 956-968-2173.

Vali-Ho, conveniently located between Harlingen and McAllen, has 37 basic rooms at affordable rates. $

Vieh's Bed-and-Breakfast

Route 4, Box 75A, San Benito, TX 98586; tel: 956-425-4651.

This inn, 45 minutes from Santa Ana National Wildlife Refuge and 80 minutes from Bentsen-Rio Grande Valley State Park, offers three rooms and serves a full breakfast. Guests are welcome to bird the property, a 15-acre tree farm on a lake. Some 130 bird species have been observed in various habitats. $$

TOURS AND OUTFITTERS

Santa Ana National Wildlife Refuge

Route 2, Box 202A, Alamo, TX 78516; tel: 956-787-3079.

Naturalists and volunteers at the refuge lead tours and nature walks Monday through Saturday.

SPECIAL EVENTS

Rio Grande Valley Birding Festival

Harlingen Area Chamber of Commerce, 311 East Tyler Street, Harlingen, TX 78550; tel: 800-531-7346 or 956-423-5440.

This mid-November festival offers instruction on birding basics, discussions of conservation issues, and seminars on hummingbirds, vireos, shorebirds, and raptors. Numerous field trips take participants to Bentsen-Rio Grande Valley State Park, Santa Ana National Wildlife Refuge, and other birding hot spots on the Gulf Coast.

Texas Tropics Nature Festival

McAllen Chamber of Commerce, P.O. Box 790, McAllen; TX 78505; tel: 877-622-5536.

Lectures by birding luminaries and seminars on optical equipment and bird behavior fill this four-day festival in mid-April. Field trips visit nearby destinations, including Bentsen-Rio Grande Valley State Park, Santa Ana National Wildlife Refuge, and the Gulf Coast.

Excursions

High Island

Houston Audubon Society, 440 Wilchester, Houston, TX 77709; tel: 713-932-1639.

An oasis of woodlands, this coastal town sees legendary "fallouts" of northbound songbirds. Having flown across the gulf from the Yucatan Peninsula and other points south, warblers, orioles, buntings, tanagers, and thrushes pause here before continuing their journey. Birders arrive in mid-April to mid-May and head for two Audubon sites: Louis Smith Bird Sanctuary and Smith Oaks Sanctuary.

Big Thicket National Preserve

3785 Milam, Beaumont, TX 77701; tel: 409-839-2689.

Eastern hardwood forests and southeastern swamps meet the central plains and arid desert at this significant ecological crossroads. Within the preserve's 86,000 acres are nine parcels of land and four rivers and lakes. The mix of habitats sustains equally varied bird life: eastern bluebird, greater roadrunner, Louisiana waterthrush, anhinga, and pileated woodpecker.

Sabal Palm Audubon Center and Sanctuary

P.O. Box 5169, Brownsville, TX 78523; tel: 956-541-8034.

Sabal palms once grew along the Rio Grande for 80 miles, beginning at the Gulf of Mexico. The last remnant of this native forest, preserved in the sanctuary along with Texas ebony, provides habitat for plain chachalacas, olive sparrows, pauraques, long-billed thrashers, green jays, and other wildlife such as bobcats, armadillos, and perhaps the endangered jaguarundi.

Aransas National Wildlife Refuge

P.O. Box 100, Austwell, TX 77950; tel: 512-286-3559.

This Gulf Coast refuge, part of the 625-mile Great Texas Coastal Birding Trail, is one of the best places in North America to observe the endangered whooping crane. After nesting in Canada, whoopers start arriving in mid-October, when they can be seen from an observation tower or by boat. The 115,000-acre refuge is also host to roseate spoonbills, reddish egrets, and white-faced and white ibises. At least three dozen warbler species stop here during migration.

Big Bend
National Park
Texas

CHAPTER **15**

There is a magical place in West Texas known as Big Bend Country. It's where the Rio Grande makes a sweeping southward arc through arid desert dominated by striking formations of ancient volcanoes and sedimentary rock. At the heart of this tumbled landscape are the **Chisos Mountains**, the southernmost mountain range in the continental United States, rising to the summit of 7,835-foot **Emory Peak**. These mountains are the centerpiece of **Big Bend National Park**, more than 800,000 acres of river floodplain, desert, grassland, woodland, and mountain habitats, with flora and fauna more typical of Mexico than the United States. Among the park's abundant wildlife is one bird, the Colima warbler, that occurs nowhere else in the United States.   ◆   Big Bend National Park is not easily reached. Park headquarters is almost 100 miles south of Highway 90, the nearest major road. As a result, the park receives fewer than 400,000 visitors annually. But the folks who do visit, particularly birders, are seldom disappointed. Some 450 species have been recorded at Big Bend, more than any other national park and many of them unknown or rare elsewhere in the country: flammulated owls, blue-throated hummingbirds, Mexican jays, black-capped and gray vireos, painted redstarts, hepatic tanagers, and the aforementioned Colima warblers. The height of the spring season is from mid-April to early May, but the birding is excellent from late March through September along trails leading from the **Chisos Basin.**   ◆   Two favorite trails that start at the basin, **Laguna Meadow Trail** and **Pinnacles Trail**, lead birders on a nine-mile, round-trip hike over steep and rocky terrain. Circling **Emory Peak**, the two routes

A remote park tucked into a bend in the Rio Grande boasts a checklist of more than 450 species.

A white wing patch and a short, rounded tail help distinguish the white-winged dove from the similar mourning dove.

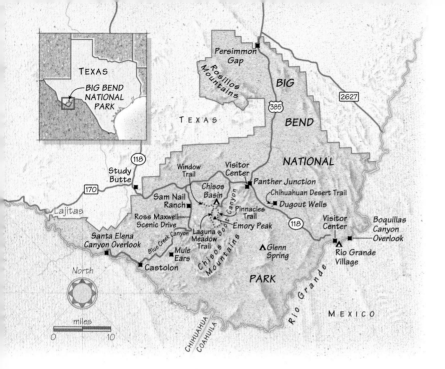

fast-flying white-throated swifts, as well as the occasional zone-tailed hawk soaring with the abundant turkey vultures. At first glance, these Mexican hawks even look like turkey vultures, soaring with their bicolor wings held in a slight V pattern and rocking from side to side. Remember that zone-tails possess feathered rather than bare red heads and have dark tails with narrow white bands.

On reaching Boot Canyon, you'll find a moist environment filled with Arizona pines, Arizona cypress, various oaks, and mountain maples, and surrounded by rocky slopes and dense pinyon-juniper woodlands. Your reward for the climb will be the ascending song of Colima warblers from the oaks and maples, and then the bird itself – rather large for a warbler at more than five inches. Canyon wrens will treat you to their "waterfall" song, a series of liquid, descending notes. And blue-throated hummingbirds streak up and down the canyon, calling loud *seep* notes. Finding a flammulated owl or a whip-poor-will, both nocturnal species, requires an overnight stay at one of the canyon's campsites.

meet in **Boot Canyon**, the only sure place for finding Colima warblers. Along the way, watch and listen for other highland species. Mexican jays and the black-crested form of the tufted titmouse make themselves known by their loud calls. Tiny bushtits, usually in flocks, can be detected by their constant high-pitched call notes as they pick insects from the foliage. Hepatic tanagers sing robinlike songs from the pines, and acorn woodpeckers perch on high snags. Hutton's vireos and black-headed grosbeaks prefer the oak-dominated side canyons, and black-chinned sparrows sing their descending "Ping-Pong-ball" songs from the brushy slopes.

Be sure to scan the open sky for flocks of

The **Window Trail**, a moderately steep and rocky hike starting in the Chisos Basin campground, offers many of the same birds, as well as several others. Violet-green and barn swallows and common ravens soar overhead. Listen for the distinct songs of black-capped and gray vireos, often present at about the halfway point of the two-mile trail. Both vireo species are skulkers best detected by their songs. Black-cappeds are

The blue-throated hummingbird (right), at five inches long, is one of the larger hummingbirds seen in North America.

Indigo buntings (opposite, top) usually arrive in Big Bend in late April and May.

The Chisos highlands (opposite, bottom) offer spectacular views south toward the mountains of Mexico.

listed as endangered elsewhere in Texas, but the Big Bend population has increased steadily since the species was first found in the 1960s. Scott's orioles, commonplace along the trail, issue melodious whistle-songs. Stop at brushy sites to listen and watch for the varied bunting, one of the park's specialties and aptly named for the male's rust, black, and blue head, orange eye rings, red patch on the throat and upper breast, purplish blue back and underparts, and blue-violet rump.

Blue Creek Canyon is a midelevation (4,000 to 4,600 feet) birding site off the **Ross Maxwell Scenic Drive** on the west side of the Chisos Mountains. Birding is best in the first two miles. In spring, the blooming penstemons, desert willows, and tree tobaccos attract orioles and hummingbirds, among

them the Lucifer hummingbird, another Big Bend specialty. Simply locate a flowering plant, find a comfortable rock to sit on, and wait. The noticeably decurved bill and the male's long, purple gorget and exceedingly long, black tail help separate this lovely creature from the other 12 hummers found in the park. You can also expect poor-wills at dawn and dusk, little black-tailed gnatcatchers issuing distinct buzzing songs, and phain-opeplas with their tall crest – the blood-red eyes of the males contrasting with their coal-black plumage.

Watering-Hole Hot Spots

The park's oases are good desert birding sites. The **Sam Nail Ranch**, along the Ross Maxwell Scenic Drive, features a working

windmill where water flows onto the ground for several feet, providing a place where resident birds and migrants can drink and bathe. Just sit quietly on the bench provided for birders and marvel at the parade: varied buntings, Bell's vireos, yellow-breasted chats, summer tanagers, black-chinned hummingbirds, ash-throated flycatchers, curve-billed thrashers, and blue grosbeaks.

At **Dugout Wells**, an oasis on the east side of the park below Panther Junction, trails take you through a small cottonwood-willow grove where you can spot ladder-backed woodpeckers, western kingbirds, Bell's vireos, yellow-breasted chats, summer tanagers, and Bullock's orioles. If you are visiting from late March to May, be sure to take the **Chihuahuan Desert Trail** to view the variety of blooming cactuses. Four kinds of prickly pears bear magenta, red, and yellow flowers. Scaled quail scurry through the cactuses and creosote bushes, and tiny verdins and black-tailed gnatcatchers perch atop nearby ocotillo. Cactus wrens and curve-billed thrashers sometimes construct their nests among the sharp cactus spines. Pyrrhuloxias – those cardinal look-alikes – are common, and black-throated sparrows are the most numerous of all desert sparrows.

Four kinds of owls frequent the cottonwoods at the oasis: the huge great horned and the tiny elf along with eastern and western screech-owls. At least two pairs of elf owls reside here from April through September, using abandoned woodpecker nests. They begin their evening songfest soon after sunset.

Warbler of the Highlands

Most birders sooner or later make a pilgrimage to Big Bend National Park for the Colima warbler. Named for a state in Mexico, these warblers migrate north of the border in mid-March to mid-April, nest and raise their young during the summer, then head south to their wintering grounds in the lush montane woodlands in Sinaloa south to Jalisco and Colima in southwest Mexico.

Spotting the warbler in its Big Bend habitat requires a daylong hike to **Boot Canyon**. Although Colimas are usually seen foraging for insects among the canyon's deciduous trees, they often are detected first by their rather distinct song: a musical trill that ascends slightly and ends with one or two lower notes.

When you do spot one of the warblers, you'll see that it possesses olive-brown upperparts, a yellow rump and undertail coverts, a gray head, and a complete, white eye ring. Its reddish brown head patch is usually not visible. Colimas build their nests on the ground, using grass, leaves, and hair. Surveys in the Chisos Mountains since 1967 have found as many as 83 pairs nesting in Boot Canyon and other high-elevation sites.

Falcons along the River

Rio Grande Village, the park's most popular winter campground, is also the park's best birding area, except in the very hot summer months. Two of Big Bend's most colorful songbirds, the vermilion

A peregrine falcon (left) perches on a snag; the Big Bend region supports one of the largest populations south of Alaska.

Northern mockingbirds (opposite, top) are found in nearly all of Big Bend's habitats. Some are year-round residents. Others only breed in the park.

Colima warblers (opposite, bottom) were first observed nesting in Big Bend in the 1930s.

Greater roadrunners (below) are fast on their feet and have been clocked at 15 miles per hour.

flycatcher and the painted bunting, can be found here with minimal effort. While the brilliant red-and-black flycatcher is common year-round in the campground, the buntings – the male's patchwork of shiny red, purple, chartreuse, and black must be seen to be believed – are summer residents only. Also expect to see yellow-billed cuckoos, summer tanagers, and three orioles: orchard, hooded, and Bullock's. These colorful birds often chase each other about the cottonwoods, to the delight of campers. Year-round birds that frequent the campground include white-winged, mourning, and Inca doves, and golden-fronted woodpeckers, which nest in the abundant cottonwoods.

The **Nature Trail** gives you easy access to the river floodplain and its active beaver pond. Green herons and green kingfishers perch along the edge or on snags, searching for frogs, fish, and other prey. From the rocky ridge above the beaver pond, you get a magnificent view of the Chisos Mountains to the west and the Rio Grande below. Peregrine falcons hunt along the river for waterfowl and shorebirds to feed their nestlings, tucked away on the high cliffs of nearby Boquillas Canyon. More than any other species, these marvelous raptors symbolize the remoteness of Big Bend National Park. Even when most peregrine populations in the United States were decimated by DDT in the 1950s and 1960s, those in Big Bend Country thrived. Then and now, more than a dozen productive eyries exist in the river and mountain canyons and on the high cliffs of the Chisos Mountains.

TRAVEL TIPS

DETAILS

When to Go

Mid-April through early May is the height of spring migration. Birders visiting from late August through mid-October will catch the fall migration. Spring through summer is the time to see nesting species. Wintering birds are plentiful from November to March. Temperatures in spring are comfortable, with highs ranging from 75° to 90°F and lows from 45° to 60°F. Summer is considerably hotter, over 100°F, though the humidity is low. Winter temperatures often drop below freezing. Expect temperatures up to 10°F cooler at high elevations. Thunderstorms are heavy but usually brief during the rainy season, mid-June through October. Snowfall is rare.

How to Get There

The nearest commercial airports are in Odessa and Midland, 230 miles northeast of Big Bend, and El Paso, 325 miles northwest of the park. There is no public transportation to the park.

Getting Around

An automobile is a necessity for birding Big Bend. Car rentals are available at all airports.

Handicapped Access

Chisos Basin and Rio Grande Village have accessible campsites. The park's visitor centers are also wheelchair accessible.

INFORMATION

Big Bend National Park

Big Bend National Park, TX 79834; tel. 915-477-2251.

Big Bend Natural History Association

P.O. Box 196; Big Bend National Park, TX 79834; tel: 915-477-2236.

Rare Bird Alerts

Tel: 713-369-9673 (statewide).

CAMPING

The national park has three campgrounds available on a first-come, first-served basis: Chisos Basin with 63 sites, Cottonwood with 31 sites, and Rio Grande Village with 100 sites. For information on these campgrounds and others outside the park, call 915-477-2251. A permit is required for all overnight backcountry camping and must be obtained in person up to 24 hours in advance of the trip. Visitors also need a permit to use backcountry roadside campsites, many of which require a high-clearance or four-wheel-drive vehicle to reach.

LODGING

PRICE GUIDE – double occupancy	
$ = up to $49	$$ = $50–$99
$$$ = $100–$149	$$$$ = $150+

Big Bend Motor Inn/ Mission Lodge

P.O. Box 336, Terlingua, TX 79852; tel: 915-371-2218.

This inn just west of the park has 80 rooms, some with kitchenettes. A restaurant, a gas station, and tent sites are also on the property. $$

Chisos Mountains Lodge

Basin Station, Big Bend National Park, TX 79834; tel: 915-477-2291.

Situated in the Chisos Mountains in the center of the park, this concessionaire has four types of accommodations: Casa Grande Motor Lodge with 38 rooms; a motel with 20 rooms; a small lodge with eight rooms; and five stone cottages. All are available year-round. A restaurant is also on the property. $$

Heath Canyon Guest Ranch

Box 386, Marathon, TX 79842; tel: 915-376-2235.

Two bunkhouses at the ranch each have three bedrooms, a kitchen, and a dining room. A bunkroom, also equipped with a kitchen, can accommodate five guests. The guest ranch is located 30 miles from the north entrance of the park and 60 miles from park headquarters. $$

Lajitas Resort

HC 70, Box 400, Terlingua, TX 79852; tel: 800-944-9907 or 915-424-3471.

This sizable resort occupies much of Lajitas, a former calvary post established in 1915. Today visitors can stay in the Old West-style Badlands Hotel or in other accommodations ranging from three motels, cabins, and bunkhouses to one- and two-bedroom condos and apartments and three-bedroom homes. The resort has a restaurant, store, and swimming pool. $$–$$$$

Terlingua Ranch

HC 65, Box 220, Alpine, TX 79830; tel: 915-371-2416.

This ranch with 31 motel rooms is one hour from the park. A restaurant and swimming pool are on the premises. $

TOURS AND OUTFITTERS

Big Bend Natural History Association

P.O. Box 196, Big Bend National Park, TX 79834; tel:915-477-2236.

For a modest fee, visitors can participate in seminars held year-round in the national park and ranging from one to three days. A variety of topics are covered, including wildflowers and cacti, geology and history, and wildlife, all taught by seasoned naturalists who know the park well. Most birding trips take place in spring and fall. Seminars, generally limited to 15 participants, tend to fill up fast;

reservations should be made up to three months in advance.

Big Bend River Tours

P.O. Box 317, Lajitas, TX 79852; tel: 800-545-4240 or 915-424-3219.

This outfitter specializes in float trips down the Rio Grande and tours of the backcountry, including several of the canyons in and around Big Bend National Park. Trips range in length from a half day to 10 days and emphasize the region's bird life, geology, and history.

Far Flung Adventures

P.O. Box 377, Terlingua, TX 79852; tel: 800-359-4138 or 915-371-2489.

Canoe or raft trips on the Rio Grande run from one to 10 days. Far Flung has access to 225 miles of river, including five stretches of canyon. The outfitter provides all of the equipment needed for multiday trips.

Rio Grande Adventures

P.O. Box 229, Terlingua, TX 790852; tel: 800-343-1640 or 915-371-2567.

Travelers may choose from river floats with hiking in remote canyons or four-wheel-drive tours of the backcountry. All equipment and food, as well as guides, are provided. Rio Grande Adventures also rents camping gear, canoes, and rafts, and offers a shuttle service. Custom guided and self-guided trips can be arranged.

Texas River and Jeep Expeditions

P.O. Box 583, Terlingua, TX 79852; tel: 800-839-7238 or 915-371-2633.

Guides take visitors into the backcountry by Jeep to explore the natural history of Big Bend National Park. Birders can also arrange to float the Rio Grande for a different view of the park's topography and wildlife.

Excursions

Guadalupe Mountains National Park

HC 60, Box 400, Salt Flat, TX 79847; tel: 915-828-3251.

Contributing to the rugged terrain of this 86,416-acre park is Guadalupe Peak, the highest point in the state at 8,749 feet. Also here is a stretch of Capitan Reef, buried eons ago beneath an ancient sea and now fossilized and exposed to view. Nearly 300 species of birds have been recorded in the park's deserts, highlands, and other habitats. Among the species that nest in the park are northern spotted owls, golden eagles, canyon wrens, and black-chinned sparrows.

Davis Mountains State Park

P.O. Box 1458, Fort Davis, TX 79734; tel: 915-426-3337.

The park encompasses grasslands, juniper and pinyon woodlands, and other habitats and is laced with hiking trails. Many birders come here to see the striking Montezuma quail, formerly known as the harlequin quail because of the male's bold facial patterning. Other sightings in and around the park may include common black-hawk, scaled quail, greater roadrunner, Cassin's kingbird, Scott's oriole, hepatic tanager, and Grace's warbler.

Bosque del Apache National Wildlife Refuge

P.O. Box 1246, Socorro, NM 87801; tel: 505-835-1828.

In late fall and winter, nearly 15,000 sandhill cranes take up residence in this 57,000-acre refuge. Extensive marshes fed by the Rio Grande attract tens of thousands of snow and Ross's geese, numerous ducks and shorebirds, bald eagles, and a small group of endangered whooping cranes. During the Festival of the Cranes, held in mid-November, special guided tours cover areas of the refuge generally closed to the public.

Southeast
Arizona

CHAPTER **16**

Distinctive and metallic, the whirring of a broad-tailed hummingbird is the first sound you hear on arriving at Ramsey Canyon. It's a harbinger of what's to come here in hummingbird heaven. On an early morning in late August, birders have already gathered at the benches in front of feeders, where black-chinned and Anna's hummingbirds dart in to sip sugar water through slender bills. Others arrive in an unceasing barrage until the feeders seem bejeweled by the tiny birds. ◆ People from all over the world visit the Nature Conservancy's **Ramsey Canyon Preserve** to view these diminutive dynamos, especially in late summer at the peak of their southward migration. A row of painted tile plaques in front of the feeders illustrates the dazzling array of hummers known to visit here from late spring through summer: berylline, blue-throated, broad-billed, broad-tailed, calliope, Costa's, magnificent, rufous, violet-crowned, and white-eared, in addition to black-chinned and Anna's. ◆ As a preserve naturalist

Desert canyons bathed by summer rains invite hummingbirds to a nectar banquet and host rarities like the elegant trogon.

gathers a group of visitors for a walk along the creek, the *tweek, tweek, tweek* of a male blue-throated steals everyone's attention. This is one of the biggest hummingbirds around, so named for the male's gorget, or throat patch, that shimmers like a turquoise mosaic. The magnificent hummingbird is slightly larger, and its colors – purple crown and green gorget – are much different. ◆ The naturalist explains that Ramsey is one of several canyons that spill down the east side of the Huachuca Mountains. Southeast Arizona in general and the **Huachuca Mountains** in particular host such a diversity of hummingbirds for several reasons: warm,

A magnificent hummingbird feeds on a cactus flower. The birds can be very protective of their feeding territories. They also hawk small insects and raid spider webs.

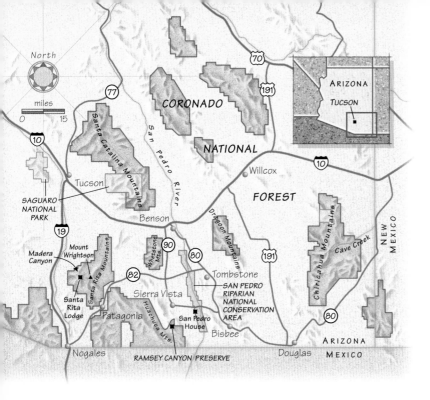

The following map labels appear on the map:

North

miles
0   15

77

CORONADO

70

191

ARIZONA

TUCSON

NATIONAL

Willcox

10

FOREST

Santa Catalina Mountains

San Pedro River

Tucson

10

SAGUARO
NATIONAL
PARK

19

Benson

Dragoon Mountains

Chiricahua Mountains

Cave Creek

NEW
MEXICO

Madera
Canyon

Mount
Wrightson

Whetstone
Mts.

90

80

191

Santa Rita Mountains

82

Tombstone

80

Santa
Rita
Lodge

Patagonia

Sierra Vista

Huachuca Mts.

San Pedro
House

SAN PEDRO
RIPARIAN
NATIONAL
CONSERVATION
AREA

Bisbee

ARIZONA

MEXICO

Nogales

RAMSEY CANYON PRESERVE

Douglas

moist climate; varied topography; and the confluence of four major biogeographic provinces. The Chihuahuan and Sonoran Deserts, the Rocky Mountains, and the Sierra Madre all converge in the region, nurturing a richness of life known in few other places in the temperate world and providing birders with an opportunity to experience subtropical species that aren't seen elsewhere in the United States.

Late-Summer Bloom

By late August, monsoon rains have been in full swing for more than a month. Cumulonimbus clouds pile up in the sky,

Male vermilion flycatchers (right) display for females by raising their crests, puffing their breast feathers, and hovering high in the air.

The Mexican jay (opposite, top) is more common than the western scrub-jay in the highlands of southeast Arizona.

Cacti make protected nest sites for curve-billed thrashers (opposite, below) and other desert birds.

lightning lashes the mountain peaks, and by afternoon strong winds whip the dust, and sheets of rain rake the earth. Normally dry washes rage with frothy brown water and the damp air is redolent with the scent of creosote bush. The monsoons usually continue through early September, nourishing a "rebirth" of life in this otherwise arid land.

For hummingbirds, a profusion of blooming wildflowers means a plentiful supply of nectar, especially from penstemons and other red, tubular flowers they prefer. Agave flowers, though pollinated primarily by bats, are also an important source of nectar. In concert comes a fresh crop of insects and spiders, providing hummingbirds with essential protein. The monsoons also sponsor a big influx of butterflies, such as the delicate cloudless sulphurs that flutter in the breeze like saffron leaves. The presence of water and the narrow tunnel of willows, cottonwoods, maples, and magnificent old sycamores along the stream draw lots of other creatures, including the rare Ramsey Canyon leopard frog and the coatimundi, or chulo, a tropical cousin of the raccoon.

The group continues to stroll up the old road built by the early miner whose name is given to the creek. With the naturalist's help, they see or hear bridled titmice, Strickland's woodpeckers, lesser goldfinches, western wood-pewees, and squawking flocks of Mexican jays. To everyone's delight, a sulphur-bellied fly-catcher, a bird that winters in the Amazon Basin, makes a coveted appearance before disappearing into an oak. On the way back down the trail, a pair of painted redstarts, summer residents here, display handsome red, white, and black plumage.

By late afternoon, the visitors have their binoculars up, scanning all the feeders. There's a male broad-tailed again, that trilling sound made by a quirk of wing anatomy. Lots of black-chins and Anna's, and a rare sight of the two big ones, the magnificent and the blue-throated. In a single day, the group has seen more than the most dedicated birder could ask for.

Irreplaceable Avian Corridor

Ramsey Canyon is only the beginning for bird lovers touring southeast Arizona. A few miles to the east is the **San Pedro River**, listed as a "Globally Important Bird Area" by the American Bird Conservancy. The river flows north more than 100 miles from northern Sonora to its confluence with the Gila River. The 40-mile, 56,000-acre stretch from the Mexican border to the Arizona town of St. David has been designated the **San Pedro Riparian National Conservation Area**. More than 100 species of birds breed here, while another 250 species migrate through or spend the winter. Each year, an estimated one million to four million songbirds crowd the corridor of cotton-woods, willows, and mesquites as they travel between southern wintering grounds and northern breeding areas.

Williamson, who works at a shaded picnic table. Williamson carefully examines each impossibly tiny bird, then deftly attaches a paper-thin numbered band to one leg. The bands will allow birds to be identified if recaught and to compile data on their longevity, nesting habits, and other behaviors. After attaching the band, Williamson measures length of bill and tail, then examines the bird for fat content. The bird weighs 3.3 grams, a little more than a penny. She lets the bird take a sip of nectar and releases it.

Meanwhile, Wood discusses hummingbird behavior. Do they mate for life, as some birds do? Not hummingbirds. "They hardly even mate for an afternoon," he quips. Once breeding is over, the male is out of the picture entirely, with the female bearing responsibility for building the nest, incubating the two eggs (each about the size of a black-eyed pea), and feeding the young. The nests are beautiful structures of spider webs, plant down, and lichens that can actually expand as the young grow.

On river's edge east of **Sierra Vista** stands an old ranch building, transformed into a visitor center called the **San Pedro House**. A trail leads to a pond where green kingfishers are sometimes seen. Gray hawks and a small bird with a preposterously big name – the northern beardless-tyrannulet – are other specialties. Weekly from April through May and from July through September, the public can stop by and watch Tom Wood and Sheri Williamson, founders of the Southeastern Arizona Bird Observatory, band hummingbirds as part of a long-term migration study. Wood sets up a mist net around the feeders and brings the birds to

Hummingbirds live life on the edge. Their metabolism requires that they eat constantly, consuming nectar for quick energy and insects for protein and other essential nutrients. These tropical birds cannot tolerate cold, so nearly all of them head for southern climes by early fall. At night, if air temperatures drop too low, they may save energy by entering torpor, a hibernation-like state in which their body temperature, heart rate, and breathing drop to minimal levels. The San Pedro provides critical habitat for migrating and nesting hummingbirds and other species. It's one of the last and most extensive riparian areas left in the desert Southwest, and, sadly, it's endangered. Groundwater pumping for residential development and irrigation threaten to suck it dry. Should the San Pedro be "dewatered," the lush ribbon of green will turn into stark gray skeletons.

Birds of Paradise

So enamored of hummingbirds are southern Arizonans that they graciously open their backyards to the world. At the Paton home in the small town of **Patagonia**, signs welcome visitors to a lovely yard along **Sonoita Creek**. All the owners ask is a modest donation to the "sugar fund." Folding chairs provide ringside views of eight feeders hanging from the eaves of the house. Like traders at the opening bell on the stock exchange, a horde of hummingbirds dives, zips, and flashes into the feeders, refueling after a long night. Two rufous hummingbirds fan their tails and assault the black-chins and Anna's. The birds are three deep at one feeder, all bullying their way in and feeding voraciously for at least an hour.

No birding trip to southeast Arizona is complete without a stop at **Madera Canyon**. The canyon cuts down the

Condors Fly Free

It's a bird. It's a plane ... No, it *is* a bird. The ominous dark shadow belongs to a California condor, a very large bird, indeed. Its 10-foot wingspan dwarfs that of an eagle. Visitors to the Grand Canyon and southeast Utah have a good chance of seeing these immense vultures soaring overhead.

Condors once ranged throughout the West, but by the early 1980s the species was on the verge of extinction. Biologists caught the remaining wild birds and began a captive breeding program. In 1996, nine birds were released at Arizona's **Vermilion Cliffs** near the **North Rim of the Grand Canyon**. By 1998, that group totaled 14 healthy birds. In late 1998, another eight young condors were let go at the Hurricane Cliffs, northwest of the Vermilion Cliffs. The long-term goal is to reestablish three separate reproducing populations in the Southwest and California.

The area is remote yet accessible enough to allow biologists to track the birds' movements and to supply these carrion eaters with cow carcasses until they start finding their own food. The cliffs also provide caves and rock outcrops for nest sites and open takeoff and landing platforms. Though condors typically cover 50 to 100 miles a day as they forage, one frequent flier from the Vermilion Cliffs group has traveled 200 to 300 miles. Most of the birds have remained closer to home, where visitors have seen them up and down the Colorado River, from the lodge on the North Rim, and from the parking lot at Bryce Canyon.

California condors (left) once ranged as far north as the Canada border and as far east as Texas.

Bullock's orioles (above) weave long, sacklike nests that are suspended from tree branches.

Saguaro cacti (opposite, top) bloom in spring, attracting hummingbirds, orioles, and doves.

Phainopeplas (opposite, bottom) are flycatchers whose diet also includes mistletoe berries.

Nightlife

At nightfall in the deserts and mountains of southeast Arizona, the star-spangled darkness comes to life as owls fill the canyons and woods with their unearthly hooting, booing, and barking.

The region's two screech-owls are readily identified by ear. The western utters a series of short accelerating whistles, or a short trill followed by a longer trill. The whiskered sounds a series of short whistles, or a succession of even more distinctive irregular hoots resembling Morse code.

Two tiny owls inhabit the region only in summer. The sparrow-sized elf owl, the world's smallest owl, is easiest to locate from late March to mid-July when its chuckling laughter is heard coming from cavities in sycamores and saguaro cacti. On moonlit nights in upper **Madera Canyon** and in **Cave Creek**, flammulated owls hoot softly or call with a two-note *boo-BOOT*. Rare and coveted is the large spotted owl, an uncommon resident of steep wooded canyons in the forested mountains. Its main call is three or four doglike barks or cries.

Other denizens of the night belong to the goatsucker family. Whip-poor-wills, the most familiar, loudly and repetitively advertise their name. Common nighthawks slice through the evening sky, announcing their presence with a booming whoosh as they enter a steep dive. The common nighthawk also utters frequent, loud, piercing calls, while the lesser nighthawk issues a soft, low *chuck, chuck*.

The buff-colored nightjar, kin to the nighthawks, is a rare local summer resident. Florida Wash on the way into Madera Canyon is an accessible place to find them. Birders are advised to arrive before sunset, walk up a short path, and sit and wait for their calls – a delicate, high *cuk-cuk-cuk-cuk-cukachee*, more like an insect than a bird. In Mexico, the nightjar's voice gives it the melodious Spanish name *preste-me-tu-cuchillo*.

Flammulated owls (above) bring their owlets large insects such as moths, caterpillars, crickets, and beetles.

Elegant trogons (opposite, top) that breed in southeast Arizona leave in fall for wintering grounds in Mexico.

A hooded oriole (opposite, bottom) uses its long, slightly curved bill to feed on nectar.

northwest side of the steep, forested slopes of the **Santa Rita Mountains** in **Coronado National Forest** south of **Tucson**. It is a deservedly famous birding locale because there's so much to see in such a small area. In only about a dozen road miles, travelers rise from the low valley of saguaro cactus and palo verde trees, through desert grassland dotted with the occasional mesquite, into evergreen oaks and alligator junipers. At road's end, trails head up through pine forest to the top of **Mount Wrightson**, at 9,453 feet elevation.

Rufous-winged, Botteri's, and Cassin's sparrows frequent the grasslands. A quartet of tanagers – summer, hepatic, western, and the rare flame-colored – present themselves as you continue uphill through different plant communities. In the heart of Madera Canyon reposes the peaceful Santa Rita Lodge, where a bulletin board reports recent avian sightings. Acorn woodpeckers chuckle in the trees, and guests sit outside to watch hummingbirds. This is the place to learn if any elegant trogons have been seen recently.

Trogons have been called "birds of paradise" for their bright colors. Males sport a vivid scarlet breast and an iridescent emerald back and head; females are a duller gray-brown overall. Both sexes have long, metallic, coppery tails that account for nearly half the birds' length and which earned them their former name of coppery-tailed trogons. Now, they are officially elegant trogons, a moniker that does indeed do justice, as no drawing or photograph can, to these gorgeous birds of the borderlands.

Trogons are most obvious during the spring breeding and nesting season, when the males are out to impress females. Once they've mated, the male and female engage in counterpoint duets. The distinctive call – *co ah, co ah* – gives the trogon its Mexican name, the coa. After young trogons are in the nest, the birds keep a lower profile. Still, in a sycamore tree beside Madera Creek in late summer, a male is quite visible as it feeds two youngsters. The first hint of the nest is a yellow beak and two eyes staring out from a round cavity in the sycamore. In a few minutes, the adult male swoops in low and stuffs a very large insect, probably a walkingstick, into the mouth of the cheeping young bird. Silence returns as he flies off to fetch more. The male returns three more times within the hour.

Deep, protected, water-bearing canyons like Madera are the preferred home ground of the rare trogons. Primarily a species of the tropics, elegant trogons were first recorded in Arizona in 1884 in the Santa Catalina Mountains north of Tucson, inching their range northward. One of the largest breeding populations known today in Arizona – up to 12 pairs – is in **Cave Creek** on the eastern side of the Chiricahua Mountains, nearly in New Mexico. Nesting trogons have also been reported in other canyons in the Huachuca Mountains and nearby ranges.

The first trogon nest found in the United States was in Madera Canyon, discovered in 1939 by Dr. Arthur Allen of Cornell University. Trogons show great fidelity to the same nest site year after year. Nests are especially vulnerable to

disturbance; watchers should remain quiet and not use recordings to attract the birds. Even observing these rules, trogons seem fully aware when people are around. "I have never seen a trogon that I felt had not already seen me," writes trogon expert Richard Cachor Taylor. "Trogons allow themselves to be observed." How fortunate that they do, for elegant trogons are one of the greatest avian delights in a region already rich beyond imagining.

TRAVEL TIPS

DETAILS

When to Go

Optimum birding occurs from April through September, especially late July through early September. Spring temperatures range from lows in the upper 40s to highs in the mid-70s. June, the hottest month, is subject to highs above 100°F, though most days remain in the upper 80s, with lows in the mid-60s. Evening thunderstorms in summer and fall often bring cooler temperatures.

How to Get There

Commercial airlines serve Tucson International Airport, less than 100 miles northwest of Ramsey Canyon Preserve.

Getting Around

A car is essential for birding this region. Car rentals are available at the airport. Parking at Ramsey Canyon Preserve is limited to 19 spaces, available on a first-come, first-served basis.

Handicapped Access

The visitor center and nearby hummingbird-viewing area at Ramsey Canyon Preserve are accessible, as are the visitor center and picnic area at San Pedro Riparian National Conservation Area.

INFORMATION

Coronado National Forest

Sierra Vista Ranger District, 5990 South Highway 92, Hereford, AZ 85615; tel: 520-378-0311.

Metropolitan Tucson Convention and Visitors Bureau

130 South Scott Avenue, Tucson, AZ 85701; tel: 800-638-8350 or 520-624-1817.

Ramsey Canyon Preserve

27 Ramsey Canyon Road, Hereford, AZ 85615; tel: 520-378-2785.

San Pedro Riparian National Conservation Area

Bureau of Land Management, 1763 Paseo San Luis, Sierra Vista, AZ 85635; tel: 520-458-3559.

Rare Bird Alert

Tel: 520-798-1005 (Tucson area).

CAMPING

Coronado National Forest has 35 campgrounds with a total of 603 campsites. Most sites are available on a first-come, first-served basis; others may be reserved by calling 800-280-2267.

Backcountry Travel

Permits are not required for backcountry hiking or camping in Coronado National Forest.

LODGING

PRICE GUIDE – double occupancy	
$ = up to $49	$$ = $50–$99
$$$ = $100–$149	$$$$ = $150+

Beatty's Miller Canyon Apiary and Orchard

2173 East Miller Canyon Road, Hereford, AZ 85615; tel: 520-378-2728.

This retreat occupies an apple orchard (elevation 5,800 feet) adjacent to the Miller Peak Wilderness Area. Accommodations include two apartments and one cabin, each with a bedroom, sitting room, and full kitchen. Visitors have access to the hummingbird and butterfly gardens. $$

Casa de San Pedro

8933 South Yell Lane, Hereford, AZ 85615; tel: 520-366-1300.

Located next to the San Pedro Riparian National Conservation Area, this bed-and-breakfast has 10 rooms with private baths. A full breakfast is served. A two-night minimum stay is required. $$$

Ramsey Canyon Inn

27 Ramsey Canyon Road, Hereford, AZ 85615; tel: 520-378-3010.

The inn, managed by the Nature Conservancy, borders Ramsey Canyon Preserve. Two apartments have kitchens; the bed-and-breakfast has six guest rooms, each with a private bath. A full breakfast is served. There is a three-night minimum stay in the apartments and a two-night minimum in the inn. $$$

San Pedro Bed-and-Breakfast

3123 Thistle Road, Sierra Vista, AZ 85636; tel: 520-458-6412.

The bed-and-breakfast is set on five acres in the San Pedro Riparian National Conservation Area. The ranch house's suite has a sitting room, refrigerator, and balcony. A separate guest house offers a room with refrigerator. Guests are treated to a full Southwestern-style breakfast. $$

San Pedro River Inn

8326 South Hereford Road, Hereford, AZ 85615; tel: 520-366-5532.

Four adobe guest houses are spread out on the inn's 20 acres, whose cottonwood trees attract a variety of birds. Each adobe has a living room, kitchen, and private bath; two- and three-bedroom units are available. A continental breakfast is served. The San Pedro Riparian National Conservation Area is a five-minute walk away. $$$

Santa Rita Lodge

HC 70, Box 5444, Sahuarita, AZ 85629; tel: 520-625-8746.

Set in the heart of Madera Canyon, the lodge has four one-room cabins and eight one-room efficiency units, all with kitchens. During spring and summer, lodge staff offer an extensive program of morning bird walks.

A two-night minimum is required from March through May. $$

TOURS AND OUTFITTERS

Southeastern Arizona Bird Observatory

P.O. Box 5521, Bisbee, AZ 85603; tel: 520-432-1388.

The observatory schedules field trips to the San Pedro Riparian Natural Conservation Area, various locations in the Huachuca Mountains, and other birding spots. Personalized guide services are available.

Tucson Audubon Society

300 East University Boulevard, Suite 120, Tucson, AZ 85705; tel: 520-578-1330.

Volunteers lead free field trips to various locations in southeast Arizona.

Upper San Pedro Ecosystem Program

Ramsey Canyon Preserve, 27 Ramsey Canyon Road, Hereford, AZ 85615; tel: 520-378-2640.

Naturalists lead excursions to the preserve and other birding spots.

SPECIAL EVENTS

Southeast Wings Birding Festival

P.O. Box 3432, Sierra Vista, AZ 85636; tel: 800-946-4777 or 520-378-0233.

Activities during this four-day festival in mid-August include field trips to see the specialties of southeast Arizona.

Wings Over Willcox Sandhill Crane Celebration

Willcox Chamber of Commerce, 1500 North Circle I Road, Willcox, AZ 85643; tel: 800-200-2272 or 520-384-2272.

Nearly 10,000 sandhill cranes winter in southeast Arizona, and birders have an opportunity to see many other species of wading birds and waterfowl during the three-day festival, held in mid-January.

Excursions

Chiricahua National Monument

Dos Cabezas Route, Box 6500, Willcox, AZ 85643; tel: 520-824-3560.

A volcanic eruption followed by 25 million years of compression and erosion shaped this area's imposing spires and towering rock formations. These moist "sky islands" rise from the desert, forming one of the continent's most biologically diverse regions. In the highlands, birders see Mexican chickadees and olive, red-faced, and Virginia's warblers. Sycamore-shaded Cave Creek is the place to spot several species of hummingbird, plus elegant trogons and painted redstarts.

Organ Pipe Cactus National Monument

Route 1, Box 100, Ajo, AZ 85321; tel: 520-387-6849.

Twenty-eight types of cacti grow in this 329,000-acre preserve on the Mexican border, including the monument's namesake, a species rarely found elsewhere in the United States. Many desert specialties – caracaras, vermilion flycatchers, black vultures, curve-billed thrashers – are among the nearly 300 bird species recorded here. Late spring and early summer, during the efflorescence of night-blooming cactuses, are good times to see elf owls and other nocturnal wildlife.

Saguaro National Park

3693 Old Spanish Trail, Tucson, AZ 85730; tel: 520-733-5153.

The park's abundant saguaro cacti, which rise to 50 feet, are a magnet for bird life. Elf owls, cactus wrens, Gila woodpeckers, and red-tailed hawks build their nests on and in these thick-armed giants, sometimes called the monarchs of the Sonoran Desert. The 91,400 acres of mixed conifer woodlands and desert scrub host other avian residents, such as Mexican Jays, curve-billed thrashers, and Gambel's quail.

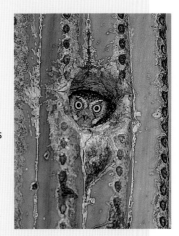

Pawnee National Grassland
Colorado

CHAPTER **17**

At first glance, the short-grass prairie appears altogether desolate. With barely enough grass to hide your ankles, there is next to nothing in the way of cover as the flat, virtually treeless landscape, shaded in muted greens and browns, stretches out to the horizon. As you look west on a clear day, the simple uniformity is emphasized by a distant view of jagged Rocky Mountain peaks. What is it about the prairie that enchants a birding connoisseur? Subtlety. Small movements in a large place; cryptic coloration in a deceptively plain but enormously rich landscape. It's a place whose inhabitants reveal themselves slowly. ◆ Situated two hours northeast of Denver, **Pawnee National Grassland** sprawls over a roughly 30-by-60-mile rectangle. Most of the land was acquired by the federal government in the 1930s when **Adapted to life on the** dust bowl conditions forced many ranchers **prairie, songbirds serenade** and farmers into bankruptcy. Today, **from sky perches, and** about one-fourth of the acreage is federally **raptors thrive on an** owned, the remainder having returned to **abundance of prey.** private ownership. The grassland is crisscrossed by a network of dirt roads that, weather permitting, allows birders easy access to most of the area. ◆ Begin by taking the 36-mile auto birding tour that originates at the **Crow Valley Recreation Area** near **Briggsdale**, where you can pick up a map of the route and a bird checklist at the grassland headquarters. Before starting off, spend some time birding the 50-acre recreation area; the park has been planted with deciduous trees and acts as a migrant trap in spring. Of the more than 290 species recorded in the grassland, about 200 have been seen in the recreation area alone.

Ferruginous hawks patrol wide, open spaces, seeking small mammals such as ground squirrels and rabbits. When they spot their prey, they hover overhead, then swoop down suddenly to claim their meal.

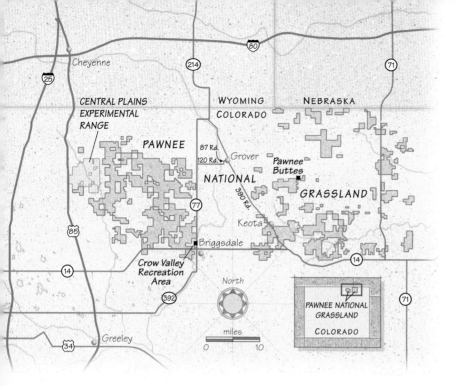

foraging for insects.

As you continue along this route, you'll witness displays of evanescent beauty by the "skylarking" birds of the prairie. Abundant McCown's longspurs in the short grasses, less-common chestnut-collared longspurs in the slightly taller grasses, Cassin's sparrows along fencerows, and horned larks and lark buntings everywhere rise up from the ground, floating and fluttering in the air with wings and tails fanned, filling the prairie with a cascade of song. Lacking trees from which to sing, they create their own "sky perches" to serenade prospective mates and declare their territorial superiority.

Perhaps this is the essence of the prairie's charm: everything happens at ground level, unhidden, right there for the patient birder to observe. A small sparrow-sized bird, its brown and beige feathers blending perfectly with the short grasses, hops along the sandy road's edge, chasing its father and

Skylarking Songbirds

The real excitement begins as you head north on Weld County Road 77, the prairie opening up before you. You'll see American kestrels and loggerhead shrikes perching on roadside fenceposts, and western meadowlarks will extend their flutelike greetings.

As you turn west onto Road 96 and enter the heart of the grasslands, carefully scan for motion in the very short grasses, favored habitat of one of the pearls of the prairie: the mountain plover. Perfectly camouflaged, these pale brown shorebirds (which, ironically, are never found at the shore or in the mountains) always stick close to the ground. Early to mid-April is the best time to see these prairie wraiths, when they establish their nesting territories and before the grasses get too long. They're often spotted in June and July, too, when they take their precocial young

Male and female Brewer's sparrows (left) are similar in appearance. The male is an enthusiastic songster, especially at dawn and dusk.

Prairie dogs (opposite, top) dig tunnels that, when abandoned, are occupied by burrowing owls.

An American kestrel (opposite, bottom) scans the terrain. The birds are often seen hovering over the prairie searching for prey.

begging loudly for its next meal. The adult McCown's longspur, nattily clad in bold black, white, and rust breeding plumage, scans the terrain from its perch on a small tussock and dives into the grass, emerging with a large grasshopper. It violently shakes the insect until parts start flying. First the wings are gone, then the hard exoskeleton, leaving a neatly peeled hot-dog-shaped morsel for its progeny. The young one, now beside itself with excitement and gape flaring, pursues its parent until the adult stuffs the insect down its throat.

Swainson's and ferruginous hawks stand on the ground, hunting ground squirrels from a "perch" that is little more than a slight rise in the terrain. Numerous prairie-dog towns, with mounds of earth piled around burrow entrances, house colonies of burrowing owls. Sit in your car and watch. Soon a head appears, then a few more. When the young start emerging, a dozen or more birds can be seen standing around, heads rotating comically as they examine their world. A lark bunting – so black that you can't see its ebony eye, its wing patch so white you can't see the feather detail – perches on a weed head

next to the road, beak full of insects, and then disappears into the grass to feed its young. A delicate Brewer's sparrow, sitting low in a saltbush, throws back its tiny head in song. And while you are watching the birds, perhaps a swift fox will lope across the flats or a herd of pronghorns appear on the next rise.

Prairie Raptors

Here and there a stunted tree has managed to survive the prairie winds. Almost every one holds a raptor's nest. Nesting space is

Pawnee Buttes in the eastern half of the grassland. The buttes, several hundred feet in length and from 200 to 300 feet high, were carved from the sandstone caprock by millions of years of erosion. An easy 1.5-mile trail leads to vantage points from which the raptors' courtship and nesting activities can be observed. Between March 1 and June 30, however, the primary overlook is closed to avoid stressing the nesting birds, and foot traffic is restricted to the marked trail. During this time, raptors can be viewed with spotting scopes from other scenic vistas. Cliff swallows, white-throated swifts, and rock wrens are common around the buttes, and the cascading liquid song of the canyon wren reverberates from the rock walls of the escarpment.

The **Central Plains Experimental Range** in the northwest corner of the grassland offers a change in habitat and bird species. A mixture of shrubby plants, taller grass, salt-sage bush, and yucca attracts sage thrashers, Brewer's and Cassin's sparrows, chestnut-collared longspurs, and loggerhead shrikes. Say's phoebes usually nest in the buildings on the site, and common nighthawks often spend the day sleeping on fenceposts.

Scattered across the grasslands are small ponds and reservoirs, most of them intermittent in nature and dependent on rainfall. Many migrant shorebirds pass through the region each spring, often pausing at these snack bars to refuel for their journey north. Water holes edged with reeds or tall grasses are likely to hold breeding American avocets or Wilson's phalaropes.

April through June is the best time of year to enjoy the breeding birds of the prairie. Courtship, establishment of territories, and nest building can be observed early in this period. By June, adult birds are feeding their young, and hawklets are stretching their wings in overcrowded nests, ready to fledge. An abundance of wildflowers completes this magnificent prairie landscape.

so limited that one small tree was found to hold a double-decker nest, with ferruginous hawks on top and a family of Cooper's hawks underneath. Occasionally, a great horned owl will usurp a hawk's nest and force the occupant to build elsewhere. Many nest trees are near the road, and birds will allow you to approach as long as you remain in your vehicle. Nesting sites may be at a premium, but there is food enough for all the young birds in the grassland's vast population of small mammals.

Cliff-dwelling raptors such as prairie falcons and golden eagles inhabit the

roadsides, watch for northern shrikes, plus pine siskins, various sparrows, and an occasional common redpoll, often feeding on sunflower heads. Huge flocks of horned larks may contain a few Lapland longspurs or a rare snow bunting.

There is an aura to the Pawnee National Grassland, a sense of well-being, of environmental health so powerful that being part of this magical place makes you feel good to be alive. Experience the prairie by getting out of your car and walking out of sight of the road. Sit down and breathe deeply. Listen to the sounds of this seemingly simple but wonderfully complex ecosystem. Let your spirit rise with the music of the meadowlark.

Winter on the prairie is also a birder's delight, as raptors take center stage. Prairie falcons, merlins, golden eagles, and rough-legged, ferruginous, and red-tailed hawks dominate the scene, preying on the year's crop of thirteen-lined and spotted ground squirrels and other small rodents. Along the

Plover of the Prairie

Almost imperceptibly, something moves on a patch of bare earth amid short prairie grasses. A careful look reveals a bird resembling a killdeer, but paler and more delicate, methodically probing small cracks in the soil for tiny insects. Its softly shaded feathers so closely match its surroundings that the bird appears to have sprung from the earth itself.

Requiring vast expanses of open prairie with sparse, very short grasses and exposed earth, the mountain plover traditionally nested in areas populated by vast herds of bison. Elimination of the bison and widespread farming profoundly reduced the plover's habitat and numbers. Ironically, introduction of cattle that heavily graze the prairie much as the bison once did have helped preserve the conditions necessary for the bird to breed successfully. Plovers often seek out these disturbed areas, where they feed on insects attracted to cattle and manure.

Alas, over the past 40 years, there has been a precipitous decline in mountain plover populations. Even the weather seems to be conspiring against them. Rainfall on the Colorado prairie was 25 percent greater than normal during the mid-to-late 1990s, leading to the growth of denser and taller grasses, which presents unsatisfactory plover breeding habitat. In some isolated areas, such as **Comanche National Grassland** in southeast Colorado, an aggressive program of prescribed burns has reclaimed habitat, and the plovers are doing well. There hasn't been extensive burning in Pawnee National Grassland due to the proximity of populated areas, and plover numbers have been reduced substantially. A return to normal rainfall combined with continued grazing of livestock on the grassland may help restore their numbers.

The mountain plover (above), unlike other plovers, is seldom seen near the seashore.

Young burrowing owls (top) remain with adults for nearly six weeks.

American avocets (opposite, top) swing their long bills side to side as they search for food in shallow water.

Western meadowlarks (opposite, bottom) use their flutelike songs to define and defend their territory.

DETAILS

When to Go

Eastern species of warblers migrate through Pawnee in May. Short-grass specialties breed here in June and July. Birders also visit from November through February to observe wintering hawks. Daytime temperatures reach the 70s in May and the 90s in July. Nighttime lows are in the 40s. Winter temperatures range from highs in the 40s and 50s to lows near 0°F. Snowfall, though infrequent, is often accompanied by high winds.

How to Get There

The nearest airports are in Cheyenne, Wyoming, a 90-minute drive from the grassland, and Denver, Colorado, a two-hour drive.

Getting Around

An automobile is necessary for birding the grasslands. Cars may be rented at the airports. Pawnee is remote, filling stations scarce; travel with a full tank of gas, ample water, and other supplies. Mountain bikes are permitted on the 36-mile auto-tour route.

Handicapped Access

Accessible areas offer fine birding at Crow Valley Recreation Area, near Briggsdale.

INFORMATION

Pawnee National Grassland/Crow Valley Recreation Area

660 O Street, Greeley, CO 80631; tel: 970-353-5004.

Greeley Convention and Visitors Bureau

902 Seventh Avenue, Greeley, CO 80631; tel: 800-449-3866 or 970-352-3566.

Rare Bird Alert

Tel: 303-424-2144 (statewide).

CAMPING

The grassland has developed campsites at Crow Valley Recreation Area. Some sites are available on a first-come, first-served basis, others by reservation. For information, call 970-353-5004.

LODGING

PRICE GUIDE – double occupancy

$ = up to $49 $$ = $50–$99

$$$ = $100–$149 $$$$ = $150+

German House Bed-and-Breakfast

1305 Sixth Street, Greeley, CO 80631; tel: 970-356-1353.

Built in 1885, this brick Queen Anne Victorian has four guest rooms, each with private bath. Visitors begin the day with a German-style breakfast. A swimming pool is on the premises. $$

Greeley Guest House

5401 West Ninth Street, Greeley, CO 80634; tel: 800-314-3684 or 970-353-9373.

The Greeley offers three types of accommodations. Sixteen rooms, two of which have Jacuzzis, have a gas fireplace, a refrigerator, and a microwave. Two suites have a living room, fireplace, refrigerator, microwave, and Jacuzzi. An apartment-style suite has a full kitchen. Breakfast is included. $$$

Greeley Inn

721 13th Street, Greeley, CO 80631; tel: 970-353-3216.

Set in the center of Greeley, the inn has 38 rooms. A swimming pool is on the premises. $–$$

Plover Inn

Box 179, Grover, CO 80729; tel: 970-895-2275.

This inn, 15 miles from Pawnee Buttes, offers three suites with a living room, kitchen, and bath; one suite has no kitchen. Two smaller rooms share a bath. Birders are served a light breakfast before early-morning excursions and a full breakfast upon return. $$–$$$

Sod Buster Inn Bed-and-Breakfast

1221 Ninth Avenue, Greeley, CO 80631; tel: 888-300-1221 or 970-392-1221.

Built in the late 1890s, this three-story octagonal building with a wraparound veranda has 10 guest rooms, each with a private bath. A full breakfast is served. $$–$$$

West Pawnee Ranch Bed-and-Breakfast

29451 Weld County Road 130, Grover, CO 80729; tel: 970-895-2482.

This active ranch, four miles from the national grassland and 30 miles from Pawnee Buttes, occupies 7,000 acres of prairie. Two of three accommodations have living rooms. In addition to birding, guests are invited to ride horses and mountain bikes, and tag along with ranch hands. A full breakfast is served; lunch and dinner are available upon request. $$

TOURS AND OUTFITTERS

Bellbird Safaris

P.O. Box 158, Livermore, CO 80536; tel: 800-726-0656.

The operator leads a 12-day tour of Colorado locales, including the national grassland, during the spring migration in early May. Birders may also book guides for day trips to the grassland and other top birding locations in Colorado.

SPECIAL EVENTS

Eagle Days Festival

Colorado Division of Wildlife, 6000 Reservoir Road, Pueblo, CO 81005; tel: 719-561-4909 or 719-561-9320.

About 130 bald eagles winter in southeast Colorado. Field trips to see these eagles, as well as western and mountain bluebirds, northern and loggerhead shrikes, and scaled quail, are led during the Eagle Days Festival, a one-day event held the first week in February. Renowned wildlife experts also share photography tips and discuss birds of prey.

Monte Vista Crane Festival

1035 Park Avenue, P.O. Box 585, Monte Vista, CO 81144; tel: 719-852-3552.

Birders who attend this three-day event in mid-March enjoy views of sandhill cranes, 20,000 of which inhabit the San Luis Valley. A handful of whooping cranes may also be seen. The festival includes workshops and guided field trips.

Excursions

Cheyenne Bottoms Wildlife Management Area

56 Northeast 40 Road, Great Bend, KS 67530; tel: 316-793-7730 or 316-793-3066.

Thousands of northbound waterfowl – green-winged and blue-winged teals, northern pintails, common goldeneyes, Canada geese – stop at this 19,000-acre management area in spring. Following these birds are long-billed dowitchers, Hudsonian godwits, and various species of sandpipers, including Baird's, white-rumped, least, and pectoral. The white-faced ibis, little blue heron, and American bittern are among the wading birds seen in these wetlands. Autumn birding is also productive. A 7,000-acre Nature Conservancy preserve adjoins Cheyenne Bottoms.

Comanche National Grassland

P.O. Box 127, Springfield, CO 81073; tel: 719-523-6591.

Wide-open canyons and stretches of short- and mid-grass prairie characterize this 445,000-acre grassland in the high plains. The various habitats, whose elevations range from 4,000 to 8,000 feet, attract 275 species of birds. Spring is the breeding season for lesser prairie chickens, Cassin's sparrows, and other prairie birds. Golden eagles and Swainson's hawks prefer the canyonlands. A seasonal lake hosts abundant waterfowl. Some species seen at Comanche, such as the scaled quail and greater roadrunner of the Southwest, are at the extremes of their normal range.

Rocky Mountain National Park

Estes Park, CO 80571; tel: 970-586-1206.

Snow-capped peaks, high-altitude tundra, lushly forested valleys, and wildflower-carpeted meadows make this park a spectacular birding destination. The best way to experience the wildlife is on the park's many trails. White-tailed ptarmigans are camouflaged by the sparse tundra vegetation, while Clark's nutcrackers boldly announce themselves as they forage for seeds to cache for winter. Golden eagles soar overhead on the lookout for a meal.

South-Central Nebraska

CHAPTER 18

Against the spring or autumn skies, long skeins of water-fowl undulate over the somber prairie, each wave like a thin band of smoke. Dawn reverberates with the primitive tremolo of sandhill cranes as they rise clamoring from the river shallows and swarm out to feed. The marshland mudflats are a lacework of shorebird tracks, the air full of swift darting and *peen*tings. ◆ This is south-central Nebraska, and as a drain collects water, so this region collects birds. ◆ The causes are readily explained. As a rule, prairies in the central United States are much drier than the pothole-laden breeding grounds to the north. The central prairies are also much drier than the waterfowl wintering areas to the south. However, in this part of Nebraska, bounded on the west by the burg of **Elwood** and on the east by **David City**, lies a critical expanse of wetlands known as the **Rainwater Basin**. Situated at the 35-degree isotherm – an invisible line that separates the late-thawing wetlands of the Dakotas from the early-thawing basins of Nebraska – they provide an essential migration habitat. ◆ That alone would be enough to make this a birder's paradise, but the area is doubly blessed. Just to the north runs the bright ribbon of the **Platte River**. Rising in Colorado, this broad, shallow, swift river races east across the width of Nebraska toward its confluence with the Missouri River. On its journey, it provides crucial habitat for migrating sandhill cranes, with the most favored roosting area along the section of the Platte just north of the basin. The combination of these two distinct but closely associated ecosystems, aided by the relative dearth of

Seasonal wetlands and a prairie river nourish migrating geese and ducks and the world's largest gathering of cranes.

Three subspecies of sandhill crane concentrate at the Platte River before continuing north to their breeding grounds.

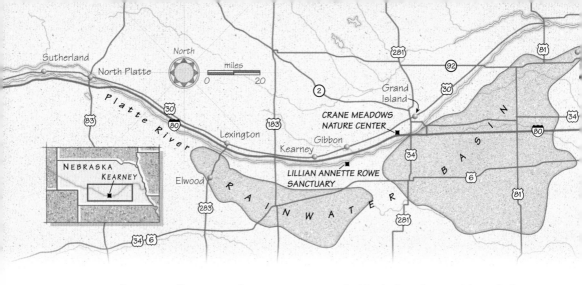

water in surrounding areas, draws water-dependent birds not by the tens or hundreds of thousands but by the millions.

Potholes They're Not

Most birders have heard of the prairie pothole region – glacier-created wetlands that lie in a broad swath from northwest Iowa to central Saskatchewan. Perhaps the most important breeding habitat for ducks

in North America, prairie potholes are most frequently found in rolling hill country known as the Missouri or Prairie coteaus.

Nebraska's rainwater basins, though similar in appearance, were created by different forces. Cataclysmic winds 20,000 years ago shaped the gentle undulations of this landscape, and over the succeeding years, rain and snowmelt caused the clay particles in the soil to settle, forming a clay lens impermeable to water. Unlike prairie potholes, which frequently lie at the bottom of steep (by prairie standards) basins, the slope of a rainwater basin is almost imperceptible. Nonetheless, the basins retain significant water resources that attract myriad waterfowl, cranes, and shorebirds.

Known locally as "lagoons," the basins have dwindled dramatically as agriculture has modified the landscape: Less than 10 percent of the original wetlands remains. Yet even in this compromised state, they continue to collect birds in amazing numbers in both spring and fall.

Fall migration is good, beginning in September, peaking in November, and ending in December. But spring is sensational. Thanks to the latitude at which the Rainwater Basin lies, the area is ice-free long before the potholes to the north. This halts the birds for a six-week period that peaks in March as they await the warmth that will open northern waters.

Surveys indicate that two to three million waterfowl are present each spring – and that doesn't include cranes and shorebirds.

Some basins hold nearly a million waterfowl at a time, the birds resting and feeding before resuming their flight. Birds that haven't already chosen a mate, such as northern pintails and green-winged teals, can be observed engaging in pair selection and nuptial displays.

Dense vegetation (left) provides a natural blind for observing birds of the central prairie.

Male yellow-headed blackbirds (opposite) show a striking contrast of yellow and black. Females are more brown, with a pale yellow throat.

Northern pintails (below) not yet paired up for the breeding season find mates at Rainwater Basin.

Of the ducks, pintails arrive earliest, then mallards, wigeons, and green-winged teals. A second wave of mallards is followed by redheads, scaups, gadwalls, blue-winged teals, and northern shovelers. At times, 50 percent of the mid-continent breeding population of mallards and 30 percent of the breeding population of pintails are concentrated in the basins.

Geese – Canada, white-fronted, lesser snows, and Ross's – also pile into the basins in March. By some estimates, 90 percent of the entire mid-continent population of white-fronted geese migrate through here

in a three-week period. More than three million snow geese and nearly one million Canada geese also pass through.

The drama continues with the eleven species of herons and bitterns, white-faced ibis, two species of cranes, six species of rails and coots, six species of plovers, seventeen species of sandpipers and phalaropes, eight species of gulls and terns, American avocet, American white pelican, and double-crested cormorant. Add to that a spring influx of raptors, and the air is alive with birds.

Prairie Courtships

Two closely related grouse of the prairies – the greater prairie-chicken and the sharp-tailed grouse – perform spring mating rituals that are nothing short of amazing.

From mid-March through mid-April, as dawn first paints the prairie, male grouse gather in groups on traditional dancing grounds known as leks. There, each defending its own small dance space, the birds inflate the purple air sacs on each side of their necks and begin to strut, heads low and wings cupped outward, rapidly pounding their legs into the prairie turf. Spinning and whirling like frantic windup toys, they ardently seek to convince the watching females that they are suitable mates.

Male prairie-chickens perform much the same routine. For their part, they have yellow-red air sacs and also boast long erectile feathers on the side of the neck. While dancing, males of both species utter loud mating calls reminiscent of children's laughter.

Birders can witness the courtship dances of these two species at **Valentine National Wildlife Refuge**, 90 miles north of Interstate 80 at **North Platte**. At over 70,000 acres, the refuge is the largest remaining tract of mid- and tallgrass prairie in North America. Both the prairie chicken and the grouse are abundant here, though the prairie-chicken population is severely declining across much of its range. Observation blinds should be reserved in advance.

Greater prairie-chickens (below), once common in the Great Plains, are now restricted to pockets of tallgrass prairie.

Geese and ducks (bottom) in Rainwater Basin exceed two million in spring.

Sedge wrens (opposite, top) nest in marshes and meadows along the Platte River.

Dark wedges under the inner wings of prairie falcons (opposite, bottom) help separate them from other raptors, especially in flight.

The bustling little city of **Grand Island** is probably the best place to base your explorations and also offers quick access to the Platte River. Be careful while driving the dirt roads of the basin region. When wet, they are very slippery, and even four-wheel-drive vehicles get stuck. Many of the basins are federally owned Waterfowl Production Areas, purchased with proceeds of hunter's duck stamps, and are open to the public. Others, acquired by the state, are managed as Wildlife Management Areas. Maps are available from the U.S. Fish and Wildlife Service or the Nebraska Game and Parks Department in Kearney.

Cranes of the Platte

While the pleasures of the Rainwater Basin are relatively unknown to birders, the show put on by the Platte River cranes is famed as one of the top wildlife spectacles in North America. The spring staging of sandhill cranes along a 60-mile stretch of river between **Grand Island** and **Lexington** and a 20-mile segment from **North Platte** to **Sutherland** brings together the greatest concentration of any crane species in the world. Although there are five subspecies of sandhill cranes, only greater, Canadian, and lesser sandhills gather on the Platte. A very few rare and endangered whooping cranes can be found among the flocks.

Like the basins, the Platte has been sorely abused by mankind. The siphoning of water for settlement and agriculture has reduced its peak flows to the point where trees and brush, once annually stripped away by spring floods, choke the banks – and in some places constrict the river itself. This, of course, deters the cranes. Only in the two 60-mile and 20-mile sections does the river retain its historic open, sandbar-filled character.

Of the sandhill crane subspecies, the lesser is by far the most common, and during the five or so weeks of staging, some 70 percent of the population crowds into this small slash of habitat. Overall, an estimated 500,000 cranes pause here during the five weeks. The first waves appear in late February, and staging peaks during the month of March.

Attracted by the broad flats, the cranes roost each night in the protection of the river. Before dawn, a cacophony of calling begins, and, sensing the rising sun, the nervous birds begin to depart in small groups. At first light, tens of thousands of

cranes lift from the river. Flying short distances to the wet meadows along the river or farther inland to farm fields, these omnivorous birds spend the day feeding on waste grain or probing moist soils for tubers, shoots, worms, and grubs. Even small animals, such as toads, frogs, and snakes, are consumed with relish.

Blinds near the river for crane watching and tours to see the cranes are provided by state and private groups, including the National Audubon Society's **Lillian Annette Rowe Sanctuary** and the **Crane Meadows Nature Center**. But not to worry if you find them booked. At any place along the roosting sections where roads pass near or cross the Platte, you can observe the coming and going of cranes at dusk and dawn. During leisurely drives along country roads or even as you cruise down busy Interstate 80, cranes are visible nearly all the time. They parachute down in spiral clouds on six-foot wings and feed in fields or meadows, where you are bound to see them erupt into their wonderful hopping, wing-fanning nuptial dances.

TRAVEL TIPS

DETAILS

When to Go

The largest concentrations of birds occur in the spring, from late February through mid-April, peaking in March. September through December is a good period to visit Rainwater Basin. Temperatures range from highs in the 50s to lows around -5°F. Mornings, the prime time to see cranes and waterfowl, are cold; wet and blustery weather is not uncommon.

How to Get There

Major airlines serve airports in nearby Grand Island and Kearney, as well as airports in Lincoln and Omaha, 125 miles and 160 miles east of Grand Island, respectively.

Getting Around

Car rentals are available at the airports. An automobile is essential for birding the area. Many bird species can be seen from the shoulder of county roads.

Handicapped Access

Handicapped assistance at the Lillian Annette Rowe Sanctuary (308-468-5282) and the Crane Meadows Nature Center (308-382-1820) may be arranged in advance. Many portions of the Rainwater Basin may be birded by automobile.

INFORMATION

Grand Island/Hall County Convention and Visitors Bureau

309 West Second Street, P.O. Box 1486, Grand Island, NE 68802; tel: 800-658-3178 or 308-382-4400.

Kearney Visitors Bureau

P.O. Box 607, Kearney, NE 68848; tel: 800-227-8340 or 308-237-3101.

Nebraska Game and Parks Commission

1617 First Avenue, Kearney, NE 68847; tel: 308-865-5310.

U.S. Fish and Wildlife Service

2610 Avenue Q, Kearney, NE 68847; tel: 308-235-5015.

Valentine National Wildlife Refuge

Fort Niobrara/Valentine National Wildlife Refuge Complex, HC14, Box 67, Valentine, NE 69201; tel: 402-376-3789.

Rare Bird Alert

Tel: 402-292-5325 (statewide).

CAMPING

Fort Kearney State Recreation Area

1020 V Road, Kearney, NE 68847; tel: 308-865-5305.

This 152-acre area on the Platte River has 110 campsites available on a first-come, first-served basis. Visitors observe cranes and other birds from the Fort Kearney Hike-Bike Trail, which begins here, crosses both channels of the Platte River, and ends at the Bassway Strip State Wildlife Management Area.

Mormon Island Recreation Area

RR 2, Box 19, Doniphan, NE 68832; tel: 308-385-6211.

Surrounded by channels of the Platte River, the island has 34 campsites available on a first-come, first-served basis.

Windmill State Recreation Area

P.O. Box 427, 2625 Lowell Road, Gibbon, NE 68840; tel: 308-468-5700.

The recreation area, between Kearney and Grand Island, has year-round camping facilities near small lakes. The 69 sites are available on a first-come, first-served basis.

LODGING

PRICE GUIDE – double occupancy

$ = up to $49 $$ = $50–$99
$$$ = $100–$149 $$$$ = $150+

Aunt Betty's Bed-and-Breakfast

804 Grand View Avenue, Ravenna, NE 68869; tel: 800-632-9114 or 308-452-3739.

Originally a boardinghouse, this impressive Victorian has four guest rooms, each furnished with antiques. Guests share two baths and enjoy breakfast before their day of birding. $–$$

Country Inn and Suites by Carlson

105 Talmadge Street, Kearney, NE 68847; tel: 800-456-4000 or 308-236-7500.

The inn has 56 standard rooms and 17 suites with sitting areas. Amenities include a restaurant and an indoor pool. $$

Grandma's Victorian Inn

1826 West Third Street, Hastings, NE 68901; tel: 402-462-2013.

Built in 1886, this restored Victorian is situated less than two miles from the Hastings Museum. Five guest rooms offer queen-sized beds, antique furniture, and private baths with clawfoot tubs. $$

Kirschke House

1124 West Third Street, Grand Island, NE 68801; tel: 800-381-6851 or 303-381-6851.

The bed-and-breakfast, a brick Victorian with stained-glass windows, has four guest rooms with shared baths, one with a private bath, and a two-level bridal suite with a private bath, fireplace, four-poster bed, veranda, and refrigerator. A hot tub is on the premises. $$–$$$

TOURS AND OUTFITTERS

Crane Meadows Nature Center

9325 South Alda Road, Wood River, NE 68883; tel: 308-382-1820.

Naturalists lead sunrise and afternoon tours during the spring crane season and conduct other nature-related programs throughout the year. Exhibits emphasize Platte River ecology, crane migration, and the region's endangered species.

Lillian Annette Rowe Sanctuary

44450 Elm Island Road, Gibbon, NE 68840; tel: 308-468-5282.

From early March to early April, guides at this National Audubon Society sanctuary conduct crane-viewing excursions to wooden blinds. Tours are available by reservation; birders planning weekend visits should book three months in advance. Photo blinds are also available.

U.S. Fish and Wildlife Service

2610 Avenue Q, Kearney, NE 68847; tel: 308-235-5015.

Birders observe cranes from blinds on these predawn and dusk tours, which depart from Kearney in March. Reservations are accepted a month in advance.

SPECIAL EVENTS

Rivers and Wildlife Celebration

Audubon Nebraska, P.O. Box 117, Denton, NE 68339; tel: 402-797-2301 or 308-468-5282.

This festival includes guest speakers, children's programs, and field trips to Rainwater Basin, the Platte River, and other birding spots. The three-day event, held in mid-March, is sponsored by Audubon Nebraska and the Lillian Annette Rowe Sanctuary.

MUSEUMS

Hastings Museum

1330 North Burlington, Hastings, NE 68902; tel: 800-508-4629.

The museum displays specimens of most resident and migratory bird species found in Nebraska. Also displayed is the world's largest exhibit of whooping cranes, shown in a lifelike habitat.

Excursions

Buffalo Gap National Grassland

Wall Ranger District, 704 Main Street, P.O. Box 425, Wall, SD; tel: 605-279-2125.

More than 230 bird species have been recorded at this 591,000-acre preserve, whose prairies, marshlands, woodlands, and open water snake across southwestern and central South Dakota. Burrowing owls nest in homes vacated by black-tailed prairie dogs. Bald and golden eagles, prairie and peregrine falcons, and ferruginous and Swainson's hawks sweep over the grassland. Songbirds such as western meadowlarks and horned larks breed here, and waterfowl visit in autumn and spring.

DeSoto National Wildlife Refuge

1434 316th Lane, Missouri Valley, IA 51555; tel: 712-642-4121.

In autumn, 350,000 migrating snow geese stop in the Missouri River Valley en route to the Gulf Coast. Joining them on DeSoto Lake are 75,000 ducks, mostly mallards. As many as 120 eagles winter in the refuge, roosting in the lakeside cottonwoods. The lake's steep banks provide nesting habitat for a colony of bank swallows, and wood ducks nest in nearby tree cavities or manmade boxes. Warblers, pheasants, bobwhites, and red-headed woodpeckers inhabit the prairie and woodlands.

Long Lake National Wildlife Refuge

12000 353rd Street SE, Moffit, ND 58560; tel: 701-387-4397.

This shallow lake swells during the spring runoff, which coincides with the arrival of abundant birds. Large groups of Franklin's gulls, American avocets resplendent in breeding plumage, and numerous species of shorebirds pause here on northward migrations. Wading birds and nine ducks, including blue-winged teals and gadwalls, nest at Long Lake. Birders in the uplands see Baird's, sharp-tailed, grasshopper, and Le Conte's sparrows, as well as ring-necked pheasants and sharp-tailed grouse.

Grand Teton National Park
Wyoming

CHAPTER **19**

Dark visitors often pass up Grand Teton for the much larger and better-known Yellowstone National Park just to the north. Yet those who stop to explore **Grand Teton National Park** become ardent admirers. The 310,443-acre park contains the **Teton Range**, one of the world's most impressive fault-block formations. A series of ancient uplifts pushed immense blocks of rock strata skyward, producing these mountains that rise starkly out of the surrounding lowlands like a mammoth wall. Of the 11 principal peaks over 10,000 feet in elevation, the highest is the **Grand Teton** itself at 13,770 feet. ◆ The birds match the scenery. A succession of habitats, from glacial cirques and lush coniferous forests to abundant lakes and ponds and extensive sagebrush flats, sustains almost 300 species. More than half are known to nest in the park, including no fewer than 21 birds of prey – more than in any of America's other national parks – and 34 species of waterbirds. Some, such as bald

Summer in the northern Rockies is prime time for nesting raptors, songbirds, and waterbirds, including the fabulous trumpeter swan.

and golden eagles, ospreys, northern goshawks, peregrine and prairie falcons, great gray owls, and trumpeter swans, serve as important indicators of the park's remote and wild status within the deteriorating global environment. ◆ Each ecosystem in the Teton highlands has its distinct bird life in summer. For the widest assortment of highland species, birders head for the mixed conifer forest, which includes scattered aspen groves in areas of old burns. This forest habitat is easily reached from the paved **Teton Park Road** along the base of the mountains and by numerous trails, such as those around **Jenny**, **String**, and **Leigh Lakes**, and the **Hermitage**

White downy feathers on young great horned owls make them easy to spot when they explore outside their nest. Two months after hatching, they make their first flight.

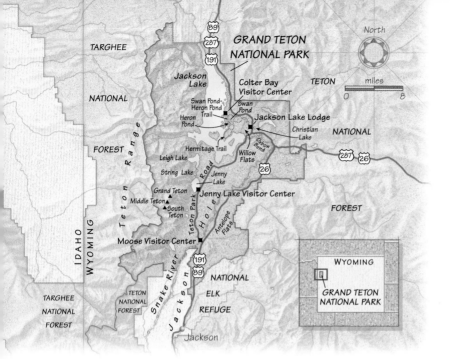

Grand Teton National Park map showing Targhee National Forest, Jackson Lake, Colter Bay Visitor Center, Teton National Forest, Swan Pond-Heron Pond Trail, Heron Pond, Swan Pond, Jackson Lake Lodge, Christian Lake, Hermitage Trail, Oxbow Bend, Willow Flats, Leigh Lake, String Lake, Jenny Lake, Grand Teton, Middle Teton, South Teton, Jenny Lake Visitor Center, Moose Visitor Center, Antelope Flats, Teton Range, Teton Park Road, Jackson Hole, Snake River, Jackson, Teton National Forest, National Elk Refuge, Idaho/Wyoming border, with an inset map of Wyoming showing the location of Grand Teton National Park.

fourth to sixth notes.

The loveliest sounds come from the two thrushes, Swainson's and hermit, that occur throughout the forest, even in areas adjacent to the park's principal campgrounds. Their flutelike songs are commonplace, though you may not know where the wonderful renditions originate. Swainson's thrushes sing an ascending spiral of mellow whistles, while hermit thrushes repeat a series of warbling notes at different pitches. Both may sing for long periods, especially during morning and evening.

Highland Highlights

Most birds of the mixed conifer forest can be seen or heard on the **Hermitage Trail** or the **Swan Lake-Heron Pond Trail**. You may also have an opportunity to spot a great gray owl, one of the species most sought after by birders. The largest of the North American owls, this huge hunter with a five-foot wingspan is a year-round resident in years of low snowfall. Preferring meadowlike areas within the forest, the owl perches on snags both day and night to watch for prey, particularly voles and pocket gophers.

Swift-flowing streams in and below the mountain canyons are home to the American dipper. This large, wrenlike songbird with dark gray plumage dips up and down – hence its name – as it stands on rocks and logs before submerging itself underwater in search of aquatic insects. Dippers build large, grassy nests in streamside crevices just above the rushing water.

At about 8,500 feet, you enter the habitat of Steller's and gray jays, Clark's nutcrackers, and pine grosbeaks. Clark's nutcrackers are

Trail near the **Colter Bay Visitor Center**.

Dark-eyed juncos and house wrens are commonly found foraging at ground level. Aerialists such as tree and violet-green swallows hawk insects. Among the arboreal species are hairy woodpeckers, mountain chickadees, red-breasted nuthatches, ruby-crowned kinglets, western tanagers, and pine siskins. The yellow-rumped warbler, one of the most numerous and colorful species, is easy to identify though it usually stays high in the trees. Male yellow-rumps possess a black face, back, and chest, and five bright yellow spots, on their cap, throat, sides, and rump. One of the most vocal forest birds, it sings *che che che che che che*, with a slight inflection on the

identified by their gray, black, and white plumage and their loud, rather distinct calls – very nasal, grating, and drawn-out *kraa-a-a* notes. To locate the rarer pine grosbeaks, listen for their whistled *pui pui pui* flight call. The gorgeous males sport grayish plumage with a red back, head, and underparts, and black wings and tail. Hiking into the backcountry is the best way to find American pipits and black rosy-finches, the only birds that nest above treeline in the alpine zone of bare rocks and low-growing shrubs.

Pine siskins (left), members of the finch family, are often seen in trees looking for seeds and insects.

A Clark's nutcracker (opposite) stores food for the winter in caches that contain as many as 33,000 seeds.

Grand Teton (below) rises above the Snake River, an ideal place to observe white pelicans, common loons, and ducks.

Grand Teton Waterways

Fed by 25,540-acre **Jackson Lake**, largest of the many lakes, **Snake River** flows southwest through the park. The river, along with its numerous oxbow ponds, provides special habitats for several of the area's most notable birds, including trumpeter swans and bald eagles. Float trips, led by outfitters several times daily in summer, will give you fine views of these great birds, as well as ospreys, often carrying fish caught by diving into the water from as high as 30 feet overhead. You may see a Cooper's hawk, the powerful northern goshawk, and the much smaller American kestrel. River guides will point out the nests of these species as you glide by.

Belted kingfishers lope up and down the river, pausing to dive for fish. As many as six species of swallows – tree, violet-green, northern rough-winged, bank, cliff, and barn – chase down flying insects, often coming so close that rafters feel they could reach up and touch one of the graceful creatures. From the cottonwood groves along the river, western wood-pewees sing their nasal *pee-er* notes, black-capped

common in areas of willows and aspens, is often referred to as a "keystone" species for its habit of maintaining sap wells used by other birds. Hummingbirds, kinglets, and warblers drink sap oozing from the wells, and insects attracted to the sap become food for other birds.

Ponds, with their quiet water and surrounding cover, contain very different bird life. Among the most productive and accessible is **Christian Pond**, across from Jackson Lake Lodge, where most of the park's nesting waterbirds can be found. Along with

chickadees proclaim *chick-a-dee-dee-dee*, and American robins and black-headed grosbeaks serenade birders with their rich melodies. Warbling vireos continue their rambling warbles throughout the day, and yellow warblers join the chorus with their lively *tseet-tseet-tzeet sitta-sitta-sitta*.

Scan the riverside groves and thickets for downy and hairy woodpeckers, northern flickers, and white-breasted nuthatches inspecting the trunks and branches for insects. The red-naped sapsucker, fairly

pied-billed grebes, numerous American coots, and various ducks – American wigeon, ring-necked and ruddy ducks, green-winged and cinnamon teals – a pair of nesting trumpeter swans resides here each summer. Sitting above the pond, you can study these majestic birds as they go about their daily routine (be sure to remain behind the signs to avoid disturbing the swans while they are nesting or caring for their young). **Oxbow Bend**, a meandering portion of the Snake River east of Jackson Lake Junction, hosts many of these same waterbirds. This is also a good location to see white pelicans, common loons, common mergansers, and Barrow's goldeneyes, among the park's handsomest ducks.

A few pairs of sandhill cranes nest at **Willow Flats**, open wetlands west of the lodge. Their nests, mounds of marsh grasses, can be five feet across. You can observe them from the **Willow Flats Overlook** along the main highway. In early summer, you will also see courting yellow-headed blackbirds. The males, with their black plumage, bright yellow head, and white wing patch, sing a marvelous song, beginning with a few harsh, rasping noises, like cacophonous scraping or strangling, and ending with a long, descending buzz. The blackbirds construct their nests using wet grasses woven around the stems of cattails and reeds. Common yellowthroats and red-winged blackbirds dwell among the cattails, while yellow warblers prefer the willows. Broad-tailed and rufous hummingbirds zip by en route to favorite feeding sites in or adjacent to Willow Flats.

The sagebrush community, dominating the eastern portion of the park, is the driest of the Grand Teton habitats and supports sage thrashers, green-tailed towhees, Brewer's, vesper, and savannah sparrows, and western meadowlarks. It is most accessible at **Antelope Flats**, east of **Moose** and park headquarters. Birders come here particularly for the sage grouse. These large grouse are fairly easy to find in very early spring during courtship, when the males strut their stuff on leks and make loud popping sounds with their inflated neck sacs. They become very difficult, even impossible, to spot after mid-June, when they wander away from the leks.

Northern harriers, holding their wings in a shallow V, quarter slowly back and forth over the flats in their characteristic pattern of hunting. At dusk and dawn, common nighthawks fly overhead, "booming" over their nest sites, and short-eared owls hunt the flats for small rodents and insects.

Plan to explore all of Grand Teton's habitats, from the high forests to the sparkling waters and sagebrush flats. By the end of your visit, you will have experienced almost all the bird life to be found in the northern Rocky Mountains.

The Trumpeter Swan

No other bird, of any size, is as charismatic as the magnificent trumpeter swan. But just a century ago, the species was thought to be extinct in the contiguous United States, the victim of mindless slaughter for its feathers, down, and meat.

A survey in 1932 found 69 birds in the tri-state region of Wyoming, Montana, and Idaho, most in **Yellowstone National Park** and **Red Rock Lakes National Wildlife Refuge**. With protection, the population increased to about 400 swans by 1998.

These graceful large birds depend mostly on quiet, undeveloped areas where they can nest and raise their young, called cygnets, without stress. Beginning in late winter, trumpeters stake out an extensive nesting territory of about 30 acres, even if the site is still covered with ice. Nest building usually commences in April, egg-laying occurs in May, eggs hatch by late June, and flying lessons begin in September or October. Swan families remain together until the next nesting season.

At Grand Teton, the swan population is most affected by water levels, human disturbances, and limited wintering sites. Too much rainfall or snowmelt can flood nests, and too little rain can create dry conditions that leave young swans stranded and vulnerable to predators. An unusually cold spring can result in inadequate food supplies, since an adult bird will consume up to 20 pounds of wet herbage every day.

More than 3,000 trumpeters from Canadian nesting areas winter with the local population in the Greater Yellowstone region. Many swans from Canada and from a healthy Alaska population have been transplanted to Oregon, southern Idaho, Utah, and other Wyoming sites in hopes of broadening the species' distribution and rebuilding migrations to more southerly wintering sites.

Trumpeter swans (above), up to five feet long with an eight-foot wingspan, are the largest of North America's waterfowl.

Golden-crowned kinglets (opposite, top) have noticeable white and black head stripes that help distinguish them from ruby-crowned kinglets.

Lazuli buntings (opposite, bottom) breed in the park, often building their nests in thickets along streams.

TRAVEL TIPS

DETAILS

When to Go

The best time for birders to visit is late spring through mid-summer, when breeding activity is at its height. Daytime summer temperatures are in the 70s and 80s. Nights are cool, often in the 40s. Thunderstorms and brief periods of rain are common; the first heavy snowfall usually starts by November 1 and continues through March. Snow and frost are always possible at high altitudes.

How to Get There

The nearest airport is in Jackson, Wyoming, 30 miles south of the park.

Getting Around

An automobile is necessary for traveling in the park. Rental cars are available at the airport. Visitors can bicycle Teton Park Road and other car routes. Bikes are not permitted on trails or in the backcountry.

Handicapped Access

Asphalt trails in the Jenny Lake area are accessible.

INFORMATION

Grand Teton National Park

P.O. Drawer 170, Moose, WY 83012; tel: 307-739-3300.

Jackson Chamber of Commerce

P.O. Box 550, Jackson, WY 83001; tel: 307-733-3316.

Rare Bird Alert

Tel: 307-265-2473 (statewide).

CAMPING

The park's five campgrounds have a combined 850 campsites. The sites, available on a first-come, first-served basis, often fill up by noon in summer. For information, call 307-739-3300.

Backcountry Travel

Overnight stays in the backcountry require a free permit. Reservations are accepted for backcountry camping. For information, call 307-739-3300.

LODGING

Coulter Bay Village

Grand Teton Lodge Company, Box 240, Moran, WY 83013; tel: 800-628-9988.

The village is open mid-May through mid-October and has 166 cabins and a restaurant. $$-$$$

Dornan's Spur Ranch Cabins

Box 39, Moose, WY 83012; tel: 307-733-2522.

Dornan's, open year-round, has 11 one- and two-bedroom cabins with kitchens. Minimum stays of one week are required. $$$–$$$$

Flagg Ranch

Box 187, Moran, WY 83013; tel: 800-443-2311.

The ranch's four motels offer a total of 92 rooms. A campground with 150 sites is also on the property. $$$

Huff House Inn

P.O. Box 1189, 240 East Deloney, Jackson Hole, WY 83001; tel: 307-733-4164.

Huff House has nine guest rooms, each with a private bath, some with whirlpools. A full breakfast is served. $$$–$$$$

Jackson Lake Lodge

Grand Teton Lodge Company, Box 240, Moran, WY 83013; tel: 800-628-9988.

The lodge, which sits on Jackson Lake and faces Grand Teton, has 385 rooms, including suites with sitting areas, many with porches or patios. A restaurant is on the premises. The lodge is open from mid-May through mid-October. $$$–$$$$

Jenny Lake Lodge

Grand Teton Lodge Company, Box 240, Moran, WY 83013; tel: 307-733-4647.

More like a resort than a lodge, this facility in the park has 37 cabins. Breakfast and dinner, bicycling, and horseback riding are included in the price. Open from early June through mid-October. $$$$

Signal Mountain Lodge Co.

Box 50, Moran, WY 83013; tel: 307-543-2831.

Open year-round, the lodge has 79 guest rooms, plus a number of rustic cabins. $$-$$$

Teton Tree House Bed-and-Breakfast

P.O. Box 550, Wilson, WY 83014; tel: 307-733-3233.

Ninety-five steps lead up to this bed-and-breakfast, 10 miles from the nearest park entrance. Six guest rooms are available, most with private balconies, some with window seats. Breakfast is included. $$$–$$$$

Teton View Bed-and-Breakfast

2136 Coyote Loop, P.O. Box 652, Wilson, WY 83014; tel: 307-733-7954.

The bed-and-breakfast has three guest rooms. One room, the Grand View, overlooks Grand Teton. Guests are served a full breakfast. $$-$$$

Triangle X Dude Ranch

Moose, WY 83012; tel: 307-733-2183.

Guests choose from 21 cabins, which offer one, two, or three bedrooms. Minimum stays range from two nights in winter to one week in summer. The price includes meals and horseback riding. $$$–$$$$

TOURS AND OUTFITTERS

Barker-Ewing Scenic Tours

P.O. Box 100, Moose, WY 83012; tel: 800-365-1800 or 307-733-1800.

Float trips through the park on the Snake River are available mid-May through September. Several daily trips cover 10 miles of the river. Guides share information about birds, animals, botany, and geology.

Grand Teton National Park

P.O. Drawer 170, Moose, WY 83012; tel: 307-739-3300.

In summer, the park offers daily programs and walks that emphasize wildlife, including birds.

Heart Six Float Trips

P.O. Box 70, Moran, WY 83013; tel: 888-543-2477 or 307-543-2477.

Float trips depart on mornings and afternoons, Monday through Saturday, and cover 10 miles of the Snake River. The season lasts from late May to early September.

Signal Mountain Lodge Floats

P.O. Box 50, Moran, WY 83013; tel: 307-543-2831.

Wildlife watching is the emphasis on these Snake River float trips, available from the end of May to September. Two trips, one in the morning and one in the evening, are offered daily.

Excursions

Medicine Lake National Wildlife Refuge

223 North Shore Road, Medicine Lake, MT 59247; tel: 406-789-2305.

The fourth-largest breeding population of white pelicans in the United States inhabits this northeastern Montana lake. About 2,000 young, raised here on an island, may be viewed from an observation deck or canoes and kayaks. The refuge's forests and meadows host other breeding birds: piping plovers, Baird's sparrows, lark buntings, chestnut-collared longspurs, sharp-tailed grouse, and ring-necked pheasants. Sandhill cranes stop here in fall.

Bear River Migratory Bird Refuge

58 South 950 West, Brigham City, UT 84302; tel: 435-723-5887.

The Bear River flows into the Great Salt Lake and feeds a large wetland. Here nest more than 60 bird species, including black-necked stilts, Clark's and western grebes, American avocets, Wilson's phalaropes, and white-faced ibis. White pelicans occupy an island in the lake and forage in the refuge. Birding is also excellent in fall and early winter, with the arrival of numerous raptors and hundreds of thousands of waterfowl, among them 40,000 tundra swans. A 12-mile auto loop is open year-round.

Snake River Birds of Prey National Conservation Area

Bureau of Land Management, 3948 Development Avenue, Boise, ID 83705; tel: 208-384-3334.

The Snake River canyon and surrounding plateaus support the densest concentration of nesting raptors in North America. Golden eagles, prairie falcons, American kestrels, northern harriers, and ferruginous, Swainson's, and red-tailed hawks build nests and hunt squirrels, rabbits, and other prey. Owls, including western screech, burrowing, long-eared, and short-eared, also nest in the area. Birders may observe raptors from various viewpoints along an auto tour loop or on river float trips.

Point Reyes
National Seashore
California

CHAPTER **20**

Ridge-top forest with commanding views. Secluded lagoons and shaded streams. Estuaries and mudflats flushed by the tides. Temperate winter climate. All the rodents, snakes, insects, shrimp, clams, and worms you can eat. Such are the enticements of this prime piece of avian real estate. Nature doesn't need to advertise the directions; birds instinctively know how to make their way to **Point Reyes Peninsula**. Tracing ancestral migratory routes, they home in on this attenuated 100-mile-long triangle of land that kicks a double-lobed heel westward into the Pacific Ocean. Migrants passing through and birds that overwinter, along with year-round residents, are all nourished by its tapestry of habitats. ◆ Most of the peninsula's saltwater estuaries, coastal scrub, freshwater wetlands, riparian corridors, and coniferous forests, largely contiguous and unfragmented, lie within **Point Reyes National Seashore**, isolated from the ever-increasing urban sprawl of the San

With every season, waves of migratory birds pass through a peninsula surrounded by the waters of the Pacific.

Francisco Bay Area. The seashore's hundreds of acres of marshes are of special value in an area where many historic wetlands have been siphoned off or filled. Limantour Estero, Drake's Estero, and the other tidal wetlands host thousands of the shorebirds that winter in or migrate through the Bay Area. Also under seashore protection is Olema Marsh, the largest freshwater marsh in Marin County. ◆ Nesting species, numbering over 120, span the entries in a field guide, from herons, egrets, and wood ducks, to ospreys and northern spotted owls, to six species of woodpeckers and equal numbers of swallows and warblers. Veteran observers are always alert for new sightings: in the late 1990s, a pair of least bitterns and their

Cedar waxwings usually travel in flocks, issuing whistling sounds in flight. They arrive at Point Reyes in fall, when madrone and toyon berries begin to ripen.

Yellow flowers of native lupine (right) drape a hillside overlooking the Point Reyes coast.

Northern harriers (below) fly low to the ground, holding their wings in a slight V, using both hearing and sight to locate prey.

Long-billed dowitchers (opposite), dunlins, sanderlings, and other sandpipers are attracted to the seashore in winter by abundant food.

in the distance, just above the horizon. Be prepared to spy far larger creatures as well: In December and January, gray whales, up to an impressive 50 feet long, pass by on their way from Alaska to Baja, then return from mid-March to May.

Classic Migrant Trap

The peninsula itself is on the move. The San Andreas Fault threads southeast to northwest through the Olema Valley and Tomales Bay, forming an invisible boundary between the peninsula and its continental anchor. The legendary quake of 1906 was a dramatic indication of the millions of years of seismic activity that have pushed Point Reyes northward for 300 miles and continue to nudge it toward Oregon at a rate of about two inches a year. You would need to go to the Tehachapi Mountains in southern California to find granite that matches the outcrops on the peninsula's forested ridge, location of the

young were spotted in Olema Marsh – the first breeding pair in more than two decades.

A number of the more than 460 species recorded at the national seashore are oceanic and do not tarry on land. About 100 miles of coastline define the peninsula, from the Pacific Ocean on the west to Tomales Bay on the east. Scanning the open Pacific, you may see scoters and loons riding the swells and northern fulmars and shearwaters flying

treetop eyries of nesting osprey. Chances are slim, however, that you will feel the Earth move as you bird Point Reyes. It's more likely that you'll see such eastern warbler species as the chestnut-sided or magnolia at this western edge of the continent.

The opportunity to observe rarities, or accidentals, is just one of the prime draws for birders, especially in September and October and to a lesser extent in early June. Buoyed by a northwest wind, these migrants travel at night, but they drop down to the peninsula when clouds obscure the stars. Wind-blown stands of Monterey cypress along **Sir Francis Drake Boulevard** may hold a foraging blackburnian or prothonotary warbler, or a rose-breasted grosbeak. A report on the local bird alert brings dedicated birders to the two lobes at the point – the **Point Reyes Lighthouse** to the west and the **Fish Docks** to the east – to glimpse an off-track painted redstart, prairie warbler, least flycatcher, or Baltimore oriole.

Catching vagrants at the point requires a little strategy and a lot of luck. If the weather has cleared and the rarities have resumed their flight, it's still worth lingering at the seashore's heel. To the east, the wide expanse of **Drake's Bay** spreads out before you, rimmed with beach and sandstone cliffs that look as if they were sliced by a giant cleaver. In early September, sooty shearwaters, gull-size seabirds numbering in the thousands, pause just inside the bay before they continue their circumnavigation of the Pacific. From early summer through fall, brown pelicans lumber in, never seeming in much of a hurry as they survey the water before pulling in their seven-foot wingspans and plunging into the bay to scoop up fish. They are shadowed by Heerman's gulls seeking left-overs. Parasitic jaegers, other harassers on the avian food chain, venture into the bay in fall to pester gulls and terns into disgorging their food.

On land, great horned owls roosting in the trees wait for evening to swoop down on

grebes or scoters. As elsewhere on the peninsula, eucalyptus trees, imports from Australia, grow vigorously and may be spangled in fall with monarch butterflies migrating south.

Fall is ideal for slowly birding along **Sir Francis Drake Boulevard**. Small flocks of Pacific golden-plovers camouflage themselves within the short-grass pasture, and flocks of horned larks or American pipits occasionally contain Lapland longspurs. Clusters of dried seed-heads serve as perches for western

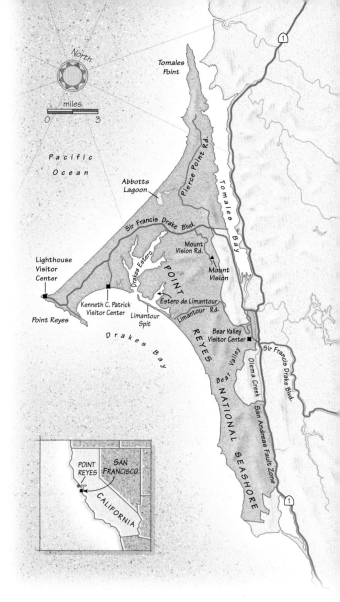

North

miles

0   3

Pacific
Ocean

Tomales
Point

Abbotts
Lagoon

Pierce Point Rd.

Tomales Bay

Sir Francis Drake Blvd.

Mount
Vision Rd.

Lighthouse
Visitor
Center

Drakes Estero

P O I N T

Mount
Vision

Kenneth C. Patrick
Visitor Center   Limantour
Spit

Estero de Limantour

Limantour Rd.

Point Reyes

R E Y E S

Bear Valley
Visitor Center

Sir Francis Drake Blvd.

D r a k e s   B a y

Bear Valley

N A T I O N A L   S E A S H O R E

Olema Creek

San Andreas Fault Zone

POINT
REYES   SAN
FRANCISCO

CALIFORNIA

Marin County, where they will be counted on **Hawk Hill** by teams from the Golden Gate Raptor Observatory. Preferring to migrate over land rather than ocean, they converge at the Golden Gate, where the water crossing is only two miles and a good tailwind will propel them south.

Shorebird Refuge

California quail greet birders at **Abbotts Lagoon**, off **Pierce Point**

bluebirds, their blue plumage standing out against autumn's tawny hues.

Overhead, red-tailed hawks, facing into the steady wind, seem tacked to the sky until they pivot their wings or angle their tails slightly to adjust their position. Above open fields hover white-tailed kites, their breasts and tails as white as puffs of cotton, listening and looking for voles. Some of the raptors are headed to the southern tip of

Road north of Sir Francis Drake Boulevard. They call *chi-CA-go*, *chi-CA-go*, a city they'll never see, against the background sound of surf hitting the beach, a mile away beyond the coastal scrub and dunes. Coyote bush, bearing silky tufts of seeds after the summer bloom, spreads out on either side of the trail to the shore. These widespread and hardy native shrubs and the profuse bush lupine offer cover and lookout perches for resident white-crowned and song sparrows, and wintering Lincoln's sparrows. You will likely see large flocks of blackbirds take to the sky and shift in unison in one direction, then another, before settling onto the nearest pasture. Though they may all sound and look like red-wings, inspect the flock closely for tricoloreds, whose red epaulets are edged in white instead of yellow.

The northern and more sheltered of the two arms of Abbott's Lagoon invites American wigeons, ruddy ducks, and buffleheads, as well as a quintuple of grebes – pied-billed, eared, horned, western, and Clark's. Amid the tules along the far shore, great blue herons and great egrets step slowly and deliberately, freeze, then plunge their daggerlike bills into the water to capture a frog or fish. The wider southern arm holds an inventory of western shorebird life, from least and western sandpipers, sanderlings, dunlins, and willets probing the lagoon's edge to godwits and dowitchers standing up to their bellies in the water. In early fall, a new crop of western snowy plovers, a threatened species, works the shore, walking a few steps, stopping, feeding, then resuming the sequence again. Each nesting season, the Point Reyes Bird Observatory fences off snowy plover habitat to protect the eggs, laid in a small depression in the sand, from predators such as common ravens.

As single-minded as the shorebirds seem, the flocks explode into the air at any sign of danger and circle over the water, seeking refuge in numbers. Maybe the threat was a turkey vulture, largely harmless to shorebirds. The next time it could be a peregrine falcon or merlin jetting across the lagoon to pluck a dunlin or sandpiper from the wheeling flock.

Shorebirds, having settled throughout the peninsula by the end of October, find a winter banquet among the ribbons of shallow water that snake through Limantour Estero. Standing on the three-mile sand spit that protects the estero from the ocean, you can watch willets, yellowlegs, godwits, and dowitchers feeding on the opulent menu of invertebrates. Sanderlings, dunlins, and sandpipers forage at water's edge, chased by the advancing and receding waves. Paths will take you along ponds and lagoons with cinnamon teals, northern shovelers, gadwalls, and ring-necked ducks. Marsh wrens scold from their hiding places, and an elusive sora or Virginia rail may briefly show itself before slipping back into dense vegetation.

Trails from **Limantour Estero** head north and inland, where in the fall of 1995 a fire burned a 12,000-acre swath from 1,300-foot Mount Vision to the Limantour Spit. The fire's heat, followed by winter rains, seeded a fine crop of Bishop pines.

Going Out to Sea

Passengers gather at the railing as the skipper eases his boat out of the harbor. The coast gradually fades into the early-morning fog, and the boatful of birders heads for the Pacific Ocean – the realm of seabirds often impossible to see from land – for a day of pelagic birding.

Some of the most rewarding pelagic trips on the continent are in the waters off Northern California, where a combination of submarine geology and ocean currents creates rich upwellings of nutrients for a wealth of seabirds and marine mammals. Flocks of sooty shearwaters seem to hug the waves as they fly by. Bobbing in the water are Cassins's and rhinoceros auklets, chunky seabirds that nest on the Farallon Islands. Common, elegant, and arctic terns wheel through the air, along with ubiquitous California and western gulls and the beautiful, migratory Sabine's gull.

Powerful pomarine jaegers, with a 48-inch wingspan, terrorize shearwaters and gulls until they give up their catch. Shearwaters are also the target of another kleptoparasite – fierce south polar skuas, a rare but coveted sighting.

Pelagic trips into **Monterey Bay**, south of San Francisco, are ideal for novices, who can count on seeing birds just after leaving the harbor. The **Farallon Islands**, 30 miles west of San Francisco, are popular in summer, nesting time for some 200,000 seabirds, including tufted puffins, common murres, cormorants, and auklets. Advanced birders join trips leaving **Bodega Bay** for the **Cordell Banks**, two hours into the Pacific, hoping to see black-footed or Laysan albatrosses or, on rare occasions, a black storm-petrel or short-tailed albatross.

Common terns (left) migrate along the Pacific Coast in spring and from late summer to fall.

A rhinoceros auklet in breeding plumage (below) wears pairs of white head plumes.

White-breasted nuthatches (opposite, top) move down tree trunks as they pick insects from the bark.

Brown pelicans (opposite, bottom) plunge into the water to catch fish, then toss their head back to swallow the meal.

Flashing iridescent orange and green, they tear through **Bear Valley**, sounding like tiny, high-pitched motors in overdrive. Waves of other birds – warbling vireos, Swainson's thrushes, and lazuli buntings – return in spring, each according to their own genetic timetables. **Olema Creek**, flowing along the San Andreas Fault, is dense with alders, where Wilson's warblers squabble over breeding sites. Violet-green, tree, cliff and barn swallows, also nesting in the valley, trace arabesques in the sky as they chase flying insects.

Manzanita, berry-laden toyon, wild lilac, and shrub-size monkeyflower fill the understory. With the renewed habitat came the birds: mixed flocks of golden- and ruby-crowned kinglets, chestnut-backed chickadees, brown creepers, and pygmy nuthatches, all gleaning insects from the trees. Listen for wrentits fencing off their territories with song and cedar waxwings carrying their soft whistles across the sky.

Spring in the Valley

In January and February, as northern breeders such as varied thrushes and golden-crowned sparrows await their cues to depart the seashore, one of the earliest spring arrivals shows up. Allen's hummingbirds return from Mexico to join the year-round Anna's.

Across from the valley's visitor center, a resident tribe of raucous acorn woodpeckers tends to their remaining cache of acorns stuffed into holes drilled in the Douglas firs. They also begin maintenance on their tree-hole nests in the 100-foot firs, pulling out morsels of pulp from the holes and tossing them like confetti into the air. You are also guaranteed to come across a pair of California towhees scratching in the leaf litter. At first, they seem drab and brown but reveal rich rufous undertail feathers and a delicate stippled necklace. Each spring, a pair of red-shouldered hawks reclaims a nest high in the crotch of a eucalyptus and repairs any winter storm damage. By May, they are busy ferrying food to the nestlings – a mouse, a small bird, a garter snake – and sometimes pause on a nearby branch to subdue or display the prey.

With spring well under way, wintering shorebirds have left the seashore, trailed by others in breeding plumage that have stopped briefly at the seashore to refuel. Birders gather again at the point to search for this season's scattering of accidentals, hoping for a bay-breasted warbler, or a northern parula, or a clay-colored sparrow. They will feel compelled to return again, when the next wave of migrants heads south and their itinerary takes them to Point Reyes.

A California quail (above) acts as a sentinel ready to warn its covey of impending danger.

Western gulls (right) crack open mollusks by dropping them from the air onto a hard surface.

Western bluebirds (opposite) nest in tree cavities, sometimes using holes vacated by woodpeckers.

TRAVEL TIPS

DETAILS

When to Go

Birding is productive year-round, with the greatest abundance of species present during fall and spring migration and in winter. Winter is cool, windy, and rainy, with daytime temperatures in the 40s and 50s. Summer is warm and dry, though often foggy, with temperatures in the 60s and 70s.

How to Get There

San Francisco and Oakland International Airports are two hours south of the Point Reyes Peninsula.

Getting Around

A car is necessary for birding Point Reyes. Rental agencies are available at the airports.

Handicapped Access

Visitor centers, the Earthquake Trail at Bear Valley, and a paved trail at Limantour Beach are accessible. A wheelchair with balloon tires for use on beaches and unpaved trails is available by reservation at Point Reyes National Seashore Association, 415-663-1200.

INFORMATION

Point Reyes National Seashore

Point Reyes Station, CA 94956; tel: 415-663-1092.

West Marin Chamber of Commerce

P.O. Box 1045, Point Reyes Station, CA 94956; tel: 415-663-9232.

Rare Bird Alerts

Tel: 415-681-7422 (Northern California) or 415-561-3030, ext. 2500 (fall raptors).

CAMPING

The seashore's four hike-in campgrounds offer 10 individual and 30 group sites. Visitors, who must obtain a free permit, may reserve sites up to two months in advance by calling 415-663-1092. Car-accessed camping is available at Samuel P. Taylor State Park, seven miles southeast of seashore headquarters. Call 415-488-9897 for information, 800-444-7275 for reservations.

LODGING

PRICE GUIDE – double occupancy

$ = up to $49 $$ = $50–$99
$$$ = $100–$149 $$$$ = $150+

Blackthorne Inn

P.O. Box 712, Inverness, CA 94937; tel: 415-663-8621.

The inn has five rooms, including Hideaway, a room with a private entrance and bay window, and Eagle's Nest, an octagonal glass-enclosed tower. A buffet breakfast is served in the dining room. $$$$

Dancing Coyote Beach

P.O. Box 98, Inverness, CA 94937; tel: 415-669-7200.

Guests stay in four cottages overlooking Tomales Bay. Each cottage has a fireplace and a full kitchen stocked with breakfast supplies. $$$–$$$$

Golden Hinde Inn

P.O. Box 295, Inverness, CA 94937; tel: 415-669-1389.

Some of the inn's 35 rooms face scenic Tomales Bay. All rooms have private baths; some have fireplaces and kitchenettes. The Golden Hinde also has a restaurant and a marina. $$

Holly Tree Inn

P.O. Box 642, Point Reyes Station, CA 94956; tel: 415-663-1554.

The inn has four guest rooms in the main house and a two-room cottage tucked into the edge of a large garden. A country breakfast is served. Amenities include a hot tub. The inn has two additional cottages: Sea Star, at Tomales Bay, and Vision, inland. $$$–$$$$

Manka's Inverness Lodge

P.O. Box 1110, Inverness, CA 94937; tel: 415-669-1034.

Originally a hunting lodge, this small compound includes two cabins and 11 guest rooms, as well as a gourmet restaurant. A cottage, built in the 1850s, is available for rent on Tomales Bay. $$$–$$$$

Olema Inn

P.O. Box 37, Olema, CA 94950; tel: 415-663-9559.

This 1876 inn has six guest rooms, each with a private bath. The inn serves a continental breakfast. A restaurant is on the premises. $$$

Vineyard Inn

P.O. Box 1177, Point Reyes Station, CA 94956; tel: 415-663-1011.

The inn's four guest rooms overlook a pond, which attracts a variety of wading birds and other species. Breakfast is included. $$$–$$$$

TOURS AND OUTFITTERS

Oceanic Society Expeditions

Fort Mason Center, Building E, San Francisco, CA 94123; tel: 800-326-7491 or 415-474-3385.

Pelagic trips to view seabirds and marine mammals depart San Francisco for the Farallon Islands from June through November.

Point Reyes Bird Observatory

4990 Shoreline Highway, Stinson Beach, CA 94970; tel: 415-868-1221.

Observatory staff lead bird walks to various habitats in the seashore. Birders may also visit the observatory's field station to see researchers band birds and to learn about observatory programs.

Point Reyes National Seashore Association

Point Reyes National Seashore, Point Reyes Station, CA 94956;

tel: 415-663-1155.

Year-round field trips and seminars led by naturalists and ornithologists cover prime birding areas throughout the national seashore. Call for schedules and reservations.

Shearwater Journeys

P.O. Box 190, Hollister, CA 95024; tel: 831-637-8527.

Guides lead summer pelagic trips to the Farallon Islands to see nesting species, including tufted puffins. Other trips leave from Bodega Bay, north of San Francisco, and from Monterey and Santa Cruz, south of the city.

SPECIAL EVENTS

Annual Point Reyes National Seashore All-Day Fall Birding Blitz

Birders often identify as many as 100 species during this seashore event, held on a Saturday in mid-October. For information about the blitz, sponsored by the Golden Gate Audubon Society and the National Park Service, call 510-843-2222 or 415-663-1155.

Bird-A-Thon

Point Reyes Bird Observatory, 4990 Shoreline Highway, Stinson Beach, CA 94970; tel: 415-868-1221.

In mid-September, teams of birders compete to identify the most species in 24 hours in the seashore and neighboring areas. Donors sponsor counters, and proceeds help fund the observatory's conservation projects. Birders of all levels are welcome to participate.

Excursions

Mono Lake

Mono Lake Tufa State Reserve, P.O. Box 99, Lee Vining, CA 93541; tel: 760-647-6331.

Environmentalists fought hard to preserve this saline lake east of the Sierra Nevada, with its curious and craggy towers of limestone deposits called tufa. As a result, Mono Lake remains an important habitat for breeding and migrating birds. Nearly 50,000 California gulls nest here, feeding on an ample supply of brine flies and brine shrimp. Tens of thousands of red-necked phalaropes and the largest population of eared grebes in the world – up to 1.8 million – stage at the lake prior to migration.

Sonny Bono Salton Sea National Wildlife Refuge

906 West Sinclair Road, Calipatria, CA 92233; tel: 760-348-5278.

Bursting through a manmade canal, the Colorado River flooded an ancient seabed to create this inland sea. Large numbers of waterfowl and shorebirds stop over during migration. Brown pelicans, American avocets, mountain plovers, long-billed curlews, and rough-winged and bank swallows winter at Salton Sea. The species checklist numbers 384, one of the highest counts of any national refuge. The Salton Sea International Bird Festival is held annually in mid-February; call 760-344-5359 for details.

Yosemite National Park

P.O. Box 577, Yosemite, CA 95389; tel: 209-372-0200.

This famed park is best visited in spring and summer, when the Sierra Nevada's birds court and nest amid granite domes, alpine lakes, and surging waterfalls. White-headed woodpeckers and red-breasted sapsuckers nest in tree holes, dippers excavate holes in streambanks, and golden eagles perch on cliff ledges. Other montane species include mountain chickadees, pine grosbeaks, Clark's nutcrackers, Townsend's solitaires, calliope hummingbirds, and mountain quail. Patient birders may spot great gray owls or northern pygmy-owls.

Klamath Basin
California and Oregon

CHAPTER **21**

When the first white trappers and explorers penetrated the **Klamath Basin**, they found a vast tessellated landscape of marsh, tule prairies, and shallow lakes, all teeming with wildlife. The basin was an oasis of plenty, a groaning board in a sere and hungry country of high plain and arid woodland. Water formed the foundation for an extravagantly generous food web that began with algae and freshwater plankton, progressed through successive levels to the tule elk and mule deer that dined on the rich and abundant sedges and reeds, and culminated in grizzly bears and cougars.　◆　But it was the waterfowl that undoubtedly created the strongest impression on the mountain men: immense flocks of migratory ducks and geese that darkened the autumnal sky with their multitudes. At least six million waterfowl packed the 185,000 acres that composed the historic marsh. The basin was the most significant stopover for ducks and geese between Canada and California's Central Valley.　◆　**Millions of migrating waterfowl and the greatest number of wintering bald eagles outside Alaska seek out these historic wetlands.** These marshes straddling south-central Oregon and northeastern California are greatly reduced today due to an ambitious reclamation project that began in 1905. Most of the lakes, potholes, water meadows, and swamps have been drained, dried, and given to the plow. Where Canada geese and wigeon once fed and preened, potatoes, wheat, horseradish, and pasturage grow. Only about 25 percent of the original wetlands remains.　◆　But the reduced physical scope of the basin's wetlands has in no way diminished their significance to migratory ducks and geese, as well as sundry other species. A total of 433 species of

Snow geese begin to arrive at Klamath Basin in fall. By midwinter, more than one million waterfowl are concentrated on the refuges.

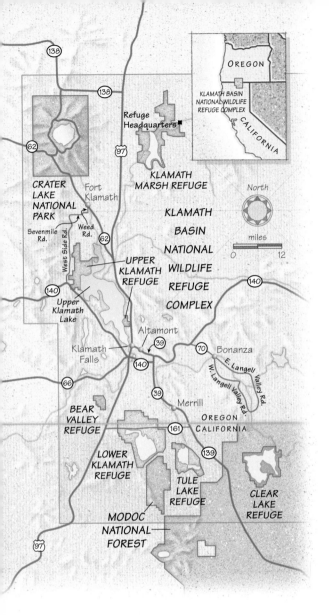

migrations typically exceed one million birds, and in the late 1990s, with continental waterfowl populations at a five-decade high, autumn numbers approached the two million mark.

Migratory Magnet

Six national refuges have been established as the **Klamath Basin National Wildlife Refuge Complex** to protect the basin's legacy: **Lower Klamath**, **Tule Lake**, and **Clear Lake** in California, and **Bear Valley**, **Upper Klamath**, and **Klamath Marsh** in Oregon. The 178,000 acres encompass a wide array of habitats ranging from deep tule marsh through grassy uplands to old-growth coniferous forest. The best refuges to see waterfowl are Lower Klamath and Tule Lake. Both have auto tour routes that cover a variety of habitats, and both offer opportunities to study birds pursuing diverse activities, from foraging in grain fields to preening in quiet backwaters. Maps and bird checklists are available at the refuge headquarters on Hill Road, in the northwest corner of Tule Lake refuge, five miles west of the town of Tulelake.

Given the basin's significance as a fall and winter migratory pit stop for everything from least sandpipers to bald eagles, October through March are the best months to visit. The first birds, northern pintails and white-fronted geese, start arriving in early September. Their ranks are joined later in the fall by dabbling ducks such as northern shovelers, mallards, and the three North American teals, green-winged, blue-winged, and cinnamon. Snow geese, Ross's geese, and all the various races of Canada goose show up at the same time. The basin is also an excellent place to view migrating swans, both

wildlife are believed to inhabit or visit the basin, including several that are rare, threatened, or endangered. The basin is as important to Pacific waterfowl now as it was at the end of the Pleistocene – more important, actually: the diminution of marsh in other portions of the Pacific Flyway has made the losses of the basin look minor in comparison. There's still a good deal of high-quality marsh, and many of the agricultural fields, particularly those planted to potatoes, grain, or alfalfa, also serve as feeding and resting sites for waterfowl. Many ducks and geese migrating south lay over in the basin, and some spend the entire winter. Peak fall

the relatively common tundra swan and the larger, and much rarer, trumpeter swan. The two species can be difficult to tell apart in flight; their forms are almost identical, and even their calls are somewhat similar. But as its name implies, the trumpeter's cry is louder and far more resonant.

Fall is also noteworthy for birds of prey, especially bald eagles. The first eagles arrive in late fall, and their numbers can swell to 1,000 by late winter. The basin now has the largest overwintering population of balds in the Lower 48 states. Tule Lake and Lower Klamath refuges are excellent places to spot feeding or hunting eagles. Simply follow the self-guided tour routes and scan the countryside carefully. By late December or early January, when most of the basin's lakes are frozen over, waterfowl concentrate on the few remaining patches of open water, and this, in turn, draws the eagles. About 300 eagles roost at the **Bear Valley** refuge in Oregon, established in 1978 to provide a secure sleeping area for the birds. The eagles find ample room on this 4,200-acre parcel of old-growth incense

cedar, ponderosa pine, white fir, and Douglas fir. Visitors are barred from Bear Valley, but an observation point about one-half mile east of the refuge off Highway 97 allows birders to watch the eagles leave their roosts in force at dawn to forage in the other refuges.

Assiduous birders will also spot a great variety of hawks, from red-tailed and rough-legged hawks in the marshland margins to northern goshawks and Cooper's hawks in the upland timber. Probably the most common sighting will be the northern harrier. These long-winged, white-rumped hawks

Male blue-winged teals (above) sport white crescents on either side of their heads. The females have more subdued markings.

Cinnamon teals (opposite) are one of three teal species that inhabit Klamath Basin in fall; the other two are green-winged and blue-winged.

A northern shoveler (left) in fall, or eclipse, plumage can be identified by its long, spatula-like bill.

aquatic insects and crustaceans to fuel their northward migrations. Many Canada geese and ducks – mallards, gadwalls, wigeons, cinnamon teals, and blue-winged teals – also nest here, qualifying as year-round residents. Large numbers of neotropical migrant songbirds come through during the spring, each in its season, each in its place. Different warblers, vireos, and thrushes find abundant cover and food in the variegated habitats of the basin and surrounding uplands. A call to refuge naturalists will give some idea of the schedules of commonly seen species and the best places to find them.

swoop low over the marshes, pouncing on coots and wounded or sick ducks. In autumn, birders often spot a northern harrier sitting by the side of a road, contentedly shredding the breast feathers from a dead coot.

Refuge Nesters

Early spring is also a busy time in the basin for birds and birders. Waterfowl, still extraordinarily numerous, power-load on

In summer, birders can watch the ducks brood their young and observe the numerous other aquatic birds of the basin, particularly herons, egrets, and bitterns, as they fish in the marshes or stalk the fields for mice, voles, and other rodents. Some white-faced ibises breed in the basin, arriving in the spring and staying through the summer. A dark-plumaged bird with an elegant curving bill, the ibis flies with outstretched neck and legs, sometimes forming long, wavering formations with its fellows.

Summer is the

Return of the Eagle

Of all the birds of prey that suffered from the use of DDT and related pesticides in the 1950s and 1960s, the bald eagle perhaps constitutes the most dramatic success story. Eagles that ingested the pesticides produced eggs with shells too thin and weak to sustain the weight of incubating females. Since the ban on DDT in 1972 – five years after the species was classified as endangered or threatened in the Lower 48 states – the bald eagle has rebounded impressively. From a low of 450 nesting pairs in the 1960s, the population in the Lower 48 states stands at about 4,000 nesting pairs, along with an unknown but presumably large cohort of juveniles.

The best place to see these magnificent birds is Alaska. Elsewhere, options for eagle viewing aren't quite as good, with one notable exception: the Klamath Basin refuges. Like the birders and the hunters, the eagles generally come for the millions of wintering waterfowl, an abundant and easily exploited food source. Opportunistic feeders, eagles will take a dead, ill, or crippled bird. They also take live, healthy prey, and at least a handful of birders each year are fortunate enough to witness a mature, white-headed bald seizing a big mallard or pintail in flight. Communal feeding is also common, with two or more eagles dining simultaneously on the same carcass.

Agricultural fields are also a good place to spot eagles. Basin farmers typically flood their fields in winter, sending great numbers of mice and voles fleeing. The eagles pounce on these displaced rodents like chickens on junebugs.

Mule deer (top) and elk are found in the uplands of the refuge and surrounding wilderness.

Bald eagles (left) leave their roosts at dawn to feed on waterfowl in the basin's lakes.

Loggerhead shrikes (opposite, top) are predatory songbirds that hunt rodents, small birds, and insects, sometimes storing them on thorns or barbed-wire fences.

Mallards (opposite, bottom) are abundant at the refuge in winter. They are among the ducks that breed in the basin.

best time for white pelicans, a bird that is emblematic of the basin. Unlike the brown pelican, these are birds of the inland waterways rather than the coast (though flocks often overwinter on saltwater estuaries). Their feeding methods differ from those of their marine cousins. Brown pelicans dive from flight, crashing spectacularly into the water to fill their pouches with fish. White pelicans usually feed in flocks on lakes, cooperatively herding fish into the shallows, synchronously dipping their bills as they swim. At a distance, flying white pelicans are sometimes mistaken for snow geese, since both species are white with black wing tips. Within a few hundred yards, however, their massive orange bills are obvious. **Upper Klamath** refuge is a nesting and brood-rearing site for these colonial-nesting birds.

The basin's wetlands justifiably get most of the attention, but the adjacent upland areas are well worth exploring. National forests border Clear Lake, Upper Klamath, and Klamath Marsh refuges, and lie due south of Lower Klamath and Tule Lake refuges. There are virtually no restrictions on hiking these woodlands. Mule deer are common, and Rocky Mountain elk are sometimes found near Klamath Marsh refuge. Pronghorn antelope and the rare sage grouse are occasionally seen in the juniper and sagebrush lands of the **Modoc National Forest** near Clear Lake refuge (the refuge itself is generally off-limits to visitors to prevent wildlife disturbance). Great gray owls are present, but rarely seen.

Though the refuges encompass most of the marshland left in the basin, they are by no means secure havens for wildlife. Agriculture continues to hold the big stick in this region, and the needs of waterfowl are essentially considered secondary. With 80 percent of the basin's original wetlands gone, waterfowl and other aquatic species can ill afford to lose more habitat. Indeed, the remaining marshes are at their effective holding capacity. Plagues of avian cholera and botulism periodically sweep through the wintering flocks, a result of overcrowding and attendant water contamination. The basin is a wildlife site of international significance; as it goes, so goes the fate of the birds of the Pacific Flyway. Even in its diminished state, the Klamath Basin will thrill and inspire – but it should also infuse the visitor with a sense of alarm. It can all be lost so very quickly.

TRAVEL TIPS

DETAILS

When to Go

Most birders visit from November through March to see wintering waterfowl and bald eagles. Migratory songbirds, shorebirds, and waterfowl may be observed at the basin in April and May. Summer is the time to see breeding waterfowl and various marsh species. Autumn temperatures reach the low 60s during the day and sometimes drop into the 30s at night. Winter highs are in the upper 30s, with lows in the 20s. By April, days are in the 50s and nights are above freezing. Mid-summer temperatures are in the low 80s.

How to Get There

Several airlines serve Kingsley Field Airport in Klamath Falls, Oregon, in the center of the refuge complex, and Medford/Jackson County Airport in Medford, Oregon, 75 miles west of Klamath Falls.

Getting Around

An automobile is essential for visiting the refuge areas. Car rentals are available at the airports. Tule Lake and Marsh have hiking trails. Tule Lake, Upper Klamath, and Klamath Marsh have canoe trails. Canoe rentals are available at Rocky Point Resort, adjacent to Upper Klamath; call 541-356-2287 for details. Birders may also bicycle auto routes in the refuge areas.

Handicapped Access

The visitor center, the paved trail to the Discovery Marsh observation platform across from the visitor center, and the boardwalk to one of the refuge photo blinds (available by reservation) are accessible.

INFORMATION

Klamath Basin National Wildlife Refuge Complex
Route 1, Box 74, Tulelake, CA 96134; tel: 530-667-2231.

Klamath County Department of Tourism
P.O. Box 1867, 1451 Main Street, Klamath Falls, OR 97601; tel: 800-445-6728.

Modoc National Forest
Doublehead Ranger District, P.O. Box 369, Tulelake, CA 96134; tel: 530-667-2246.

Siskyou County Visitors Bureau
808 West Lennox Street, Yreka, CA 96097; tel: 800-446-7475 or 530-842-7857.

Rare Bird Alerts
Tel: 510-524-5592 (Northern California) or 503-292-0061 (Oregon).

CAMPING

Camping is not available in the refuges. The nearest campground is 18 miles south of the visitor center at Lava Beds National Monument. Contact the monument, 530-667-2282, for information.

LODGING

PRICE GUIDE – double occupancy
$ = up to $49 $$ = $50–$99
$$$ = $100–$149 $$$$ = $150+

Boarding House Inn
1800 Esplanade Avenue, Klamath Falls, OR 97601; tel: 541-883-8584.

The inn has two guest rooms, each with a kitchen and private bath, and a suite with a bedroom, living room, kitchen, and private bath. $$

Cimarron Motel
3060 South Sixth Street, Klamath Falls, OR 97603; tel: 800-742-2648 or 541-882-4601.

The Cimarron offers 163 basic units, some with refrigerators and microwaves. A swimming pool is on the premises. $–$$

Golden Eagle Motel
P.O. Box 109, Dorris, CA 96023; tel: 530-397-3114.

Of the motel's 19 rooms, seven have refrigerators and microwaves. $

Hospitality Inn Bed-and-Breakfast
P.O. Box 442, Dorris, CA 96023; tel: 530-397-2097.

Birding enthusiasts operate this European-style inn, three miles from the Lower Klamath refuge. Four guest rooms are available. A full breakfast is served. $$

Maverick Motel
1220 Main Street, Klamath Falls, OR 97601; tel: 541-882-6688.

An outdoor pool is on the premises of this 49-room motel. $

Merrill Motel
435 West Front Street, Merrill, OR 97633; tel: 541-798-5598.

The motel has nine rooms, some with kitchens. $

Olympic Lodge
3006 Greensprings Drive, Klamath Falls, OR 97601; tel: 541-883-8800.

The lodge has 29 rooms, half with kitchens and refrigerators. $$

Park Motel
Highway 139 South, P.O. Box 36, Tulelake, CA 96134; tel: 530-667-2913.

Eleven basic rooms with private baths are available. $

Rocky Point Resort
28121 Rocky Point Road, Klamath Falls, OR 97601; tel: 541-356-2287.

Situated on the northwest shore

of Upper Klamath Lake, this resort has four cabins, each with a bedroom, living area, full kitchen, and bath. Also available are five guest rooms with private baths. A restaurant is on the premises. $$

Thompson Bed-and-Breakfast

1420 Wild Plum Court, Klamath Falls, OR 97601; tel: 541-882-7938.

The bed-and-breakfast is adjacent to 400-acre Moore Park, where visitors see a variety of birds, including bald eagles. Each of the four guest rooms has a private bath; two rooms overlook Lake Klamath. A full breakfast is served. $$

TOURS AND OUTFITTERS

Klamath Basin National Wildlife Refuge Complex

Route 1, Box 74, Tulelake, CA 96134; tel: 530-667-2231.

The refuge conducts group tours by prior arrangement.

Rocky Point Guide Service

27431 Rocky Point Road, Klamath Falls, OR 97601; tel: 541-356-2287.

Canoe tours depart from Rocky Point Resort for wildlife explorations of Upper Klamath and Pelican Bay.

SPECIAL EVENTS

Klamath Basin Bald Eagle Conference

Klamath County Department of Tourism, P.O. Box 1867, 1451 Main Street, Klamath Falls, OR 97601; tel: 800-445-6728.

Organized in 1980, the mid-February conference includes workshops, lectures on raptors, and field trips to the refuges and other nearby birding spots.

Excursions

Malheur National Wildlife Refuge

HC 72, Box 245, Princeton, OR 97721; tel: 541-493-2612.

Malheur's strategic location along the Pacific migration corridor makes it the ideal stopping place for 200,000 snow and Ross's geese in spring and fall. An equally dramatic sight is the autumn gathering of 3,000 sandhill cranes, which feed in the refuge's grain fields before heading south. In spring, 250 sandhill cranes nest here, and waves of warblers, vireos, buntings, and tanagers pass through on their way north.

Ruby Lake National Wildlife Refuge

HC 60, Box 860, Ruby Valley, NV 89833; tel: 702-779-2237.

Flanked by mountains that rise above 10,000 feet, these wetlands in east-central Nevada expand to 17,000 acres in years of abundant rainfall. The vast refuge is a key breeding site for canvasbacks, cinnamon teals, gadwalls, and other ducks, and for wading birds like the white-faced ibis. Tundra swans pass through in autumn. Hike the nearby Ruby Mountains to see golden eagles, mountain bluebirds, and sage grouse. Ruby Lake is reached by car.

Stillwater National Wildlife Refuge

P.O. Box 1236, Fallon, NV 89407; tel: 702-423-5128

As winter ice thaws, migratory and breeding birds head for the wetlands of this 77,500-acre Lahontan Valley refuge. Clark's, pied-billed, and eared grebes nest here, along with Forester's terns, redhead ducks, and a colony of white-faced ibis. White pelicans forage at Stillwater, having commuted from their large colony on Pyramid Lake's Anaho Island. Thousands of shorebirds and waterfowl visit the refuge during their late-summer and fall migration.

Kenai
Peninsula
Alaska

One simple statement captures the vastness and grandeur of Alaska: once you've seen the Great Land, you will never be the same. For adventurous birders, visiting Alaska is a dream come true. But since Alaska is one-fifth the size of the entire Lower 48 states and is, for the most part, roadless, deciding where to bird can be a challenge. ◆ Fortunately, there is one beautiful, uncrowded place, accessible by road, that has it all: the **Kenai Peninsula** just south of Anchorage, Alaska's biggest city. Protruding into the storm-tossed North Pacific, the Kenai is Alaska in miniature, packed into a peninsula about 160 miles long and 130 miles wide. Here you can enjoy Alaskan birding at its best in mist-shrouded rain forests and lake-dotted boreal forests, along rushing salmon streams, in coastal marshes and mudflats, and on beaches rimmed with tide pools. Other birding adventures await you at sea along rugged Kenai coastlines with cascading waterfalls, up into deep glaciated fjords with calving glaciers,

Boreal forests alive with songbirds, coastal islands covered with seabirds, and countless bald eagles – welcome to birders' nirvana.

and around islands with world-class seabird bazaars and marine-mammal haulouts. ◆ May and June are best for finding the greatest number of migrant species in full song and bright breeding plumages. But birding is excellent year-round, particularly for seabirds and waterfowl. That's because the turbulent, nutrient-rich waters of the Gulf of Alaska fuel one of the most biologically productive marine food webs in the world. What's more, a bounty of salmon and other fish sustains an abundance of bald eagles that strains belief. ◆ Begin your explorations of the Kenai by car from Anchorage over the **Seward Scenic Byway**, with its panoramic

Breeding colonies of horned puffins are found on islands south of the Kenai Peninsula and as far north as the Bering Sea.

White-crowned sparrows (right), both males and females, have noticeably striped crowns.

Birders (below) observe gulls, kittiwakes, and other seabirds at Gull Island in Kachemak Bay.

Young winter wrens (opposite) have recently left the nest. They are permanent residents of coastal Alaska.

views of the coastal mountains. The roadway starts along narrow, 45-mile-long **Turnagain Arm**, where Captain Cook's ships "turned again" in June 1778 while in search of the Northwest Passage. The Arm is famous for having some of the highest tides in the world – up to 38.6 feet. Spectacular bore tides running at 10 knots, with six-foot-high waves, occur in spring. From mid-June through August, pods of strikingly white beluga whales can be seen following schools of salmon and hooligan, also known as candlefish, on the incoming tide. At such times, bald eagles are everywhere along the arm.

The steep slopes bordering the highway

rise into the Chugach Mountains, the second highest range in the state and the highest coastal range in the world. At the head of Turnagain Arm, you enter the 5.6-million-acre **Chugach National Forest**, second largest in the United States and encompassing the rugged mountain country of the Kenai Peninsula's eastern half. After climbing over Turnagain Pass almost to the alpine zone through forests of mountain and western hemlocks, the highway comes to a fork at milepost 90. Here, at **Tern Lake**, a viewing platform with interpretive signs allows you to scan the shallow, marshy lake for arctic terns, mew gulls, and common loons, all of which nest here, and perhaps trumpeter swans. Northern waterthrush may be heard calling from the brushy marsh edges.

At this junction, the Seward Highway continues south to Seward, while the Sterling Highway leads southwest to Homer. Well-marked trailheads on both routes provide access to forest habitats. En route to Seward, the **Crescent Creek-Carter Lake Trail** and **Lost Lake Trail** introduce you to the haunting calls of the retiring and well-camouflaged varied thrush, a bird that perhaps best represents the subdued and misty nature of the rain forest. A raucous

Steller's jay may suddenly appear, uttering its harsh and rasping *chaak! chaak!* From high in the firs and Sitka spruce, the *wheesy-wheesy-wheesy-whee* of the beautiful Townsend's warbler, wearing bright yellow and black plumage, drifts down as it flits about in search of favored insects.

A 10-mile side trip to Exit Glacier in **Kenai Fjords National Park** parallels the Resurrection River. At road's end, inconspicuously colored orange-crowned warblers, along with dark-eyed juncos, fox sparrows, and white-crowned and golden-crowned sparrows, may be heard and seen along the **Harding Icefield Trail** as it leads through dense thickets of alder, willow, and cottonwood to the foot of the Harding Glacier.

Fjords and Seabird Islands

Pelagic trips out of Seward into **Resurrection Bay** and **Kenai Fjords National Park** offer some of the finest marine wildlife viewing anywhere. After your boat departs the small harbor, it usually isn't long before playful sea otters have you scrambling on deck for a close-up look. Despite the busy summer boat traffic in Resurrection Bay, chances of sighting humpback whales or even a pod of killer whales are good, especially at **Blying Sound**. Dall's porpoises may suddenly appear alongside the boat to ride the bow-wave and create rooster tails of spray when they swim at top speed.

The favored route out of Resurrection Bay is along the west shore and its eagle nests to **Cheval Island**, where you can observe colonies of glaucous-winged gulls, double-crested and red-faced cormorants, and horned and tufted puffins. As the boat cruises near the rocky shoreline, you'll hear the loud whinnying calls of the black oystercatcher. With its outsized, flattened red bill, white eyes ringed with red, black body, and pallid feet, the oystercatcher may appear comical, but it is ideally adapted to picking and shelling limpets, barnacles, and mussels from among the slippery rocks at low tide.

After the boat rounds Aialik Cape into **Aialik Bay**, begin watching for flocks of rhinoceros auklets diving for fish and other prey. At the head of **Holgate Arm**, you can witness the calving of the Holgate Glacier. Harbor seals lounge on nearby ice floes as you wait for the next huge blocks of ice to crash thunderously into the sea. Black bears sometimes appear high on open mountain slopes, and it's not unusual to spot mountain goat nannies with their newborn kids on steep rocky recesses where they are safe from bears and wolves.

Following the Whales

Birders scanning the Kenai's coastal waters should watch for clouds of vapor marking the location of spouting whales. Circling above them are flocks of kittiwakes, gulls, and other seabirds quick to snatch up tidbits of food brought to the surface by the feeding leviathans.

Fourteen whale species, from the smallest minke whale to the 150-ton blue whale (the largest mammal on earth) find the food-rich coastal waters to their liking. Humpbacks are among the most readily observable species. Often feeding cooperatively, they concentrate their prey in a bubble net, accomplished by exhaling columns of bubbles around shoals of small fish or small crustaceans. They then lunge to the surface, mouths agape, to consume their prey in huge quantities.

Pods of slow-swimming belugas roll casually at the surface as they follow prey. The diet of these food generalists includes some 100 species of fish, shrimp, octopus, crabs, and clams. Their echolocation abilities and complex vocalizations enable them to find food in even the most turbid coastal waters.

The highly social killer whales, or orcas, have the most diverse diet of all cetaceans. Traveling in pods of three to 40 individuals, they often cooperate in hunting marine mammals, fish, and squid. Marine birds following feeding whales need to be ever alert, for the swift-charging killers are known to include birds of most any flavor in their diet.

A humpback whale (left) rises, mouth agape, engulfing large quantities of fish. Seabirds often pursue feeding whales in search of an easy meal.

Bald eagles (right) are a common sight in Alaska.

ancient murrelets, all busily feeding, are among the seabirds at the other end of the size scale.

Birding Trails

Back on land and following the Sterling Highway to Homer brings you first to beautiful **Kenai Lake**, source of the 82-mile-long **Kenai River**, Alaska's most popular salmon stream. The milky blue-green color of the lake and river is due to suspended glacial flour, or silt, produced by the grinding action of glaciers at the river's source. Bald eagles, along with mew and glaucous-winged gulls, black-billed magpies, and common ravens, are ever present when the fish are running, drawn to the abundant eggs and carcasses of spawned-out salmon. Because of the salmon and trout fry, common and red-breasted mergansers raise their families here. In winter, the river attracts both common and Barrow's goldeneyes and dapper harlequin ducks.

West of the mountains, the highway crosses the nearly two-million-acre **Kenai National Wildlife Refuge**, whose myriad wilderness lakes are inhabited by a host of waterbirds, including nesting common loons, red-necked grebes, and trumpeter swans. This is moose country, with large antlered bulls frequently seen browsing along the road or wading in lakes and ponds. The refuge's public information cabin at milepost 58 is a good place to stop for directions to current birding hot spots.

On the return to Seward, the boat's captain will try – weather permitting – to show you the **Chiswell Islands** in the **Alaska Maritime National Wildlife Refuge**. Matushka, Beehive, Natoa, and other islands in the eight-member group are a seabird lovers' paradise. Towering cliffs attract thousands of nesting black-legged kittiwakes, common murres, horned and tufted puffins, and parakeet auklets. Peregrine falcons visit the islands as well, and it's a special thrill to observe a peregrine swoop down to capture a seabird in flight. As a bonus, the captain finds gatherings of the now-endangered Steller's sea lion hauled out on rocky promontories.

Back on the open sea in **Blying Sound**, be alert for sooty or short-tailed shearwaters, pomarine jaegers, and northern fulmars. If this is your lucky day, a black-footed or Laysan albatross may sail by. Red-necked phalaropes and marbled, Kittlitz's, and

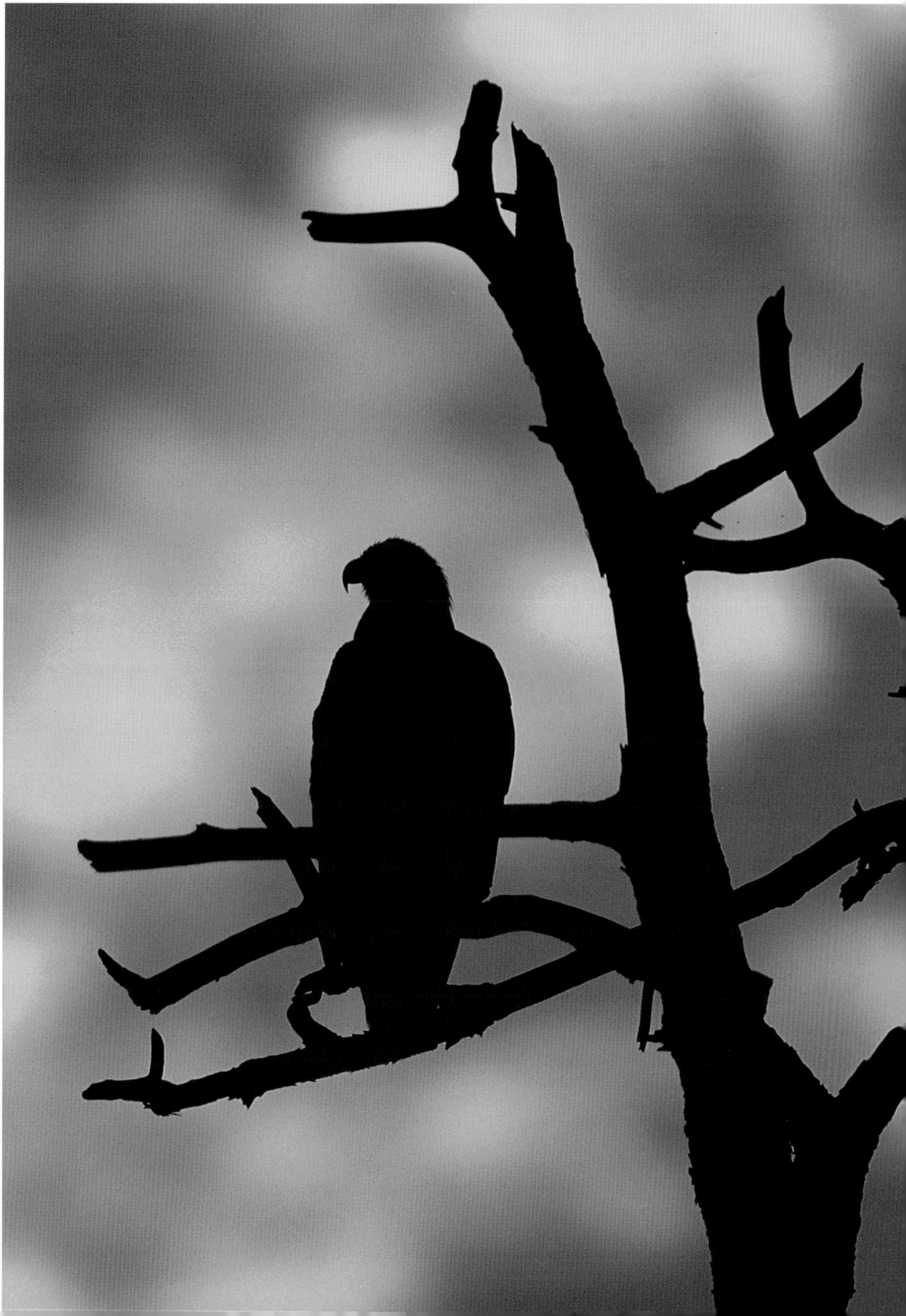

The 19-mile **Skilak Lake Road** provides access to a number of exceptional birding trails. One of these, the **Kenai River Trail**, crosses regrowth from the 1991 Pothole Lake Fire. Downy and hairy woodpeckers fly to and from their nest sites in dead trees, and alder flycatchers and western wood-pewees call from their perches on dead limbs. As the trail enters the mixed conifer-hardwood forest, listen for the *hic-three-cheers* call of the olive-sided flycatcher. The three-toed woodpecker may be seen peeling bark from beetle-invested spruce trees. Upon reaching the Kenai River Canyon, you are treated to an awe-inspiring view.

One of the most heralded vocalists of the refuge's boreal forest is the ruby-crowned kinglet. Along with its golden-crowned cousin, it is among the smallest of North American birds. Despite its size, the ruby-crowned emits surprisingly loud, attenuated warbles, punctuated by short chatters, from early spring to midsummer. It's hard to believe such a vigorous sound comes from such a diminutive creature.

View from the Spit

As you continue to **Homer** along the bluffs overlooking the waters of **Cook Inlet**, towering snow-clad volcanoes line the western horizon. Upon approaching Homer, you will be positioned for a breathtaking vista of the city of 4,500 nestled at the base of a narrow spit that extends four and a half miles into the sparkling blue waters of Kachemak Bay. The rugged snow-capped

Navigating Underwater

The birds feeding in the rich waters surrounding the Kenai Peninsula have evolved a remarkably diverse set of strategies and adaptations to exploit the bounty.

Phalaropes, kittiwakes, jaegers, and petrels glean their food items at or near the surface, while terns and kingfishers dive from the air, using momentum to reach targeted prey at shallow depths. Other birds dive much deeper and must first overcome their buoyancy, the very quality that allows them to stay afloat.

Bottom-feeding seaducks, including eiders, scoters, and harlequins, perform a sharp upward-arching plunge, then swim down to mollusk beds, propelled by powerful strokes of their feet. Murres, puffins, and other deeper-diving seabirds have heavier bones and smaller respiratory air sacs than land birds, which enable them to navigate the underwater world. Using narrow paddle-like wings powered by strong muscles, they fly swiftly through the water, with their feet and tail serving as rudders.

Cormorants go to even greater extremes to enhance their deep-diving capabilities. Raising their feathers to let water displace the trapped air, they intentionally become waterlogged. This is why you often see the birds perched on rocks with wings outstretched to warm and dry themselves in the sun.

Birds that have adapted to swim proficiently underwater may not be so skillful in the air. Puffins, murres, guillemots, and murrelets paddle furiously across the water at the approach of a tourboat, then dive if they cannot take wing. When these seabirds do propel themselves aloft, they fly low over the water on whirring wings, earning them the nickname of bumblebees of the sea.

A cygnet (top), a young trumpeter swan, emerges from its shell. Trumpeters are far more abundant on the Kenai than in the Lower 48 states.

A tufted puffin (above) catches small fish in its bill as it swims swiftly underwater.

Thick-billed murres (opposite, top) inhabit the Chiswell and Barren Islands.

A female harbor seal (opposite, bottom) guards her pup.

peaks of the Kenai Mountains rising to 4,000 feet form a magnificent backdrop across the bay.

Homer Spit qualifies as one of the most accessible birding areas in Alaska. Bald eagles are almost always within close sight year-round. Early May sees the arrival of 100,000 or more migrant shorebirds of some 20 species. The restless flocks busily probe the mudflats before tucking their heads under their wings for a brief snooze. The best time to view shorebirds is at high tide when they are crowded close to the narrow shores. As if on cue, flocks of dunlins, western sandpipers, and short-billed dowitchers suddenly take wing and, in unison, twist and turn in a dazzling display of synchronized flight. After a few circles over the water, the flock returns to another stretch of mudflat to renew their energetic feeding – or rises into the sky and makes a beeline up the coast toward distant nesting grounds.

Black-bellied and semipalmated plovers and least sandpipers may join the feeding parties as the tide recedes in **Mud Bay**. Less frequent visitors are Hudsonian godwits, whimbrels, red knots, and the rare bristle-thighed curlew.

Scanning the wind-whipped waters of **Kachemak Bay** can reveal common eiders and surf scoters riding the waves, accompanied by the occasional common loon or a loose flock of oldsquaw ducks. But the best way to enjoy the bay is to hire a local water taxi and make the six-mile trip to **Gull Island**. As many as 15,000 seabirds of eight species crowd the isle and nearby islets. Black-legged kittiwakes, the most numerous, are joined by common murres, pigeon guillemots, glaucous-winged gulls, and pelagic, red-faced, and double-crested cormorants. Tufted puffins dig nesting burrows in the sod-covered soil of the island's upper slopes. A bald eagle or peregrine falcon occasionally visits to test the vulnerability of the nesting birds and their chicks. Watch closely at the water's edge for wandering tattlers, black and ruddy turnstones, black oyster-catchers, and surfbirds.

Fortunately, most of the Kenai Peninsula and its natural wonders are within state and federal conservation systems. As long as these wild places remain protected, they will continue to provide unforgettable birding for generations to come.

TRAVEL TIPS

DETAILS

When to Go

Visitors see the greatest number of breeding birds in May and June. Birding is also good in summer and early fall. Summer temperatures range from the mid-40s to the 70s. Daytime spring and fall temperatures are in the 40s and 50s. Expect much cooler temperatures at sea and near glaciers. Annual precipitation averages 60 inches in Seward and 25 inches in Homer.

How to Get There

Commercial airlines serve Anchorage, about 35 miles from the Kenai Peninsula. The Alaska Railroad runs between Anchorage and Seward in summer. Visitors may also reach the peninsula on the Alaska Marine Highway ferry, which connects Seward and Homer.

Getting Around

Car rentals are available in Anchorage, Seward, and Homer.

Handicapped Access

The Harding Icefield Trail in Kenai Fjords National Park is accessible, as are some campgrounds in Kenai National Wildlife Refuge and Chugach National Forest.

INFORMATION

Alaska Maritime National Wildlife Refuge

2355 Kachemak Bay Drive, Suite 101, Homer, AK 99603; tel: 907-235-6546.

Chugach National Forest

P.O. Box 390, Seward, AK 99664; tel: 907-224-3374.

Kenai Fjords National Park

P.O. Box 1727, Seward, AK 99664; tel: 907-224-3175.

Kenai National Wildlife Refuge

Box 2139, Soldotna, AK 99669; tel: 907-262-7021.

Seward Convention and Visitors Bureau

P.O. Box 749, Seward, AK 99664; tel: 907-224-8051.

Rare Bird Alert

Tel: 907-338-2473 (statewide), 907-224-2325 (Seward), or 907-235-7337 (Kachemak Bay).

CAMPING

Kenai Fjords National Park has 10 walk-in sites and four public-use cabins reached by boat, kayak, or small plane; call 907-224-3175 for reservations. Kenai National Wildlife Refuge has 14 campgrounds and about 300 sites, some of which require fees and permits; call 907-262-7021 for information. Chugach National Forest has more than 150 sites and cabins; some require fees or permits. For forest information, call 800-280-2267 or 877-444-6777.

Backcountry Travel

Permits are required for some areas in the park, refuge, and forest.

LODGING

PRICE GUIDE – double occupancy

$ = up to $49 $$ = $50–$99
$$$ = $100–$149 $$$$ = $150+

Bay View Inn

P.O. Box 804, Homer, AK 99603; tel: 800-478-8485 or 907-235-8485.

The inn overlooks Kachemak Bay and has spectacular views of the Kenai Mountains. Some of the 11 rooms have kitchenettes; a suite has a living area and kitchen; a cottage has a loft, sitting room, and kitchen. $$–$$$

Breeze Inn Motel

P.O. Box 2147, Seward, AK 99664; tel: 888-224-5237 or 907-224-5238.

This motel at Seward Harbor has 86 rooms, some with harbor or mountain views. A restaurant is on the premises. $$$–$$$$

Homer-Alaska Referral

P.O. Box 1264, Homer, AK 99603; tel: 907-235-8996.

This service books accommodations in Kenai Peninsula bed-and-breakfasts and cabins, as well as tours and outfitters. Prices vary.

Ocean Shores Motel

3500 Crittenden Drive, Homer, AK 99603; tel: 800-770-7775 or 907-235-7775.

The motel is set on four ocean-front acres overlooking Kachemak Bay. Many of the 32 rooms have large picture windows, balconies, and kitchens. $$–$$$

River Valley Cabins

12770 Old Exit Glacier Road, Seward, AK 99664; tel: 907-224-5740.

Guests staying in these cabins on seven wooded acres north of Seward can bird the state forest and national park surrounding the property. One large cabin has two bedrooms and a full kitchen. Six cabins have a bedroom, sitting room, and small refrigerator. A continental breakfast is served. $$$–$$$$

TOURS AND OUTFITTERS

Central Charter

4241 Homer Spit Road, Homer, AK 99603; tel: 800-478-7847 or 907-235-7847.

Daily tours explore the wildlife of Kachemak Bay, including seabirds at Gull Island.

Rainbow Tours

P.O. Box 1526, Homer, AK 99603; tel: 907-235-7272.

Tours leave Homer twice daily for the Gull Island seabird rookery.

The following companies operate boat tours from Seward to Resurrection Bay, Kenai Fjords, and the Chiswell Islands:

Kenai Fjords Tours
P.O. Box 1889, Seward, AK 99664; tel: 800-478-8068.

Major Marine Tours
P.O. Box 101400, Anchorage, AK 99510; tel: 800-764-7300 or 907-224-8030.

Renown Charters and Tours
507 E Street, Suite 201, Anchorage, AK 99501; tel: 907-272-1961.

SPECIAL EVENTS

Kachemak Bay Shorebird Festival
Homer Chamber of Commerce, P.O. Box 541, Homer, AK 99603; tel: 907-235-7740.

Guided trips, educational programs, and children's activities are the highlights of this four-day festival, held during the early-May arrival of thousands of shorebirds in the Homer area.

MUSEUMS

Alaska SeaLife Center
P.O. Box 1329, Seward, AK 99664; tel: 800-224-2525 or 907-224-3080.

This 115,000-square-foot center, opened in 1998, has windows that open above and below the waters of Resurrection Bay. Indoor displays feature the habitats of marine mammals and birds.

Pratt Museum
3779 Bartlett Street, Homer, AK 99603; tel: 907-235-8635.

The museum displays the natural history of the Kachemak Bay and Cook Inlet areas. Three video monitors show real-time images of nesting gulls, murres, and kittiwakes on Gull Island.

Excursions

Alaska Chilkat Bald Eagle Preserve

Alaska Division of Parks and Outdoor Recreation, 400 Willoughby, fourth floor, Juneau, AK 99801; tel: 907-465-4563 or 907-766-2292.

Beginning in fall, bald eagles head for the mouth of the Chilkat River to feast with resident eagles on spawned-out salmon. A warm upwelling of water keeps the river free of ice through January. As many as 3,500 eagles have been counted here during times of peak concentration, from early November to early December. The city of Haines sponsors the Alaska Bald Eagle Festival in mid-November; for information, call 800-246-6268.

Copper River Delta

Chugach National Forest, Cordova Ranger District, P.O. Box 280, Cordova, AK 99574; tel: 907-424-7661.

The glacier-fed Copper River widens at the Gulf of Alaska into a 400-square-mile delta. This vast area sustains astounding numbers of migratory birds, including trumpeter swans, white-fronted geese, northern pintails, millions of shorebirds, and thousands of sandhill cranes. One square mile can contain 250,000 shorebirds. Some birds remain to nest. The Copper River Delta Shorebird Festival is held in nearby Cordova in early May; call 907-424-7260 for information.

Denali National Park and Preserve

P.O. Box 9, Denali Park, AK, 99755; tel: 907-683-2294.

For many visitors, this park is the ultimate symbol of Alaskan wilderness. Grizzly bears, caribou, moose, Dall sheep, and wolves wander through a landscape dominated by the majestic Alaska Range. Among Denali's numerous bird species are northern wheatears, bohemian waxwings, long-tailed jaegers, lapland longspurs, snow buntings, and raptors such as golden eagles, northern goshawks, merlins, and gyrfalcons.

Hawaii Volcanoes National Park

Hawaii

CHAPTER **23**

"Birdwatching in Hawaii is more about bird listening," advises a ranger at **Hawaii Volcanoes National Park**. The birds are mostly small and the vegetation concealing, but the songs are clear, melodious, and strong. Nine species of endemic land birds show themselves on this morning's jaunt through the vast park on the **Big Island of Hawaii**. Their names are mellifluous and usually sound like their songs: apapane, iiwi, 'io, amakihi, omao, koae kea, elepaio, nene, and black noddy. It is a lucky morning. Introduced species also make an appearance: northern cardinal, common myna, house sparrow, house finch, and the elegant Kalij pheasant. ◆ Along the way, the birders witness the act of creation itself as **Kilauea Volcano** grumpily goes about its daily business, steaming, belching, and spewing lava into the ocean at the rate of 130,000 gallons a minute, making the Big Island bigger still. Since 1983, more than 500 acres of new land have been added to this largest of the Hawaiian Islands.

Birdsong, strong and melodious, wafts through the Big Island's verdant rain forests and rises above rivers of steaming lava.

◆ The mid-ocean volcanoes that built the Hawaiian archipelago are among the largest mountains on Earth. When the islands emerged from the sea, they were barren. But lava is rich in minerals. It has everything life needs – just add water. The seeds of life arrived in ocean currents, borne on winds, and as gifts from migratory birds. It was a long flight, more than 2,400 miles over ocean in any direction. Plant and avian colonizations were largely by chance, and the biota that evolved in isolation is astonishing in its intricate beauty and diversity. Ornithologists theorize that a single species of undistinguished finch,

The iiwi uses its deeply curved bill to reach the nectar of flowering plants. Its call, resembling a door on rusty hinges, is unmistakable.

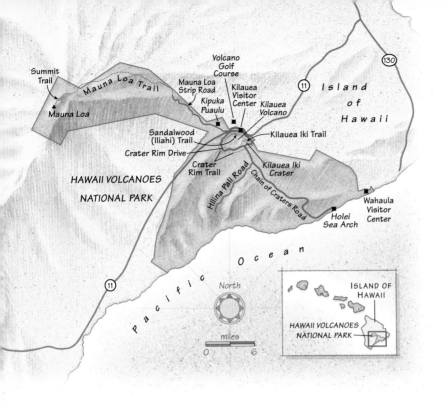

descends immediately into a lush rain forest backed up against a crater wall. It's like crossing an invisible divide and stepping back in time a million years. Enormous ferns rise from furry brown stems and tower overhead in lacy umbrellas. Dew sparkles like ice on scarlet ohia-lehua blossoms. All around is the sweet song of birds, unnoticed in the nearby parking lot, but pervasive in the quiet of the forest. The ranger puts her finger to her lips and tilts her ear to the trees. A brilliant red bird flits from the foliage, white rump feathers startling among the scarlet – an apapane. The distinctive whirring of his wings is quite audible. "He has a repertoire like Caruso," the ranger says, "about 50 songs."

The best strategy for sighting the diminutive Hawaiian birds is to stake out the flowers they feed on – the red ohia-lehua, the brilliant yellow mamane, the creamy bouquets of the giant koa trees. It also helps to get above the canopy and look down on the trees. The trail winds through the forest, into rocky crevices velvet with moss, and out to open space with just such a vantage. It is here that the grayish omao, or Hawaiian thrush, makes a debut for the birder.

In the old days, canoe makers looking for trees to carve into their great vessels would observe the elepaio with care. If the bird lingered on a koa tree and began probing for insects, the tree was deemed unsuitable. The koa forests that once dominated much of Hawaii were sharply reduced with the introduction of cattle and horses and their need for pasture. Avian populations declined with the clearing of the forests. The good news for birds, however, is that

perhaps related to a mainland crossbill or goldfinch, founded the glamorous dynasty known as Hawaiian honeycreepers, a group unrivaled for variety in any continental bird family. In the utter remoteness of the Hawaiian Islands, a process of coevolution occurred, in which the plants and birds developed mutually beneficial features, with beaks and pistils fitting like fingers in a glove.

Islands amid Lava

Across the road from the visitor center parking lot, where mynas scold and squabble in the border grass, the **Sandalwood Trail**

when pasturelands are abandoned, koa naturally springs up again.

Stands of koa line the park's **Mauna Loa Strip Road**, which makes the drive excellent for roadside birding and a chance to see the elepaio, a diminutive, brown and white flycatcher. The narrow road winds 13 miles up the slope of another volcano, currently inactive but restless 6,662-foot **Mauna Loa**. The king of this road is the Kalij pheasant, a native of Nepal imported in 1962 that saunters from one foraging spot to another disdainful of traffic. Overhead, the 'io, or Hawaiian hawk, soars gracefully in the updrafts. This imperious raptor was the symbol of Hawaiian royalty. The name of the royal palace in Honolulu is Iolani, literally "hawk of heaven."

A fine birding stop is **Kipuka Puaulu**, commonly called **Bird Park**. A kipuka is an island of vegetation spared by the vagaries of a lava flow during an eruption. These islands, with their moats of hardened black lava, make excellent, protected bird habitats. Tourists in search of rivers of fire seldom bother with the remote, undramatic Mauna

A fiddlehead (left) uncurls in the rain forest. Full-grown tree ferns can be more than six feet tall.

Nene geese (below) do not find the park's lava fields inhospitable. Unlike most waterfowl, they are seen only occasionally near water.

The Hawaiian hawk (opposite), issues a call, *eeee-oh*, that sounds like its Hawaiian name, 'io.

Loa Road. In the solitude, you may be visited by the elepaio and the apapane. You're also likely to spot introduced species: northern cardinal, Japanese white-eye, house finch, and red-billed leiothrix.

At road's end, under a brilliant sky, several birders holding tape recorders smile at the arias they are recording. Suddenly an iiwi, in scarlet splendor, flies toward them

descendant of the Canada goose and Hawaii's official state bird, is a prime example. The sole survivor of at least nine native goose species, it is a handsome gray bird with a black face and furrowed neck. The fossil record indicates that nenes once numbered in the thousands on all the major Hawaiian islands, perhaps 25,000 on the Big Island alone. Then humans arrived, destroying habitat and slaughtering the birds. Untold thousands of nenes left Hawaii salted in barrels aboard 19th-century whaling ships. By 1950, only about 30 birds remained.

A collaborative effort between local biologists and the Wildfowl Trust

and hovers momentarily overhead, its long, curved bill clearly visible, then goes on its way, singing like an old screen door on rusty hinges.

Volcano Rookery

It's not merely the beauty of Hawaii's native birds that inspires awe and affection but the knowledge that they are endangered. Some have been brought back from the brink of extinction. The nene, an evolutionary

of Slimbridge, England, has saved the nene. Three birds were sent to the trust in 1950. The trio hatched and reared offspring. In all, 268 healthy British-born nenes were sent home to form the backbone of a new breeding population. There are now more than 2,000 nenes in the wild, but they are still the world's most endangered geese. Oblivious of their plight, flocks of nene congregate on the greensward of **Volcano Golf Course**, which makes the clubhouse popular with birders having lunch. Nenes waddle right past the picture windows.

The lovely white koae kea, or white-tailed tropicbird, an endemic seabird, carries dinner seven miles from its oceanic hunting areas to **Kilauea Iki Crater**, where it nests and feeds squid to its chicks tucked away in nooks in the crater wall. A four-hour walk on the looping **Kilauea Iki Trail** will take you through rain forest singing with many of the same birds on the Sandalwood Trail, then down to the crater floor, warmed by fires in the furnace of the Earth. Steam vents hiss, old black lava crackles underfoot like potato chips, sulphur fumes waft in the breezes, and prayers rise like incense, imploring the fire goddess Pele to remain at bay. There is an exhilarating element of danger. Rock cairns mark the way. Your companions are the koae kea soaring overhead, doing their aerial dances before the next commute out to sea for squid.

Elsewhere in Hawaii's volcanic landscape, you'll find other birds equally well adapted to the environment. In the dramatic coastal section of the park, for example, stark lava cliffs are pounded by turquoise surf, and columns of steam billow from the flow of molten rock into the ocean. It's in this apparently inhospitable setting that the black noddy builds its nests, especially near **Holei Sea Arch**. Families of nene also have been spotted ambling across nearby lava fields – a testament to the persistence of life on this lush but geologically restless island.

Behold the Birds While You Can

If Charles Darwin had landed on the Hawaiian Islands instead of the Galápagos, he would have found even more dramatic evidence to support his theories of evolution.

In the remote and pristine volcanic archipelago of Hawaii, life took unexpected turns. For one thing, it relaxed. There were no natural predators. Colonizing plants lost their thorns and noxious odors. Many species of birds forgot to fly. Parent species begat an astonishing array of offspring. In the Galápagos, for instance, a total of 17 different finches evolved from a single mainland ancestor. Hawaii produced at least 40 different honeycreepers from a single finchlike ancestor. More than 90 percent of the plants, birds, insects, and other species occurring in Hawaii are endemic – that is, they are unknown elsewhere on Earth. No other landmass in the world has such a high level of endemism.

This wonderful natural heritage is in crisis. Nearly three-fourths of the documented extinctions in the United States have been Hawaiian species. More than half of Hawaii's original bird species are gone. The three leading causes are the arrival of predators, degradation of habitat, and introduction of avian malaria, carried by mosquitoes.

Conservation groups have made remarkable strides in preserving what is left of the fragile island ecosystems and in aiding stressed populations. The Nature Conservancy of Hawaii has established preserves on all the major islands. A captive breeding program pioneered by the Peregrine Fund at the **Keauhou Bird Conservation Center** on the slopes of **Kilauea Volcano** is plucking birds from the jaws of extinction. One of the notable successes was the reintroduction of the rare and endangered puaiohi, a small Kauai thrush, to its native habitat in the forests at **Kokee, Kauai**.

Elepaios (top) on the Big Island vary in color and markings; the birds fly out from tree perches to hawk insects or pick them from leaves and bark.

The endangered crested honeycreeper (above), also known as the akohekohe, is found only in Maui's rain forests.

Koa trees (opposite, top), a species of acacia, thrive in a kipuka, an island of vegetation untouched by lava flows.

The song of the amakihi (opposite, bottom) is an extended trill that crescendos before fading away.

TRAVEL TIPS

DETAILS

When to Go

Birding on the Big Island is rewarding year-round, but spring is the best time to observe breeding and nesting species. Climate varies considerably within the park. Expect cold and rain at high elevations, hot, dry, and windy conditions in the coastal area at the end of Chain of Craters Road. November through April is the rainy season, with 10 to 13 inches of precipitation per month and temperatures in the 50s and 60s. Expect temperatures in the 70s May through October.

How to Get There

Major airlines and interisland carriers serve Keahole Airport in Kona, 100 miles from the park. Interisland carriers also serve General Lyman Field in Hilo, about 30 miles from the park.

Getting Around

An automobile is necessary for birding the park. Car rentals are available at the airports.

Handicapped Access

The park visitor center and the Devastation Trail are accessible.

INFORMATION

Hawaii Volcanoes National Park

P.O. Box 52, Hawaii Volcanoes National Park, HI 96718; tel: 808-985-6000.

Big Island Visitors Bureau

250 Keawe Street, Hilo, HI 96720; tel: 808-961-5797.

CAMPING

Two park campgrounds, Namakini Paio and Kulanaokuaiki, have sites available on a first-come, first-served basis. Namakini Paio has 10 cabins with electricity and barbecue pits. To reserve a cabin, call 808-967-7321.

Backcountry Travel

A permit, obtainable one day in advance, is required for camping and backcountry travel in the park. For information, call 808-985-6000.

LODGING

All Islands Bed-and-Breakfast

463 Iliwahi Loop, Kailua, HI 96734; tel: 800-542-0344 or 808-263-2342.

The agency arranges stays at more than 700 bed-and-breakfasts throughout the Hawaiian Islands, and assists with other travel plans. Prices vary.

Carson's Volcano Cottages

P.O. Box 503, Volcano, HI 96785; tel: 808-967-7683.

Guests bird the rain forest surrounding this compound. Five cottages, two of which accommodate families, have kitchen facilities. The inn's five guest rooms have private baths. Breakfast is served in the main dining room. $$–$$$$

Country Goose Bed-and-Breakfast

P.O. Box 597, Volcano, HI 96785; tel: 800-238-7101 or 808-967-7759.

Perched at an elevation of 3,500 feet, the Country Goose offers two guest rooms, each with a private bath and entrance. Gourmet breakfasts are served. $$

Hale Ohia Cottages

P.O. Box 758, Volcano, HI 96785; tel: 800-455-3803 or 808-967-7986.

Three cottages with kitchen facilities occupy a one-acre garden filled with native plants. Four suites have private baths and refrigerators; a deluxe suite has a separate living room and bedroom. Breakfast is included. A hot tub is available for use in a private corner of the garden. $$–$$$

Kalahiki Cottage

McCandless Ranch, P.O. Box 500, Honaunau, HI 96726; tel: 808-328-8246.

Situated on a 15,000-acre ranch that stretches from the west coast of the Big Island to the slopes of Mauna Loa, this one-bedroom cottage has a kitchen and private lanai. The property, one of the largest intact forest areas on the island, supports native and introduced birds. This is the only place where the Hawaiian crow can be seen in the wild. Guests tour the ranch for a fee. $$$$

Kilauea Lodge

P.O. Box 116, Volcano, HI 96785; tel: 808-967-7366.

This 12-room lodge, one mile from the park, is set on 10 acres. Guests are encouraged to explore the grounds. A two-bedroom cottage has a kitchen and living area. A restaurant is on the premises. $$$–$$$$

Volcano House

P.O. Box 53, Hawaii Volcanoes National Park, HI 96718; tel: 808-967-7321.

Volcano House has 42 units near the rim of Kilauea Caldera, ranging from small accommodations to deluxe second-floor rooms with views of the volcano. A restaurant is available. $$–$$$$

TOURS AND OUTFITTERS

Hawaii Audubon Society

850 Richards Street, Suite 505,

Honolulu, HI 96813; tel: 808-528-1432.

The society offers monthly field trips to a variety of locations and provides information for visiting birders.

Hawaii Forest and Trail

74-5035B Queen Kaahumanu Highway, Kailua-Kona, HI 96740; tel: 800-464-1993 or 808-331-8505.

Guides lead small groups of birders to the Big Island's rain forests and "dry forests." Other trips cover various aspects of the island's natural history. Visitors may also arrange custom itineraries.

Hawaii Volcanoes National Park

P.O. Box 52, Hawaii National Park, HI 96718; tel: 808-985-6000.

Park staff lead several nature walks daily, which include opportunities to see a number of bird species.

Oceanic Society Expeditions

Fort Mason Center, Building E, San Francisco, CA 94123; tel: 800-326-7491 or 415-474-3385.

Five- and nine-day tours, conducted by naturalists and researchers, cover the birds, marine mammals, history, and ecology of Midway Atoll. The society is the only organization authorized to give natural-history programs on the atoll, where visitation is strictly controlled. Trips are scheduled for spring and early summer and for late fall and winter. The society also offers participatory research expeditions and arranges independent multiday visits.

Excursions

Hanalei National Wildlife Refuge

P.O. Box 1128, Kilauea, Kauai, HI 96754; tel: 808-828-1413.

Mudflats and freshwater ponds amid taro fields provide a sanctuary for waterbirds. Hawaiian coots, black-necked stilts (a Hawaiian subspecies of the mainland stilt), common moorhens, and black-crowned night-herons wade in the flooded patches and parade along the grassy dikes. Japanese bush-warblers, Japanese white-eyes, melodious laughing-thrushes, white-rumped shamas, and the endangered koloa, or Hawaiian duck, are also seen here. Birders can hike the refuge trails or paddle a rented kayak on the Hanalei River.

Kilauea Point National Wildlife Refuge

P.O. Box 1128, Kilauea, Kauai, HI 96754; tel: 808-828-1413.

A historic lighthouse marks the northernmost spot on Kauai, an excellent vantage for watching seabirds. Wedge-tailed shearwaters, Laysan albatrosses, red-footed boobies, and red-tailed and white-tailed tropicbirds nest in the refuge. Newell's shearwaters, with their 30-inch-plus wingspans, drop in from inland nests. Birders also see great frigatebirds, brown boobies, and reintroduced nene geese. Endangered green sea turtles, Hawaiian monk seals, and pods of Pacific spinner dolphins ply offshore waters.

Midway Atoll National Wildlife Refuge

P.O. Box 29460, Honolulu, HI 96820; tel: 808-541-1201.

More than two million birds nest on this coral atoll, 1,300 miles northwest of Honolulu. The former U.S. Navy airbase supports the largest colony of Laysan albatrosses, surpassing 380,000 pairs, and 21,000 pairs of black-footed albatrosses. In addition, 17 seabird species, including tropicbirds, frigatebirds, and boobies, nest or visit here, joined by many land birds and shorebirds. Among the marine mammals seen offshore are Hawaiian monk seals and green sea turtles.

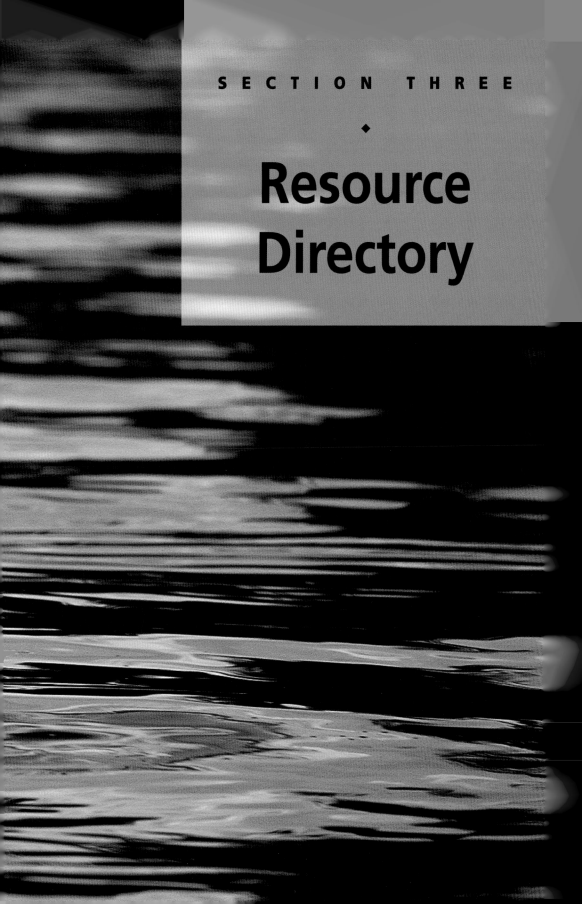

SECTION THREE

◆

Resource
Directory

FURTHER READING

Field and Identification Guides

No other book that you will acquire for your birding library is as important – and practical – as a field guide. The guide, which you'll carry with you, should offer comprehensive coverage of the places where you regularly watch birds. As your interests develop, you may want to own specialized guides such as those devoted to raptors, shorebirds, and warblers, or nests and eggs.

Advanced Birding (Peterson Field Guides), by Kenn Kaufman (Houghton Mifflin, 1990).

All the Birds of North America, by Jack L. Griggs (American Bird Conservancy, 1997).

Birds (Discovery Books, 1999).

Birds of North America: A Guide to Field Identification, by Chandler S. Robbins, Bertel Bruun, and Herbert S. Zim (Golden Books, 1983).

Eastern Birds' Nests (Peterson Field Guides), by Hal H. Harrison (Houghton Mifflin, 1975).

A Field Guide to the Birds East of the Rockies, by Roger Tory Peterson (Houghton Mifflin, 1980).

A Field Guide to the Birds of Hawaii and the Tropical Pacific, by H. Douglas Pratt, Phillip L. Bruner, and Delwyn G. Berrett (Princeton University Press, 1987).

Field Guide to the Birds of North America, Third Edition (National Geographic Society, 1999).

A Field Guide to Western Birds, by Roger Tory Peterson (Houghton Mifflin, 1990).

A Guide to the Nests, Eggs, and Nestlings of North American Birds, by Paul J. Baicich and Colin J.O. Harrison (Academic Press, 1997).

Guide to the Birds of Alaska, by Robert H. Armstrong (Alaska Northwest Books, 1995).

Hawks (Peterson Field Guides), by William S. Clark and Brian K. Wheeler (Houghton Mifflin, 1987).

Hawks in Flight: The Flight Identification of North American Migrant Raptors, by Pete Dunne, David Sibley, and Clay Sutton (Houghton Mifflin, 1988).

Ocean Birds of the Nearshore Pacific: A Guide for the Sea-Going Naturalist, by Rich Stallcup (Point Reyes Bird Observatory, 1990).

A Photographic Guide to North American Raptors, by Brian K. Wheeler and William S. Clark (Academic Press, 1995).

Seabirds: An Identification Guide, by Peter Harrison (Houghton Mifflin, 1985).

Shorebirds: An Identification Guide, by Peter Hayman, John Marchant, and Tony Prater (Houghton Mifflin, 1986).

Stokes Field Guide to Birds: Eastern Region, by Donald and Lillian Stokes (Little, Brown, 1996).

Stokes Field Guide to Birds: Western Region, by Donald and Lillian Stokes (Little, Brown, 1996).

Warblers of North America (Peterson Field Guides), by Jon Dunn and Kimball Garrett (Houghton Mifflin, 1997).

Western Birds' Nests (Peterson Field Guides), by Hal H. Harrison (Houghton Mifflin, 1979).

Regional Guides and Bird Finders

Field guides help you answer the question, What birds did I see? Birdfinding guides like those below answer another question: Where can I find birds? These and guides targeting specific areas, also included here, are invaluable for planning a trip and also make essential traveling companions.

America's 100 Most Wanted Birds, by Steven G. Mlodinow and Michael O'Brien (Falcon Publishing, 1998).

A Birder's Guide to Churchill, by Bonnie Chartier (American Birding Association, 1994).

A Birder's Guide to Colorado, by Harold R. Holt (American Birding Association, 1997).

A Birder's Guide to Florida, by Bill Pranty (American Birding Association, 1996).

A Birder's Guide to the Kenai Peninsula, Alaska, by George C. West (Pratt Museum and Birchside Studios, 1994).

A Birder's Guide to Maine, by Elizabeth C. and Jan Erik Pierson and Peter D. Vickery (Down East Books, 1996).

A Birder's Guide to Planning North American Trips, by Jerry A. Cooper (American Birding Association, 1995).

A Birder's Guide to Point Pelee, by Tom Hince (Tom Hince, 1999).

A Birder's Guide to the Rio Grande Valley of Texas, by Mark Lockwood et al. (American Birding Association, 1999).

A Birder's Guide to Southeastern Arizona, by Richard Cachor Taylor (American Birding Association, 1995).

A Birder's Guide to Wyoming, by Oliver K. Scott (American Birding Association, 1993).

Birdfinding in Forty National Forests and Grasslands (American Birding Association and U.S. Forest Service, 1994).

Birdfinding Guide to New Jersey, by William J. Boyle Jr. (Rutgers University Press, 1989).

Birding Crane River: Nebraska's Platte, by Gary Lingle, William S. Whitney, and Ernest V. Ochsner (Harrier Publishing, 1994).

Birding Northern California, by John Kemper (Falcon Publishing, 1999).

Birding Texas, by Roland H. Wauer and Mark A. Elwonger (Falcon Publishing, 1998).

The Birdwatcher's Guide to Hawaii, by Rick Soehren (University of Hawaii Press, 1996).

Enjoying Birds in Hawaii: A Birdfinding Guide to the Fiftieth State, by H. Douglas Pratt (Mutual Publishing, 1993).

A Field Guide to Birds of the Big Bend, by Roland H. Wauer (Gulf Publishing, 1996).

50 Best Places to Go Birding in and Around the Big Apple, by John Thaxton and Allan Messer (City and Co., 1999).

Finding the Birds of Jackson Hole, by Bert Raynes and Darwin Wile (American Birding Association, 1994).

Finding Birds in Southeast Arizona, by Davis and Russell (Tucson Audubon Society, 1995).

The Natural History of the Point Reyes Peninsula, by Jules G. Evens (Point Reyes National Seashore Association, 1993).

General Resources and References

Field guides need to be portable, so they can't provide in-depth information about birds and their behavior. For more detailed discussion, you'll want to turn to books such as the *Audubon Society Encyclopedia* or Kenn Kaufman's *Lives of North American Birds*. Or do you want to know more about migration? Avian flight? The link between birds and dinosaurs? Or even how to get started in birding? Check out the other titles below, which cover these topics and a host of others.

The Audubon Society Encyclopedia of North American Birds, by John K. Terres (Wings Books, 1980).

Birder's Dictionary, by Randall T. Cox (Falcon Publishing, 1996).

The Birder's Handbook: A Field Guide to the Natural History of North American Birds, by Paul R. Ehrlich, David S. Dobkin, and Darryl Wheye (Simon & Shuster, 1988).

Birding, A Nature Company Guide, by Joseph Forshaw, Steve Howell, Terence Lindsey, and Rich Stallcup (Nature Company, 1994).

Birds Asleep, by Alexander F. Skutch (University of Texas Press, 1993).

The Complete Birder: A Guide to Better Birding, by Jack Connor (Houghton Mifflin, 1988).

Dictionary of American Bird Names, by Ernest A. Choate (Harvard Common Press, 1985).

Directory of Birding and Nature Festivals, by Sharon DeCray et al (National Fish and Wildlife Foundation, 1999).

How Birds Fly, by David Goodnow (Periwinkle, 1992).

How Birds Migrate, by Paul Kerlinger (Stackpole Books, 1995).

How to Spot Hawks and Eagles, by Clay Sutton and Patricia Taylor Sutton (Chapters Publishing, 1996).

How to Spot an Owl, by Clay and Patricia Sutton (Chapters Publishing, 1994).

The Life of Birds, by David Attenborough (Princeton University Press, 1998).

Lives of North American Birds, by Kenn Kaufman (Houghton Mifflin, 1996).

Living on the Wind: Across the Hemisphere with Migratory Birds, by Scott Weidensaul (Farrar, Straus and Giroux, 1999).

The Mistaken Extinction: Dinosaur Evolution and the Origin of Birds, by Lowell Dingus and Timothy Rowe (W. H. Freeman, 1997).

The Mountain and the Migration: A Guide to Hawk Mountain, by James J. Brett (Cornell University Press, 1991).

North American Birds of Prey, by Clay Sutton and Richard K. Walton (Knopf, 1994).

The Origin and Evolution of Birds, by Alan Feduccia (Yale University Press, 1996).

The Wind Masters: The Lives of North American Birds of Prey, by Pete Dunne (Houghton Mifflin, 1995).

Essays, Personal Observations, and History

For the days when you can't go birding, the next best thing is reading about the experiences of others, from Leonard Nathan's quest for the elusive snow bunting and Marie Winn's observations in New York's Central Park to Maurice Broun's story of Pennsylvania's Hawk Mountain and Joseph Kastner's history of legendary birders.

Birdwatching with American Women: A Selection of Nature Writings, edited by Deborah Strom (W. W. Norton, 1986).

Diary of a Left-Handed Birdwatcher, by Leonard Nathan (Graywolf Press, 1996).

The Feather Quest, by Pete Dunne (Dutton, 1992).

Hawks Aloft, by Maurice Broun (Stackpole, 1999).

Kingbird Highway: The Story of a Natural Obsession that Got a Little Out of Hand, by Kenn Kaufman (Houghton Mifflin, 1997).

A Parrot without a Name: The Search for the Last Unknown Birds on the Earth, by Don Stap (University of Texas Press, 1991).

Red-Tails in Love: A Wildlife Drama in Central Park, by Marie Winn (Pantheon Books, 1998).

Season at the Point: The Birds and Birders of Cape May, by Jack Connor (Atlantic Monthly Press, 1991).

Tales of a Low-Rent Birder, by Pete Dunne (University of Texas Press, 1986).

Treasury of North American Birdlore, edited by Paul S. Eriksson and Alan Pistorius (Paul S. Eriksson, 1994).

A World of Watchers: An Informal History of the American Passion for Birds, by Joseph Kastner (Sierra Club Books, 1986).

Bird Photography

If you want to start taking photographs of birds, follow the advice of these award-winning photographers, whose books are full of inspirational images.

The Art of Bird Photography: The Complete Guide to Professional Field Techniques, by Arthur Morris (Amphoto, 1998).

Bird Photography Pure and Simple, by Arthur Morris (Tern Books, 1997).

Wild Bird Photography, by Tim Fitzharris (Firefly Books, 1996).

Wild Bird Photography, by Tim Gallagher (Lyons Press, 1994).

Books for Children

Young birders will appreciate having a field guide of their own, such as a copy of Peterson First Guides. The other books here will help stimulate their interest in birding and tell them more about what they see in the field.

Birds of North America, by Angela Royston and Paul J. Baicich (Silver Dolphin, 1995).

Birdsong, by Audrey Wood (Harcourt Brace, 1997).

Bird Watching for Kids, by Steven A. Griffin and Elizabeth May Griffin (Northward, 1995).

Birdwise: Forty Fun Feats for Finding Out About Our Feathered Friends, by Pamela M. Hickman (Perseus, 1988).

A Magpies' Nest, by Joanna Foster (Clarion, 1995).

Peterson First Guides: Birds of North America, by Roger Tory Peterson (Chapters Publishing, 1998).

The Secrets of Animal Flight, by Nic Bishop (Hougton Mifflin, 1997).

Simon & Shuster Children's Guide to Birds, by Jinny Johnson (Simon & Shuster, 1996).

Watching Our Feathered Friends, by Dean T. Spaulding (Lerner, 1997).

Magazines

Some magazines, such as *Audubon* and *National Wildlife*, include articles on birds and birding destinations as part of their coverage of the natural world and environmental issues. Others are devoted entirely to birds and birding.

Audubon
National Audubon Society, P.O. Box 52529; Boulder, CO 80322; tel: 800-274-4201 or 212-979-3000.

Bird Watcher's Digest, The Skimmer
P.O. Box 110, Marietta, OH 45750; tel: 800-879-2473.

Birders Journal
8 Midtown Drive, Suite 289, Oshawa, Ontario L1J 8L2.

Birder's World
P.O. Box 1612, Waukesha, WI 53187; tel: 800-446-5489; www.kalmbach.com/birders.

Birding, Field Notes, Winging It
American Birding Association, P.O. Box 6599, Colorado Springs, CO 80225; tel: 800-835-2473; www.americanbirding.org.

Living Bird
Cornell Laboratory of Ornithology, 159 Sapsucker Woods Road, Ithaca,

NY 14850; tel: 607-254-BIRD; www.ornith.cornell.edu.

National Wildlife
National Wildlife Federation, 8925 Leesburg Pike, Vienna, VA 22184; tel: 703-790-4000; www.nwf.org.

WildBird
P.O. Box 52898, Boulder, CO 80322; tel: 800-365-4421.

BIRDING ON THE INTERNET

These websites, in addition to those affiliated with organizations listed in this directory, offer lots of information of use to birders. Most sites provide links to the websites of birding and conservation organizations.

www.theaviary.com.
Numerous articles covering backyard birding, migration, and other subjects, plus material for children and teachers.

www.birder.com
Bird-related trivia, checklists of species, information on backyard birding, and access to lists of bird festivals and conferences.

www.birdwatching.com.
Observations by various authors, bird lore, birding tips, and reviews of optics, CDs, and birding software.

www.gorp.com/activity/birding.
Large site covering outdoor activities, including birding, and providing information on national parks, refuges, and other sites of interest to traveling birders, as well as such topics as avian songs and calls.

www.optics4birding.com
Reviews of optics, answers to frequently asked questions, sources for optics, and information on repair.

www.petersononline.com.
Background on Roger Tory Peterson, identification tips based on Peterson's system, and games to improve birding skills.

www.virtualbirder.com.
Large archive of articles on birding destinations, virtual tours of birding hot spots, up-to-date rare bird alerts, and book reviews.

BIRDING BY EAR

If you're a relatively new birder, you may be surprised at the variety of avian songs and calls – and frustrated at trying to identify them. All it takes is a little practice, with the help of songs and calls on tape or CD.

Birding by Ear: Eastern/Central (Peterson Field Guides) by Richard K. Walton and Robert W. Lawson (Houghton Mifflin, 1999).

Birding by Ear: Western (Peterson Field Guides), by Richard K. Walton and Robert W. Lawson (Houghton Mifflin, 1999).

Bird Songs of Florida, by Geoffrey A. Keller (Cornell Laboratory of Ornithology, 1997).

A Field Guide to Western Bird Songs (Cornell Laboratory of Ornithology, 1992).

Guide to Bird Sounds (Cornell Laboratory of Ornithology, 1985).

Stokes Field Guide to Bird Songs: Eastern Region, by Lang Elliott, Donald Stokes, and Lillian Stokes (Time Warner, 1997).

Stokes Field Guide to Bird Songs: Western Region, by Lang Elliott, Donald Stokes, and Lillian Stokes (Time Warner, 1999).

Voices of Hawaii's Birds (Hawaii Audubon Society, 1996).

ORGANIZATIONS

The ornithological and environmental organizations below offer a number of services for birders – they also serve birds by conducting research and advocating for species and habitat protection. Some, like the National Audubon Society and the Nature Conservancy, manage preserves known for their excellent birding. Government entities, such as the Bureau of Land Management and U.S. Fish and Wildlife Service, oversee parks and refuges, a number of which appear in this book.

American Bald Eagle Foundation
P.O. Box 49, Haines, AK 99827; tel: 907-766-3094.

American Birding Association
P.O. Box 6599, Colorado Springs, CO 80934; tel: 719-578-1614; www.americanbirding.org.

Bureau of Land Management
1849 C Street, N.W., Washington, D.C. 20241; tel: 202-452-7780; www.blm.gov/.

Cornell Laboratory of Ornithology
159 Sapsucker Woods Road, Ithaca, NY 14850; tel: 607-254-BIRD; www.ornith.cornell.edu.

George Miksch Sutton Avian Research Center
P.O. Box 2007, Bartlesville, OK 74005; tel: 918-336-BIRD; www.suttoncenter.org.

The Hummingbird Society
P.O. Box 394, Newark, DE 19715; tel: 800-529-3699 or 302-369-3699; www.hummingbird.org.

International Crane Foundation
P.O. Box 447, Baraboo, WI 53913; tel: 608-356-9462; www.baraboo.com/bus/icf.

National Audubon Society
700 Broadway, New York, NY 10003; tel: 212-832-3000; www.audubon.org.

National Bird-Feeding Society
P.O. Box 23BA, Northbrook, IL 60065; tel: 847-272-0135.

National Fish and Wildlife Foundation
1120 Connecticut Avenue, N.W., Suite 900, Washington, D.C. 20036; tel: 202-857-0166; www.nfwf.org.

National Park Service
Office of Public Inquiries, P.O. Box 37127, Washington, D.C. 20013; tel: 202-208-4747.

National Wildlife Federation
8925 Leesburg Pike, Vienna, VA 22184; tel: 703-790-4000; www.nwf.org.

National Wildlife Refuge Association
1776 Massachusetts Avenue, N.W., Suite 200, Washington, D.C. 20036; tel: 202-296-9729; www.refugenet.com.

The Nature Conservancy
4245 North Fairfax Drive, Suite 100, Arlington, VA 22203; tel: 703-841-5300; www.tnc.org.

New Jersey Audubon Society
9 Hardscrabble Road, P.O. Box 126, Bernardsville, NJ 07924; tel: 908-204-8998; www.nj.com/audubon.

North American Bluebird Society
P.O. Box 74, Darlington, WI 53530; www.cobleskill.edu/nabs.

Peregrine Fund
566 West Flying Hawk Lane, Boise, ID 83709; 208-362-3716; www.peregrinefund.org.

Trumpeter Swan Society
3800 County Road 24, Maple Plain, MN 55359; tel: 612-476-4663; www.taiga.net/swans/index.html.

U.S. Fish and Wildlife Service
Division of Refuges, 4401 North Fairfax Drive, Arlington, VA 22203; tel: 800-344-WILD or 202-857-0166; www.fws.gov.

TOUR OPERATORS

In the destination chapters of this book, you'll find the names of outfitters located at or near each destination. The tour operators listed here take birders to some of the same destinations but also offer trips to many other birding hot spots in North America and elsewhere around the world.

Borderland Tours
2550 West Calle Padilla, Tucson, AZ 85745; tel: 800-525-7753; www.borderland-tours.com.

Cheesemans' Ecology Safaris
20800 Kittredge Road, Saratoga, CA 95070; tel: 800-527-5330.

Connecticut Audubon
67 Main Street, Essex, CT 06426; tel: 800-996-8747; www.ctaudubon.org.

Eagle-Eye Tours Inc.
P.O. Box 5010, Point Roberts, WA 98281 or P.O. Box 94672, Richmond, BC V6Y 4A4, Canada; tel: 800-373-5678 or 604-948-9177; www.eagle-eye.com.

Field Guides, Inc.
9433 Bee Cave Road, Building 1, Suite 150, Austin, TX 78733; tel: 800-728-4953 or 512-263-0117; www.fieldguides.com.

Flights of Fancy Adventures, Inc.
901 Mountain Road, Bloomfield, CT 06002; tel: 860-243-2569.

Focus on Nature Tours
P.O. Box 9021, Wilmington, DE 19809; tel: 800-362-0869; www.focusonnature.com.

High Lonesome Ecotours
570 South Little Bear Trail, Sierra Vista, AZ 85635; tel: 800-743-2668, www.hilonesome.com.

Massachusetts Audubon Society Natural History Travel
South Great Road, Lincoln, MA 01773; tel: 800-289-9504.

New Jersey Audubon Society Travel
794 Rancocas Road, Mount Holly, NJ 08060; tel: 609-261-2495; www.nj.com/audubon.

Victor Emanuel Nature Tours (VENT)
P.O. Box 33008, Austin, TX 78764; tel: 800-328-8368 or 512-328-5221; www.ventbird.com.

Voyagers
P.O. Box 915, Ithaca, NY 14851; tel: 607-257-3091.

WINGS Inc.
1643 North Alvernon, Suite 105, Tucson, AZ 85712; tel: 520-320-9868; www.wingsbirds.com.

Wonder Bird Tours
P.O. Box 2015, New York, NY 10159; tel: 800-BIRD-TUR or 212-736-BIRD.

MANUFACTURERS OF OPTICAL EQUIPMENT

Although major manufacturers of optical equipment usually do not sell directly to consumers, they can provide literature about their products and help you find local dealers for binoculars, scopes, and tripods.

Bausch & Lomb/Bushnell
9200 Cody, Overland Park, KS 66214; tel: 800-423-3537 or 913-752-4300.

Bogen Photo Corp.
565 East Crescent Avenue, P.O. Box 506, Ramsey, NJ 07446; tel: 201-818-9500.

Canon USA, Inc.
One Canon Plaza, Lake Success, NY 11042; tel: 800-652-2666 or 516-488-6700.

Celestron International
2835 Columbia Street, Torrance, CA 90503; tel: 310-328-9560.

Eagle Optics
2120 West Greenview Drive, #4, Middleton, WI 53562; tel: 800-289-1132 or 608-836-7172.

Kowa Optimed, Inc.
20001 South Vermont Avenue, Torrance, CA 90502; tel: 800-966-5692 or 310-327-1913.

Leica Camera, Inc.
156 Ludlow Avenue, Northvale, NJ 07647; tel: 800-248-0223 or 201-767-7500.

Meade Instruments Corporation
16542 Millikan Avenue, Irvine, CA 92606; tel: 949-451-1450.

Mirador Optical Corporation
4040-8 Del Rey Avenue, P.O. Box 11614, Marina del Rey, CA 90295; tel: 800-748-5844 or 310-821-5587.

Nikon, Inc.
1300 Walt Whitman Road, Melville, NY 11747; tel: 800-645-6687 or 516-547-4200.

Pentax Corporation
35 Inverness Drive East, Englewood, CO 80112; tel: 800-709-2020.

Swift Instruments, Inc.
952 Dorchester Avenue, Boston, MA 02125; tel: 800-446-1116 or 617-436-2960.

PHOTO AND ILLUSTRATION CREDITS

Tom Blagden/Larry Ulrich Stock Photography, Inc. 68, 102T, 123B

R. K. Bowers/Vireo 138B

Matt Bradley/Tom Stack and Associates 141T

Shirley A. Briggs/Rachel Carson History Project 71B

Sonja Bullaty/Bullaty-Lomeo 74, 77T

Brandon D. Cole 198

W. Perry Conway/Tom Stack & Associates 93T, 155B, 159M

Rob Curtis/Vireo 149T

Mark Dietz 163T, 165T

J. Dunning/Vireo 129

Patrick Endres/Wide Angle Productions 9B, 46T, 52, 203B

Jeff Foott/Jeff Foott Productions 41B, 121M, 121B, 160, 171T, 172B, 175T

Jeff Foott/Tom Stack & Associates 133B

Sam Fried 40TL, 73M, 83T, 105T, 136, 141M, 154, 156B, 157B, 191T, 196T

Tim Gallagher 95B

John Gerlach/Tom Stack & Associates 41T, 71T, 145B, 162, back cover bottom

Francois Gohier 62T, 65B, 85B, 157T, 207T

Thomas Hallstein 193M

Randi Hirschmann 203M

George Holton/Photo Researchers Inc. 26

Joe Mac Hudspeth 18B, 48, 105BM, 114, 127B

George H. H. Huey 133BM, 137B, 146T, 151m,151b, 208T

John Hyde/Alaska Stock Images 19

Jack Jeffrey/Photo Resource Hawaii 206, 208B, 209T, 209B

Wolfgang Kaehler 58, 61B, 63B, 211M

Charles Kennedy 77B

Thomas Kitchin/Tom Stack & Associates 66, 97M, 139T, 152, 165B, 170, 173

Lee Kline 164B

Bill Lea 118b

Tom and Pat Leeson front cover, 89T, 95M, 167M, 186, 201B, 212-213

Joe McDonald/Tom Stack & Associates 69B, 103B

Colin McRae 8T, 24T, 28M

Bob Miller 182T

Bruce Montagne 102B

Arthur Morris/Birds as Art 1, 4L, 5B, 22, 24B, 25T, 27T, 27B, 28B, 29T, 34T, 34B, 38, 40TR, 46B, 53T, 53B, 55B, 65T, 79B, 82, 85T, 89M, 89B, 90, 92, 94, 97B, 98, 100, 101T, 101M, 101B, 103T, 106, 108T, 109B, 110T, 116, 119T, 119B, 120B, 121T, 126, 130T, 141B, 156T, 175M, 180B, 182B, 183, 189B, 194, 196B, 211B, back cover top

Brian Parker/Tom Stack & Associates 211T

Rich Penny/Dinosaur Man 18T

Louie Psihoyos 16

Paul Rezendes 73B

Carl R. Sams II 6-7, 10-11, 20-21, 30, 42B, 47T, 70T, 113T, 117T, 167B

John Shaw/Tom Stack & Associates 105B, 128B

Fredrick Sears 14-15

Bill Silliker, Jr. 73T, 204

Tom Soucek 8L, 111B, 179, 200B

Gene and Jason Stone/Leeson Photography 149B, 176

Tom Till 123T, 133TM

Larry Ulrich/Larry Ulrich Stock Photography, Inc. 178T

Tom J. Ulrich 63T, 164T, 175B, 181B 185B

Greg Vaughn/Tom Stack & Associates 185T, 207B

Tom Vezo 2-3, 5T, 9T, 12-13, 28T, 32T, 32B, 33, 35, 36, 39T, 39B, 40TM, 42T, 44, 47B, 49T, 49B, 50, 54, 55T, 56-57, 60, 61, 62B, 69T, 69M, 70B, 79T, 79M, 80, 83T, 84T, 84B, 86, 87, 93B, 95T, 97T, 105TM, 108B, 109T, 110B, 111T, 113M, 113B, 117B, 123M, 124, 127T, 128T, 130B, 131, 133T, 134, 137T, 138T, 142, 144, 145T, 146B, 147T, 151, 155T, 159T, 163B, 167T, 168, 172T, 178B, 180T, 181T, 188, 189T, 190B, 191B, 193B, 197, 199, 201T

Art Wolfe 43, 25B, 118T, 147B, 148, 159B, 185M, 190T, 200T

George Wuerthner 29B, 120T, 171B, 193T

Tom Walker 65M, 139B, 203

Design by Mary Kay Garttmeier
Layout by Ingrid Hansen-Lynch

Index by Elizabeth Cook

Maps by Karen Minot

T-top, B-bottom, M-middle, R-right, L-left

INDEX

Note: page numbers in italics refer to illustrations